Learning to Solve Problems with Technology

A Constructivist Perspective

Second Edition

David H. Jonassen

University of Missouri

Jane Howland

University of Missouri

Joi Moore

University of Missouri

Rose M. Marra

University of Missouri

Merrill
Prentice Hall

Upper Saddle River, New Jersey
Columbus, Ohio

Library of Congress Cataloging in Publication Data

Learning to solve problems with technology: a constructivist perspective/David H. Jonassen . . . [et al.].
   p. cm.
   Rev. ed. of: Learning with technology. c1999.
   Includes bibliographical references and index.
   1. Educational technology. 2. Teaching—Aids and devices. 3. Learning. 4. Constructivism (Education) I. Jonassen, David H., II. Jonassen, David H., Learning with technology.

LB1028.3 .J63 2003
371.33—dc21

2002070985

Vice President and Publisher: Jeffery W. Johnston
Executive Editor: Debra A. Stollenwerk
Editorial Assistant: Mary Morrill
Production Editor: JoEllen Gohr
Production Coordination: Clarinda Publication Services
Photo Coordinator: Cynthia Cassidy
Design Coordinator: Diane C. Lorenzo
Cover Designer: Thomas Borah
Cover Photo: Image Bank
Production Manager: Pamela Bennett
Director of Marketing: Ann Castel Davis
Marketing Manager: Krista Groshong
Marketing Coordinator: Tyra Cooper

This book was set in Palatino by The Clarinda Company.
The cover was printed by Phoenix Color Corp.

Photo Credits: p. 1, SW Productions, Getty Images, Inc./PhotoDisc, Inc.; p. 19, David Buffington, Getty Images, Inc./PhotoDisc, Inc.; pp. 31, 209, Anthony Magnacca/Merrill; pp. 69, 121, 134, 163, Scott Cunningham/Merrill; p. 189, University of Washington HIT Lab/Mary Levin; p. 227, Anne Vega/Merrill. All other photos supplied by the authors.

Pearson Education Ltd.
Pearson Education Australia Pty. Limited
Pearson Education Singapore Ptc. Ltd.
Pearson Education North Asia Ltd.
Pearson Education, Canada, Ltd.
Pearson Educación de Mexico, S.A. de C.V.
Pearson Education—Japan
Pearson Education Malaysia Pte, Ltd.
Pearson Education, *Upper Saddle River, New Jersey*

Merrill
Prentice Hall

10 9 8 7 6
ISBN 0-13-048403-2

PREFACE

The constructivist revolution in education is a decade or more old. It is an even newer idea to educational technology. It is so new to some educational circles that some perceive it as a fad. We think not. Constructivism is an old idea to sociology, art, and philosophy. As a way of understanding the learning phenomenon, it is ageless. People have always constructed personal and socially acceptable meaning for events and objects in the world. Since evolving from primordial ooze, humans have interacted with the world and struggled to make sense out of what they experienced; this is as natural to humans as breathing. The popular Chinese proverb about forgetting what you tell me and understanding what I do bears witness to the ageless belief that knowledge, meaning, and understanding do not exist outside of meaningful, intentional activity. People naturally construct meaning. Formal educational enterprises that rely on the efficient transmission of prepackaged chunks of information are not natural, yet they are pandemic. The modern age values understanding less than it does progress (i.e., efficient transmission of culturally accepted beliefs). It doesn't have to be that way. Modernism can support meaning-making as well. This book looks at how modern technologies such as computers and video can be used to engage learners in personal and socially co-constructed meaning-making and problem solving.

For many, constructivism represents a new way of conceiving the educational experience. Yet constructivism as a philosophy and as a pedagogy is now widely accepted. This is a time of theoretical foment, where nearly all contemporary theories of learning (constructivism, situated learning, social cognition, activity theory, distributed cognition, ecological psychology, and case-based reasoning) share convergent beliefs about how people naturally come to know (Jonassen & Land, 2000). This book is not about theory, but it shares the beliefs of these theories.

Learning to Solve Problems with Technology: A Constructivist Perspective is about how educators can use technologies to support constructive learning. In the past, technology has largely been used in education to learn *from*. Technology programs were developed with the belief that they could convey information (and hopefully understanding) more effectively than teachers. But constructivists believe that you cannot convey understanding—that can only be constructed by learners. This book argues that technologies are more effectively used as tools to construct knowledge *with*. The point is that technology is a tool to think and learn *with*.

How can technologies be used as meaning-making tools? In this book, after contrasting different conceptions of learning, we elucidate our conception of meaningful learning. Meaningful learning is active, constructive, intentional, authentic, and cooperative. How do we engage students in active, constructive, intentional, authentic, and cooperative learning activities? By asking them to solve problems. In Chapter 2 we briefly contrast different kinds of problem solving and then describe how technologies can best engage and support problem solving in schools. Technologies can effectively support information searching, modeling, decision making, and designing. Each of these is either a kind of problem solving or an important process in problem solving.

In Chapter 3 we show how learners who articulate a personally meaningful goal or intention can explore the Internet in search of ideas that help them construct their own understanding. Sharing their own understanding by constructing personal and group Web sites completes the knowledge construction cycle.

Another problematic belief of schools is that learning is always an individual endeavor, so schools focus only on assessing the knowledge that resides in individual heads. Learning in everyday and professional (non-school) contexts is rarely individual. Rather, individuals rely on peers to help them accomplish tasks and to learn. Chapter 4 provides many ideas for how the Internet can be used to foster community building within schools, districts, states, countries, and around the world.

Chapter 5 describes numerous activities in which students can use video cameras, editors, and digitizers to represent their ideas. Constructing video presentations requires that learners articulate an idea well enough to represent it through video. In this chapter, video is used not to teach students, but rather as a tool that learners can teach and learn with. Students are natural video producers.

From video, Chapter 6 adds sound, graphics, and multimedia computers as tools that students can use to represent what they know. While producing multimedia programs, students become sensitive to the needs and desires of the audience for whom they are producing. They work harder and use more skills, without complaint, than they ever would with pencil and paper. Multimedia represents a new form of literacy that students will learn only by participating in the production of multimedia.

Chapter 7 is a **new chapter** that focuses on immersive, exploratory environments. Microworlds enable learners to speculate about phenomena in a simplified representation of the real world, and to test hypotheses. This chapter also briefly introduces virtual realities, which are only beginning to find their way into educational venues. Virtual reality environments hold great promise as the most engaging, authentic, and interactive environments yet. The technology is not yet available to make these environments widely available; that will change soon.

Chapter 8 is also a **new chapter** that presents a number of environments that are designed to engage problem solving—the purpose of this book. These environments do not cover the curriculum, but where they are available, they will surely engage learners in meaningful learning.

What you sow, so also must you reap. Translated into educational vernacular, if your goal is constructive learning, and if you engage your students in meaningful constructive activities, then you are obligated to assess constructive learning. This congruence is an underlying assumption of the book. Chapter 9 shows how to develop rubrics that can be used to assess constructive learning and problem solving.

We have tried to standardize our descriptions of technology-enhanced learning activities in this book. For most learning activities, we first describe the activity and then comment briefly on the learning processes (active, constructive, intentional, authentic, and cooperative) engaged by the activity, the problem-solving processes engaged by the activity, and the role of the teacher in supporting the activity. We have tried not to be overly prescriptive. Some teachers have asked for detailed lesson plans for each of the activities. We decided on principle not to provide them, not because we are mean, but because lesson plans would violate the assumptions of the book laid out in Chapter 1. We have tried to describe activities that will allow teachers to engage learners in constructive learning. That kind of learning is unlikely to happen if we tried to script every part of the lesson. Also, lesson plans cannot account for the myriad variables that influence success in your classrooms. We have no idea who you are, what your beliefs are, what kinds of technology and technology support you have available, what your students are like, what values they bring to the classroom, what your colleagues are like, and so on. In order to write meaningful lesson plans, we would have to know all of those things. So you as a teacher must also construct your own understanding of the activities and the roles of technology by experiencing them. Some will likely be the most effective activities that you have ever tried, and others will doubtlessly fail—that is the nature of real learning. To learn to integrate technologies more effectively, you must experience successes and failures. You will quickly learn what factors are most important to you in your settings. We certainly wish you the very best of luck.

Bear this in mind as you experience these activities. We live in the information age. In order to function in that world, students must learn how to be information producers, not just consumers. This book provides a new look at how educational technologies can support knowledge construction through production rather than knowledge reproduction. When educational technologies are used as knowledge construction tools, students are naturally and necessarily engaged in meaningful learning, which should be the goal of all educators.

Acknowledgments

The authors would like to thank the following reviewers: Kara Dawson, University of Virginia; Peggy Ertmer, Purdue University; R. Scott Grabinger,

University of Colorado at Denver; M. K. Hamza, Florida Atlantic University; Joan Hanor, California State University, San Marcos; Virginia Jewell, Columbus State; Franklin R. Koontz, The University of Toledo; W. Michael Reed, West Virginia State University; Gregory C. Sales, University of Minnesota; Edna O. Schack, Morehead State University; Mark Schack, Morehead State University; Sharon Smaldino, University of Northern Iowa; Neal Strudler, University of Nevada, Las Vegas; Nancy H. Vick, Longwood College; and Connie Zimmer, Arkansas Tech University.

Reference

Jonassen, D. H. & Land S. L. (2000). *Theoretical foundations of learning environnments.* Mahwah, NJ: Lawrence Erlbaum Associates.

DISCOVER THE COMPANION WEBSITE
ACCOMPANYING THIS BOOK

THE PRENTICE HALL COMPANION WEBSITE: A VIRTUAL LEARNING ENVIRONMENT

Technology is a constantly growing and changing aspect of our field that is creating a need for content and resources. To address this emerging need, Prentice Hall has developed an online learning environment for students and professors alike–Companion Websites–to support our textbooks.

In creating a Companion Website, our goal is to build on and enhance what the textbook already offers. For this reason, the content for each user-friendly website is organized by chapter and provides the professor and student with a variety of meaningful resources.

FOR THE PROFESSOR—

Every Companion Website integrates **Syllabus Manager**™, an online syllabus creation and management utility.

- **Syllabus Manager**™ provides you, the instructor, with an easy, step-by-step process to create and revise syllabi, with direct links into Companion Website and other online content without having to learn HTML.
- Students may logon to your syllabus during any study session. All they need to know is the web address for the Companion Website and the password you've assigned to your syllabus.
- After you have created a syllabus using **Syllabus Manager**™, students may enter the syllabus for their course section from any point in the Companion Website.

- Clicking on a date, the student is shown the list of activities for the assignment. The activities for each assignment are linked directly to actual content, saving time for students.
- Adding assignments consists of clicking on the desired due date, then filling in the details of the assignment—name of the assignment, instructions, and whether or not it is a one-time or repeating assignment.
- In addition, links to other activities can be created easily. If the activity is online, a URL can be entered in the space provided, and it will be linked automatically in the final syllabus.
- Your completed syllabus is hosted on our servers, allowing convenient updates from any computer on the Internet. Changes you make to your syllabus are immediately available to your students at their next logon.

FOR THE STUDENT—

Common Companion Website features for students include:

- **Chapter Objectives**—outline key concepts from the text
- **Interactive Self-Quizzes**—complete with hints and automatic grading that provide immediate feedback for students

  After students submit their answers for the interactive self-quizzes, the Companion Website **Results Reporter** computes a percentage grade, provides a graphic representation of how many questions were answered correctly and incorrectly, and gives a question by question analysis of the quiz. Students are given the option to send their quiz to up to four email addresses (professor, teaching assistant, study partner, etc.).

- **Web Destinations**—links to www sites that relate to chapter content
- **Family Education Network**—the Pearson Family Education Network offers a wealth of additional resources to aid in their understanding and application of content.
- **Message Board**—serves as a virtual bulletin board to post–or respond to–questions or comments to/from a national audience
- **Chat**—real-time chat with anyone who is using the text anywhere in the country—ideal for discussion and study groups, class projects, etc.

To take advantage of these and other resources, please visit the *Learning to Solve Problems with Technology: A Constructivist Perspective*, Second Edition, Companion Website at

www.prenhall.com/jonassen

CONTENTS

Chapter 5 Learning by Visualizing With Technology: Recording Realities With Video   121

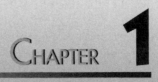

What Is Meaningful Learning?

WHAT IS LEARNING?

The first word of the title of this book is learning. Why? Because we believe that learning should be the most important outcome of schools. Learning is what humans do best, and school is supposed to foster learning. Why are humans such effective learners? Biologists, psychologists, anthropologists, and others generally agree that it has a lot to do with our relatively large brain size. So, we begin this book by briefly examining the question of what it means to learn.

There are many conceptions of learning. Based on their experiences and beliefs, people have constructed different theories about what it means to learn. These theories and their assumptions about learning and its outcomes differ. You may be tempted to ask, "Well, which one is right?" We can only tell you that they are all somewhat right. They are theories, that is, explanations by theorists about how they think the world works. Theories are too often taught as objects of truth. But everyone, from toddlers through experts, naturally constructs theories about how the world works. Some theories are just better informed. The following theories attempt to explain learning phenomena. However, no theory can explain all learning phenomena.

Learning Is Biochemical Activity in the Brain   At the most material level, learning requires the release of a neurotransmitter from the hippocampus that facilitates the transmission of minute electrical pulses between the neurons of the brain. Patterns of behavior and cognitive activity are associated with patterns of neuronal firing. So learning is a matter of engramming certain patterns of neuronal connections. CAT scans and electroencephalographs (machines that monitor brain activity) can show learning occurring, as different areas of the brain light up when people are engaged in different learning tasks. Like most people, the philosopher Descartes wasn't satisfied with this conception of learning, so he distinguished between the body and the mind. The mind, and the learning it affords, is more than the body. Most people agree that human learning depends on brain activity but cannot be adequately described in terms of it.

Learning Is a Relatively Permanent Change in Behavior   Behavioral psychologists of the late 19th and early 20th centuries believed that learning is evidenced by behavioral dispositions. When exposed to certain stimuli, people respond in predictable ways if they are reinforced for their performance. Even complex behaviors, such as language learning, can be described as behavioral tendencies. Behavioral psychologists focused their research on describing laws of human behavior. Cognitive psychologists believed that the human mind possessed intentionality and originality and so was more than a collection of reinforced behaviors. However, behaviorism very accurately describes many aspects of social learning. Most of us would not work without a paycheck. And behavioral methods work quite effectively with many special learning populations. All people respond to reinforcers on some level.

Learning Is Information Processing   The early cognitive psychologists and systems thinkers conceived of human learning as information processing. Like computers, humans take in information, then hold it briefly in short-term memory until they can find a place to store it permanently in long-term memory. When faced with a task, we retrieve information from long-term memory and shift it into working memory where we can use the information to perform some task. Learning is a matter of developing more sophisticated processing methods. Although information processing theory identified some of the mechanisms of mind, contemporary constructivist philosophers (described later in this chapter) believe that the human mind is uniquely capable of making meaning from its environment, a process that cannot adequately be explained using machine metaphors.

Learning Is Remembering and Recalling   The emphasis on information processing legitimized perhaps the oldest conception of learning, what you know. Almost all formal educational institutions have always measured knowledge in terms of what students are able to remember when given an examination. Learning is a process of "knowledge acquisition," a filling-up of the mind. If you are highlighting any of this text in preparation for an examination, then your teacher (and you, tacitly) believes that learning is remembering. However, constructivist philosophers believe that knowledge is more than remembering, that we strive to make sense out of what we are studying.

Learning Is Social Negotiation   Meaning making is seldom accomplished individually. Rather, humans naturally tend to share their meaning with others, so meaning making more likely results from conversations than cramming. Just as the physical world is shared by all of us, so is some of the meaning that we make from it. Humans are social creatures who rely on feedback from fellow humans to determine their own identity and the viability of their personal beliefs. Social constructivists believe that meaning making is a process of negotiation among the participants through dialogues or conversations. Learning is inherently a social-dialogical process (Duffy & Cunningham, 1996). People with similar experiences enjoy discussing those experiences, so they can learn from each other.

Learning Is Thinking Skills   Many theorists believe that learning is best exhibited through guile and wit, the ability to think more cleverly than others. Critical thinking as an issue emerged during the 1970s and 1980s as an antidote to reproductive, lower-order learning (Paul, 1992). There are many models of critical thinking, but most emphasize *logical* thinking (judging the relationships between meanings of words and statements), *critical* thinking (knowing the criteria for judging statements covered by the logical dimension), and *pragmatic* thinking (considering the background or purpose of the judgment and the decision as to whether the statement is good enough for the purpose) (Ennis, 1989). Learning requires showing that you can analyze and apply knowledge, according to critical theorists.

Learning Is Knowledge Construction   Individuals make sense of their world and all that they come in contact with by constructing their own representations or models of their experiences. Knowledge construction is a natural process. Whenever humans encounter something they do not know but need to understand, their natural inclination is to attempt to reconcile it with what they already know in order to determine what it means. Toddlers are constructivist machines. They constantly explore their worlds and frequently encounter phenomena that they do not understand. So they continue to explore it, familiarizing themselves with its possible functions and limitations. Parents try to intervene by teaching them lessons, but toddlers prefer to explore and learn for themselves.

Learning Is Conceptual Change   Many conceptual change theorists believe that learning is a process of making sense out of domain concepts in such a way that they develop coherent conceptual structures. In order to make meaning, humans naturally organize and reorganize their naïve models of the world in light of new experiences. The more coherent their theories of the world, the better are their conceptual structures. More contemporary conceptual change theorists (Schnotz, Vosniadou, & Carretero, 1999) emphasize the role of context in conceptual reorganization. Conceptual change, according to them, is more about embedding concepts in different contexts.

Learning Is Contextual Change   The knowledge of phenomena that we construct and the intellectual skills that we develop include information about the context in which it was experienced (Brown, Collins, & Duguid, 1989; Lave & Wenger, 1991). Information about the context is part of the knowledge that is constructed by the learner in order to explain or make sense of the phenomenon. The knowledge that is constructed by a learner consists of not only the ideas (content) but also knowledge about the context in which it was acquired, what the learner was doing in that environment, and what the knower intended to get from that environment. That is why abstract rules and laws (such as mathematical formulae), divorced from any context or use, have little meaning for most learners. If learning is embedded in a context, evidence of new learning could result from reusing that knowledge in new contexts.

Learning Is Activity   We cannot separate our knowledge of things from our experiences with them. Activity theorists (Leont'ev, 1972) claim that conscious learning and activity (performance) are interactive and interdependent (we cannot act without thinking or think without acting; they are the same). Activity and consciousness are the central mechanisms of learning. The important distinction is that in order to think and learn, it is necessary to act on some entity. Rather than focusing on knowledge states, as cognitive psychologists do, activity theorists focus on the activities in which people are engaged, the nature of the tools they use in those activities, the social and contextual relationships among the collaborators in those activities, the goals and intentions of those activities, and the objects or outcomes of those activities (Jonassen, 2002). Activity theorists readily accept the contradictions implied by these different theories of learning as a necessary part of an activity system involving many scholars trying to understand learning.

Learning Is Distributed Among the Community   As we interact with others in knowledge-building communities, our knowledge and beliefs about the world are influenced by that community and their beliefs and values. So, learning can also be conceived of as changes in our relation to the culture(s) to which we are connected (Duffy & Cunningham, 1996). Through participating in the activities of the community (Lave and Wenger, 1991), we absorb part of the culture that is an integral part of the community, just as the culture is affected by each of its members. Communities of learners, like communities of practitioners, can be seen as a kind of widely distributed memory with each of its members storing a part of the group's total memory. Distributed memory, what the group as a whole knows, is clearly more capacious than individual memories, and so the sharing of those memories makes the community more dynamic.

The group's knowledge is distributed among the participants in these communities (Salomon, 1993). When a complex task has to be performed, members of the group will contribute what they know to the performance of the whole group.

Learning Is Tuning Perceptions to Environmental Affordances
Ecological psychologists believe that learning results from the reciprocal perception of affordances from the environment and actions on the environment. That is, different environments afford different kinds of thinking and acting. As learners, we become attuned to what the environment affords us and so we act on the environment in some way. The changes in our abilities to perceive and act on an environment provide evidence of learning. Ecological psychologists emphasize the role of perception in learning.

Learning Is Chaos   Ask any middle school teacher. No, what we mean is that learning exhibits characteristics of chaos theory. Learning systems of all sizes tend to behave randomly; that is, we cannot explain the outcomes of the learning systems. When we examine the variables that describe system performance, they do not repeat regularly, so we view the systems as unstable. Learning systems tend not to resist outside disturbances, but rather over-react to changes in conditions. However, in most systems, people do learn. Learning is a self-organizing phenomenon. When people in systems need to learn, they will. As educators, we simply cannot predict it because we are not examining the phenomenon systemically.

So, What Is Learning?   It is all of these. Humans are such complex organisms that they are unable to fully understand themselves. That is, we have not yet learned who and what we are. We certainly cannot agree on what it means to learn. We have briefly described some of the theories that have been constructed to explain what learning is. They all describe some aspects of human learning.

WHAT IS MEANINGFUL LEARNING?

Our assumption in this book is that the primary goal of education at all levels should be to engage students in meaningful learning, which occurs when students are making meaning. While schools play a variety of important social, custodial, and organizational roles in communities, their primary obligation should be to help students to learn how to recognize and solve problems, comprehend new phenomena, construct mental models of those phenomena, and given a new situation, set goals and regulate their own learning (learn how to learn). Figure 1.1 illustrates the interaction of five interdependent attributes of meaningful learning. If we accept that our goal, as technology-using educators, is to support meaningful learning, then we should use technologies to engage students in active, constructive, intentional, authentic, and cooperative learning. These attributes of meaningful learning will be used throughout the book as the goals

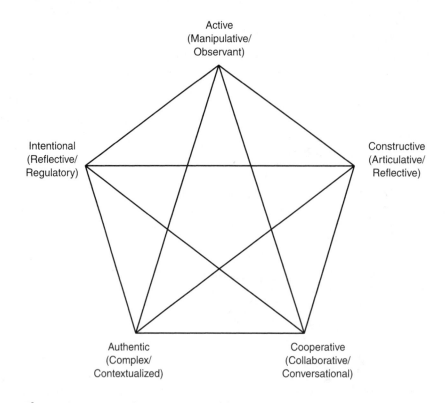

Figure 1.1 Five Attributes of Meaningful Learning

for using technologies as well as the criteria for evaluating the uses of technology. Let's examine these attributes a little more closely.

• **Meaningful Learning Is Active (Manipulative/Observant)**   Learning is a natural, adaptive human process. Humans have survived and therefore evolved because they were able to learn about and adapt to their environment. Humans of all ages, without the intervention of formal instruction, can develop sophisticated skills and construct advanced knowledge about the world around them when they need to or want to. When learning about things in natural contexts, humans interact with their environment and manipulate the objects in that environment, observing the effects of their interventions and constructing their own interpretations of the phenomena and the results of the manipulation. For instance, before playing sandlot baseball, do kids subject themselves to lectures and multiple-choice examinations about the theory of games, the aerodynamics of orbs, and vector forces of bats? No! They start swinging the bat and chasing fly balls, and they negotiate the rules as they play the game. Through formal and informal apprenticeships in communities of play and work, learners develop skills and knowledge that they then share with other members of those communities with whom they learned and practiced those skills. In all of these situations, learners are actively manipulating the objects and tools of the trade and observing the effects of what they have done. The youngster who consistently hits foul balls will adjust his/her stance and handgrip on the bat continuously in order to manipulate the path of flight and observe the effects of each manipulation. Meaningful learning requires learners who are actively engaged in a meaningful task (not just pressing the spacebar to continue) in which they manipulate objects and parameters of the environment they are working in and observing the results of their manipulations.

• **Meaningful Learning Is Constructive (Articulative/Reflective)** Activity is necessary but not sufficient for meaningful learning. It is essential that learners articulate what they have accomplished and reflect on their activity and observations—to learn the lessons that their activity has to teach. New experiences often provide a discrepancy between what learners observe and what they understand. They are curious about or puzzled by what they see. That puzzlement is the catalyst for meaning making. By reflecting on the puzzling experience, learners integrate their new experiences with their prior knowledge about the world, or they establish goals for what they need to learn in order to make sense out of what they observe. Learners begin constructing their own simple mental models to explain their worlds, and with experience, support, and more reflection, their mental models become increasingly complex. Ever more complex models will enable them to reason more consistently and productively about the phenomena they are observing. The active and constructive parts of the meaning-making process are symbiotic. They both rely on the other for meaning making to occur.

• **Meaningful Learning Is Intentional (Reflective/Regulatory)**   All human behavior is goal directed (Schank, 1994). That is, everything that we do is intended to fulfill some goal. That goal may be simple, such as satiating hunger or getting more comfortable, or it may be more complex, such as developing new career skills or studying for a master's degree. When learners are actively and willfully trying to achieve a cognitive goal, they think and learn more because they are fulfilling an intention. Technologies have traditionally been used to support teacher goals, but not those of learners. Technologies need to engage learners in articulating what their learning goals are in any learning situation and then supporting them. Learners should be required by technology-based learning systems to articulate what they are doing, the decisions they make, the strategies they use, and the answers they found. When learners articulate what they have learned and reflect on the processes and decisions that were entailed by the process, they understand more and are better able to use the knowledge that they have constructed in new situations.

• **Meaningful Learning Is Authentic (Complex/Contextualized)**   The greatest intellectual sin that we educators commit is to oversimplify most ideas that we teach in order to make them more easily transmissible to learners. In addition to removing ideas from their natural contexts for teaching, we also strip ideas of their contextual cues and information and distill the ideas to their "simplest" form so that students will more readily learn them. But what are they learning? That knowledge is divorced from reality, and that the world is a reliable and simple place. But the world is not a reliable and simple place, and ideas rely on the contexts they occur in for meaning. At the end of chapters, textbooks re-insert the ideas they presented into some artificial problem for learners to solve in some predictable ways. However, learning often fails because students learned to understand the ideas as algorithmic procedures outside of any context, so they have no idea how to relate the ideas to real-world contexts. Additionally, these textbook problems are constrained, practicing only a limited number of activities that were introduced in the chapter, so when they are faced with complex and ill-structured problems, students do not know where to begin.

Most contemporary research on learning has shown that learning tasks that are situated in some meaningful real-world task or simulated in some case-based or problem-based learning environment are not only better understood, but also are more consistently transferred to new situations. Rather than abstracting ideas in rules that are memorized and then applied to other canned problems, we need to teach knowledge and skills in real-life, useful contexts and provide new and different contexts for learners to practice using those ideas. And we need to engage students in solving complex and ill-structured problems as well as simple, well-structured problems (Jonassen, 1997). Unless learners are required to engage in higher order thinking, they will develop oversimplified views of the world.

• **Meaningful Learning Is Cooperative (Collaborative/Conversational)** Humans naturally work in learning and knowledge-building communities, exploiting each other's skills and appropriating each other's knowledge. In the real world, humans naturally seek out others to help them to solve problems and perform tasks. Then why do educators insist that learners work independently all of the time? Schools generally believe that learning is an independent process, so learners seldom have the opportunity to "do anything that counts" in collaborative teams despite their natural inclinations. When students collaborate without permission, educators may even accuse them of cheating. However, we believe that relying solely on independent methods of instruction cheat learners out of more natural and productive modes of thinking. Often, educators will promote collaborative methods of learning, only to resort to independent assessment of learning. Learners, they believe, must be accountable for their own knowledge, so even if you agree, at least in principle, with collaborative learning principles, the hardest part of applying your beliefs will be assessing learners. Throughout this book, we will provide vignettes on how groups as well as individuals may be assessed. We cannot forget that most learners are strategic enough to know "what counts" in classrooms, so if they are evaluated individually, collaborative learning activities may fail because students realize that group outcomes are not important.

Collaboration most often requires conversation among participants. Learners working in groups must socially negotiate a common understanding of the task and the methods they will use to accomplish it. That is, given a problem or task, people naturally seek out opinions and ideas from others. Technologies can support this conversational process by connecting learners in the same classroom, across town, or around the world (see chapter 4). When learners become part of knowledge-building communities both in class and outside of school, they learn that there are multiple ways of viewing the world and multiple solutions to most of life's problems. Conversation should be encouraged. In classrooms that focus on individual learning, however, conversation is too often discouraged. In those classrooms, students know that the important views are those espoused by the textbook or the teacher, so conversation is not productive.

As depicted in Figure 1.1, these characteristics of meaningful learning are interrelated, interactive, and interdependent. That is, learning and instructional activities should engage and support combinations of active, constructive, intentional, authentic, and cooperative learning. Why? Because we believe that these characteristics are synergetic. That is, learning activities that represent a combination of these characteristics result in even more meaningful learning than the individual characteristics would in isolation.

There are many kinds of learning activities that engage meaningful learning, just as there are teachers who have for years engaged students in meaningful learning. We argue throughout this book that technologies can and should become the tools of meaningful learning. Technologies afford students the opportunities to engage in meaningful learning if used as learning tools. In the next section, we explicate the assumptions about technologies that underlie their use as learning tools. The remainder of this book describes ways that technologies can be used as tools for learning *with*.

HOW DOES TECHNOLOGY FACILITATE LEARNING?

Learning From Technology

Educational technologies have been traced historically to illustrations in 17th-century books and slate chalkboards in 18th-century classrooms. Educational technologies in the 20th century include first lantern-slide projectors, later radio, and then motion pictures. Chapter 5 describes the development of educational television in the 1950s and 1960s. During the same period, programmed instruction emerged as the first true educational technology, that is, the first technology developed specifically to meet educational needs. With every other technology, including computers, educators recognized the importance of each and debated how to apply each nascent commercial technology for educational purposes. Unfortunately, educators have almost always tried to use technologies to teach students in the same ways that teachers had always taught. So information was embedded in the technology (e.g., the content presented by films and TV programs or the teaching sequence in programmed instruction), and the technology presented that information to the students. The students' role was to learn the information presented by the technology, just as they learned information presented by the teacher. The role of the technology was to deliver lessons to students, just as trucks deliver groceries to supermarkets (Clark, 1983). If you deliver groceries, people will eat. If you deliver instruction, students will learn.

The introduction of modern computer technologies in classrooms followed the same pattern of use. Before the advent of microcomputers in the 1980s, mainframe computers were used to deliver drill and practice and simple tutorials for teaching students lessons. When microcomputers began populating classrooms, the natural inclination was to use them in the same way. A 1983 national survey of computer uses showed that drill and practice was the most common use of microcomputers (Becker, 1985).

Later in the 1980s, educators began to perceive the importance of computers as productivity *tools*. The growing popularity of word processing, databases, spreadsheets, graphics programs, and desktop publishing were enabling businesses to become more productive. So students in classroom began word processing and using graphics packages and desktop publishing programs. This tool concept pervaded computer uses according to a 1993 study by Hadley and Sheingold. They showed that well-informed teachers were extensively using text processing tools (word processors), analytic and information tools (especially databases and some spreadsheet use), and graphics tools (paint programs and desktop publishing) along with instructional software (including problem-solving programs along with drill and practice and tutorials).

The development of inexpensive multimedia computers and the eruption of the Internet in the mid-1990s quickly changed the nature of educational computing. Communications and multimedia, little used according to Hadley and Sheingold, have dominated the role of technologies in the classroom ever since. But what are the students producing? Too often, they are using the technology to reproduce what the teacher or textbook told them.

Our conception of educational computing and technology use, described below, does not conceive of technologies as teachers. Rather, we believe that in order to learn, students should be teachers, *representing* what they know rather than memorizing what teachers and textbooks tell them. Technologies provide rich and flexible media for representing what students know and what they are learning. A great deal of research on computers and other technologies has shown that they are no more effective at teaching students than teachers, but if we begin to think about technologies as learning tools that students learn *with*, not *from*, then the nature of student learning will change.

Learning With *Technology*

The ways that we use technologies in schools should change from technology-as-teacher to technology-as-partner in the learning process. Students do not learn from technology, they learn from thinking. Technologies can engage and support thinking when students learn *with* technology. But, how do students learn *with* technologies? How can technologies become intellectual partners with students? If you agree with this role for technologies, then you must make a different set of assumptions about what technologies are and what they do. Throughout this book, we assume that:

- Technology is more than hardware. Technology consists also of the designs and the environments that engage learners. Technology can also consist of any reliable technique or method for engaging learning, such as cognitive learning strategies and critical thinking skills.
- Learning technologies can be any environment or definable set of activities that engage learners in active, constructive, intentional, authentic, and cooperative learning.
- Technologies are not conveyors or communicators of meaning, nor should they prescribe and control all learner interactions.
- Technologies support learning when they fulfill a learning need—when interactions with technologies are learner-initiated and learner-controlled, and when interactions with the technologies are conceptually and intellectually engaging.
- Technologies should function as intellectual tool kits that enable learners to build more meaningful personal interpretations and representations of the world. These tool kits must support the intellectual functions that are required by a course of study.
- Learners and technologies should be intellectual partners, where the cognitive responsibility for performing is distributed by the part of the partnership that performs it the best.

Traditionally, technologies have been used to teach students. That is, they have been used to deliver and communicate messages to students who, it is hoped, comprehend those messages and learn from them. The underlying assumption is that people learn *from* technology; that is, students learn from watching instructional films and television or responding to programmed instruction or computer-assisted instruction frames, just the same as they learn from listening to a lecture by the teacher. This view assumes that knowledge can be transmitted from the teacher to the student and that knowledge can be embedded in technology-based lessons and transmitted to the learner. So students learn *from* technology what the technology knows or has been taught, just as they learn from the teacher what the teacher knows.

In this book, we argue that students cannot learn what either teachers or technologies know. Rather, students learn from thinking—thinking about what they are doing or what they did, thinking about what they believe, thinking about what others have done and believe, thinking about the thinking processes they use—just thinking. Thinking mediates learning. Learning results from thinking.

How Technologies Foster Learning

If technology is used to support learning in the ways that we have described, then it will not be used as delivery vehicles. Rather, technologies should be used as engagers and facilitators of thinking and knowledge construction. Some useful roles for technologies in learning include:

- Technology as tools to support knowledge construction:
  - for representing learners' ideas, understandings, and beliefs
  - for producing organized, multimedia knowledge bases by learners
- Technology as information vehicle for exploring knowledge to support learning by constructing:
  - for accessing needed information
  - for comparing perspectives, beliefs, and worldviews
- Technology as context to support learning by doing:
  - for representing and simulating meaningful real-world problems, situations, and contexts
  - for representing beliefs, perspectives, arguments, and stories of others
  - for defining a safe, controllable problem space for student thinking
- Technology as social medium to support learning by conversing:
  - for collaborating with others
  - for discussing, arguing, and building consensus among members of a community
  - for supporting discourse among knowledge-building communities
- Technology as an intellectual partner (Jonassen, 2000) to support learning by reflecting:
  - for helping learners to articulate and represent what they know
  - for reflecting on what they have learned and how they came to know it
  - for supporting learners' internal negotiations and meaning making
  - for constructing personal representations of meaning
  - for supporting mindful thinking

As we will argue in chapter 2, technologies should be used to help learners to solve problems. Classroom technologies can best support problem solving by helping learners to access information, model the problems, and make decisions.

Each technology activity described in this book will be examined for the engagement of meaningful learning activities (active, constructive, intentional, authentic, and collaborative) as well as for their roles (accessing information, modeling the problems, and making decisions) in helping learners to solve problems.

IMPLICATIONS OF CONSTRUCTIVISM

Using technologies as constructivist tools assumes that our conceptions of education will change, that schools or classrooms (at least those that use technologies in the ways that we describe) will reform the educational process. Although few people would ever publicly admit that schools should not emphasize meaningful learning, most people in our society tacitly accept that schools do not. Intentional learning presupposes that parents, students, and teachers will realize this and demand more. They will demand change, so that thinking and problem solving (see chapter 2) are valued as much as memorizing. Technologies will not be the cause of the social change that is required for a renaissance in learning, but they can catalyze that change and support it if it comes.

Implications for Teachers

In order for students to learn *with* technology, teachers must accept and learn a new model of learning. Traditionally, teachers' primary responsibility and activity have been directly instructing students, where teachers were the purveyors of knowledge and students the recipients. That is, the teacher told the students what they knew and how they interpreted the world according to the curriculum, textbooks, and other resources they have studied. Teachers are hired and rewarded for their content expertise. This assumes that the ways in which teachers know the world are correct and should be emulated by the students. Students take notes on what teachers tell them and try to comprehend the world as their teachers do. Successful students develop conceptions more similar to teachers' conceptions. Learners will not be able to learn *with* technology in this kind of learning context. They will not be able to construct their own meaning and manage their own learning if teachers do it for them.

So, first and foremost, teachers must relinquish at least some of their authority, especially their intellectual authority. If teachers determine what is important for students to know, how they should know it, and how they should learn it, then students cannot become intentional, constructive learners. They aren't allowed. In those classroom contexts, there is no reason for students to make sense of the world—only to comprehend the teacher's understanding of it. We believe that the students' task should not be to understand the world as the teacher does. Rather, students should construct their own meaning for the world. If they do, then the teachers' roles shift from dispensing knowledge to helping learners construct more viable conceptions of the world. We said earlier that we believe that not all meaning is created equally. So the teacher needs to help students to discover what the larger community of scholars regards as meaningful conceptions and to evaluate their own beliefs and understandings in terms of those standards. Science teachers should help students comprehend the beliefs of the scientific community. Social studies teachers should examine with their students the values and beliefs that societies have constructed. In this role, the teacher is not the arbiter of knowledge but rather is a coach who helps students to engage in a larger community of scholars.

Teachers must also relinquish some of their authority in their management of learning. They cannot control all of the learning activities in the classroom. If teachers determine not only what is important for students to know, but how they should learn it, then students cannot be self-regulated learners. They aren't allowed.

Finally, teachers must gain some familiarity with the technology. They must gain skills and fluency with the technology. However, they will be most successful in helping students to learn *with* technology if they do not learn about the technologies in order to function as the expert. Rather, they should learn to coach the learning of technology skills. In many instances, teachers will be learning with the students. We have worked in many school situations where the students were constantly pushing our understanding of the technology. Often, we were barely keeping ahead of the students. They can and will learn *with* technologies, with or without the help of the teacher. That does not mean that as a teacher, you can abdicate any responsibility for learning the technologies. Rather, teachers should try not to be the expert all of the time.

These implications are very problematic for many teachers. They require that teachers assume new roles with different beliefs than they have traditionally pursued. Most teachers in most schools will find these implications challenging. We believe that the results will justify the risks. Just as teachers must assume new roles, learning *with* technology requires that students also assume new roles.

Implications for Students

If teachers relinquish authority, learners must assume it. Learners must develop skills in articulating, reflecting on, and evaluating what they know; setting goals for themselves (determining what is important to know) and regulating their activities and effort in order to achieve those goals; and collaborating and conversing with others so that the understanding of all students is enriched. Many students are not ready to assume that much responsibility. They do not want the power to determine their own destiny. It is much easier to allow others to regulate their lives for them. How skilled are students at setting their own agendas and pursuing them? Many students believe in their roles as passive recipients. However, our experience and the experience of virtually every researcher and educator involved with every technology project described in this book show that most students readily accept those responsibilities. When given the opportunity, students of all ages readily experiment with technologies, articulate their own beliefs, and construct, co-construct, and criticize each other's ideas. When learners are allowed to assume ownership of the product, they are diligent and persevering builders of knowledge.

Constructivist approaches to learning, with or without technology, are fraught with risks for students, parents, teachers, and administrators. Change always assumes risks. Many of the activities described in this book entail risks. We encourage you to take those risks. The excitement and enthusiasm generated by students while they construct their own understanding using technology-based tools are more than sufficient rewards for taking those risks.

CONCLUSIONS

An underlying assumption of this book is that the most productive and meaningful uses of technology will not occur if technologies are used in traditional ways—as delivery vehicles for instructional lessons. Technology cannot teach students. Rather, learners should use the technologies to teach themselves and others. Meaningful learning will result when technologies engage learners in:

- knowledge construction, not reproduction
- conversation, not reception
- articulation, not repetition
- collaboration, not competition
- reflection, not prescription.

After chapter 2, the remainder of this book describes how technology-based activities can support meaningful learning in schools from a constructivist perspective. While the focus of the book is K–12, most of the ideas we present are also valid for universities, corporations, and other learning agencies.

THINGS TO THINK ABOUT

If you would like to reflect on the ideas presented in this chapter, consider your responses to the following questions.

1 If learners cannot know what the teacher knows because they do not share a common knowledge and experience base, how can we be certain that students learn important things? For instance, if you want to teach students about the dangers of certain chemical reactions in the lab, how do we ensure that learners know and understand those important lessons?

2 What is your theory of learning? From your perspective, how do people learn?

3 Is it possible to learn (construct personal meaning) without engaging in some activity? That is, is it possible to learn simply by thinking about something? What are you thinking about? Can you think of an example?

4 When learners construct knowledge, what are they building? How is it possible to observe the fruits of their labor, that is, the knowledge they construct?

5 Think back to your childhood. What can you remember from your early childhood? Where did your remembrance occur? What meaning did it have at the time? How has that meaning changed over time?

6 Think about a recent controversial topic that you have heard or read about. What are the different sides arguing about? What do they believe? What assumptions do they make about what is causing the controversy? Where did those beliefs come from?

7 Radical constructivists argue that reality exists only in the mind of the knower. If that is true, is there a physical world that we live in? Prove it.

8 Some educators argue that we learn much more from our failures than from our successes. Why? They believe that we should put students in situations where their hypotheses or predictions fail. Can you think of a situation in which you learned a lot from a mistake?

9 Recall the last difficult problem that you had to solve. Did you solve it alone, or did you solicit the help of others? What did you learn from solving that problem? Can that learning be used again?

10 Can you learn to cook merely from watching cooking shows on television? What meaning do you make from the experiences that you observe? Will the experience that you have when you prepare a dish be the same as that of the television chef? How will it be different?

11 Technology is the application of scientific knowledge, according to many definitions. Can you think of a teaching technology (replicable, proven teaching process) that does not involve machines?

12 Can you calculate the exact square root of 2,570 without a calculator? Does the calculator make you smarter? Is the calculator intelligent?

13 Describe the thinking processes engaged by a short answer vs. a multiple-choice test question. Are the processes different? Are they assessing knowledge? Is that knowledge meaningful? Why or why not?

14 Can you think of an activity that makes you dumber, not smarter? Do you learn anything from that activity?

15 Have you ever produced your own video, movie, slide show, or computer program? How did it make you think? How did it make you feel?

REFERENCES

Becker, H. J. (1985). *How schools use microcomputers: Summary of a 1983 national survey.* (ERIC Document Reproduction Service No. ED 257448)

Brown, J. S., Collins, A., & Duguid, P. (1989, January–February). Situated cognition and the culture of learning. *Educational Researcher*, 32–42.

Clark, R. (1983). Reconsidering research on learning from media. *Review of Educational Research*, 53(4), 445–459.

Duffy, T. M., & Cunningham, D. C. (1996). Constructivism: Implications for the design and delivery of instruction. In D. H. Jonassen (Ed.), *Handbook of research on educational communications and technology*. New York: Scholastic.

Ennis, R. H. (1989). Critical thinking and subject specificity: Clarification and needed research. *Educational Researcher*, 18(3), 4–10.

Hadley, M., & Sheingold, K. (1993). Commonalities and distinctive patterns in teacher interation of computers. *American Journal of Education*, *101*(3), 261–315.

Jonassen, D. H. (1997). Instructional design models for well-structured and ill-structured problem-solving learning outcomes. *Educational Technology: Research and Development*.

Jonassen, D. H. (2000). *Computers as mindtools in schools*: *Engaging critical thinking*. Upper Saddle River, NJ: Merrill/Prentice Hall.

Jonassen, D. H. (2002). Learning as activity. *Educational Technology*, *42*(2), 45–51.

Lave, J., & Wenger, E. (1991). *Situated learning*: *Legitimate peripheral participation*. Cambridge, England: Cambridge University Press.

Leont'ev, A. (1972). The problem of activity in psychology. *Voprosy filosofii*, *9*, 95–108.

Paul, R. W. (1992). Critical thinking: What, why, and how. In C. A. Barnes (Ed.), *Critical thinking*: *Educational imperative*. San Francisco: Jossey-Bass.

Salomon, G. (1993). On the nature of pedagogic computer tools. The case of the wiring partner. In S. P. LaJoie & S. J. Derry (Eds.), *Computers as cognitive tools*. Hillsdale, NJ: Lawrence Erlbaum.

Schank, R. C. (1994). Goal-based scenarios. In R. C. Schank & E. Langer (Eds.), *Beliefs, reasoning, and decision making*: *Psychologic in honor of Bob Abelson*. Hillsdale, NJ: Lawrence Erlbaum.

Schnotz, W., Vosniadou, S., & Carretero, M. (1999). *New perspectives on conceptual change*. Amsterdam: Pergamon.

CHAPTER **2**

Problem Solving Is Meaningful Learning

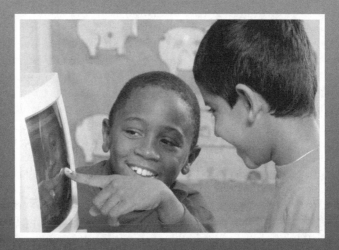

WHAT DRIVES LEARNING?

What drives learning as much or more than anything is the nature of the task or activity that learners are engaged in. Memorizing information for a test engages learners in rehearsal and perhaps some organizational activities. Writing a paper requires information seeking and organizing, thesis generation, and a host of writing processes. It is the nature of the task that students intend to perform that will best determine the nature of the learning that students will complete. In order for students to learn meaningfully, they must be willfully engaged in a meaningful task. According to our conception of learning described in chapter 1, the goal or intention of the task should require active, constructive, intentional, authentic, and cooperative learning activities. What kinds of tasks do that?

The most consistently meaningful tasks, both in school and out, require people to solve problems. People in everyday situations and professional contexts regularly solve problems. In business, professionals are paid for solving problems, not memorizing information for tests. At home, problems are everywhere (how can we afford something?; what's wrong with the heater?; which health plan do we subscribe to?; how can we keep the dog off the couch?; etc.). When people are solving problems in those settings, they are learning meaningfully because the task is meaningful. The task is meaningful because they want to solve the problem. In order to solve the problem, they must understand what the problem is about, as well as various solution options, outcomes, inferences, and so on.

Solving problems can also be the most meaningful kind of learning activity in formal educational settings. We believe that the primary, if not exclusive, purpose of all education should be to teach students to solve problems. Why? Because the nonschool world (everyday life, business, hobbies, organizations) demands competent problem solvers. Requiring learners to memorize for tests is a waste of valuable school time and an insult to learners, and it models and systemically retards intellectual development. That is, requiring students to memorize for a test ensures that they will not develop intellectually. Is that what we really want to do?

Just what is a problem? There are only two critical attributes of a problem. First, a problem is an unknown. If we have a goal and do not know how to reach that goal, there is an unknown, so we have a problem. Second, finding the unknown must have some social, cultural, or intellectual value to someone. If no one believes that it is worth finding the unknown, there is no perceived problem. Finding the unknown is the process of problem solving.

Kinds of Problem Solving

Jonassen (2000b) articulated a typology of 11 different kinds of problems, including logical problems, algorithmic problems, story problems, rule-using problems, decision-making, troubleshooting, diagnosis-solution problems, tactical/strategic performance, case/system analysis problems, design problems, and dilemmas. This range of problem types describes a continuum of problems from well-structured to ill-structured. That is, algorithms and story problems are well-structured problems.

What does that mean? Well-structured problems typically present all elements of the problem; engage a limited number of rules and principles that are organized in a predictive and prescriptive arrangement; possess correct, convergent answers; and have a preferred, prescribed solution process (Jonassen, 1997). Problems like systems analysis, design, and dilemmas are ill-structured. Ill-structured problems may have many alternative solutions, vaguely defined or unclear goals and unstated constraints, and multiple criteria for evaluating solutions. Sometimes referred to as "wicked" problems, ill-structured problems often require learners to express personal opinions or beliefs about the problem.

Within each of these categories, problems vary in their complexity. Although ill-structured problems tend to be more complex, well-structured problems can sometimes be complex as well, whereas ill-structured problems, like dilemmas, can be fairly simple. We will briefly describe each kind of problem next.

Logical Problems   Logical problems tend to be abstract tests of logic that puzzle the learner. They are used to assess mental acuity, clarity, and logical reasoning. Classic games such as Missionaries and Cannibals or Tower of Hanoi challenge learners to find the most efficient (least number of moves) sequence of action. In order to solve logic problems, learners must determine the specific method of reasoning that will yield the most efficient solution. Logic problems are used most frequently to research problem-solving processes; however, because of their abstract nature, the skills required to solve them do not generally transfer to everyday or professional problems.

Algorithmic Problems   One of the most common problem types encountered in schools is the algorithm. Most common in mathematics courses, students are taught to solve problems using a finite and rigid set of procedures with limited, predictive decisions. The calculations required to solve these problems require comprehension of the operations, execution procedures, and retrieval of arithmetic facts (McCloskey, Caramaza, & Basili, 1985). Such algorithmic approaches are also commonly used in science courses (setting up an experiment) or home economics (calculating quantities needed for recipes). Algorithmic problems are also solved in everyday settings (procedures for installing software or assembling a toy).

The primary limitation of algorithmic approaches is the overreliance on procedural knowledge structures and the lack or absence of conceptual understanding of the objects of the algorithm and the procedures engaged. Content that is learned only as a procedure can rarely be transferred because of a lack of conceptual understanding of the underlying processes.

Story Problems   In an attempt to situate algorithms in some kind of context, many textbook authors and teachers employ story problems. This usually takes the form of embedding the values needed to solve an algorithm into a brief narrative or situation. Look at the end of most textbook chapters for examples. In order to solve story problems, learners try to select the most appropriate formula for solving the problem, extract the values from the narrative, and insert them into the formula, solving for the unknown quantity. This method does not promote transfer. In order to transfer story problem solving effectively, learners need to understand the structure of the problem, the conceptual underpinnings of that structure, and how the structure relates to the situation described in the problem (Jonassen, in press). Most of the research that has been conducted about problem solving has focused on story problems, yet they are not authentic and bear little resemblance to any kind of problems that people solve in nonschool contexts.

Rule-Using Problems   Many problems have correct solutions but multiple methods and uncertain outcomes. They tend to have a clear purpose or goal that is constrained but not restricted to a specific rule-oriented procedure or method. Rule-using problems can be as simple as setting a table and as complex as completing tax return schedules. Using an online search system to locate relevant information on the World Wide Web is an example of a rule-using problem. The purpose is clear: find the most relevant information in the least amount of time. That requires selecting search terms, constructing effective search arguments, implementing the search strategy, and evaluating the utility and credibility of information found. The outcome is not certain, however; it depends on how well the learner applies the rules that define the search process—that is, how effective the search terms are, whether the terms are connected by the appropriate Boolean connectors, and so on. Given that there are multiple search strategies that are possible, rule-using problems can become decidedly more ill-structured.

Decision-Making Problems   Decision-making problems are usually constrained to decisions with a limited number of solutions. For instance, which health plan do we select? Which depreciation schedule will optimize short-term profits? Although these problems have a limited number of solutions, the number of factors to be considered in deciding among those solutions as well as the weights assigned to them can be very complex. Decision problems usually require comparing and contrasting the advantages and disadvantages of alternate solutions. Decisions are justified in terms of the weighting of those factors.

Troubleshooting Problems   Troubleshooting is one of the most common forms of everyday problem solving. Maintaining complex computer equipment or debugging a computer program requires troubleshooting skills. The primary purpose of troubleshooting is to diagnose a fault in a system and replace it. Some part of a system is not functioning properly, resulting in a set of symptoms that have to be diagnosed and matched with the user's knowledge of various fault states. Troubleshooters use symptoms to generate and test hypotheses about different fault states. Troubleshooting requires a combination of domain or system knowledge as well as troubleshooting strategies and procedural knowledge of test methods. These skills are integrated and organized by the troubleshooter's experiences. More experienced troubleshooters are generally better troubleshooters.

Diagnosis-Solution Problems   Diagnosis-solution problems are similar to troubleshooting. Most diagnosis-solution problems require identifying a fault state, just like troubleshooting. However, in troubleshooting the goal is to repair the fault and get the system back online as soon as possible, so the solution strategies are more restrictive. Diagnosis-solution problems usually begin with a fault state similar to troubleshooting (e.g., symptoms of a sick person). The physician examines the patient and considers patient history before making an initial diagnosis. In a spiral of data collection, hypothesis generation, and testing, the physician focuses on a specific problem. At that point, the physician must suggest a solution. Frequently, there are multiple solutions and solution paths, so the physician must justify a particular solution. It is this ambiguity in solution paths that distinguishes diagnosis-solution problems from troubleshooting.

Tactical/Strategic Performance   Tactical-strategic performance requires real-time, complex decision making where the performers apply a number of tactical activities to meet a more complex and ill-structured strategy while maintaining situational awareness. In order to achieve the strategic objective, such as flying a military airplane in combat or quarterbacking a professional football offense, the performer applies a set of complex tactical activities that are designed to meet strategic objectives. Strategy formation represents a systems analysis or design problem (described next). Meeting that strategy through tactical maneuvers is a tactical performance. Typically there are a finite number of tactical activities that have been designed to accomplish the strategy; however, the mark of an expert tactical performer is his or her ability to improvise or construct new tactics on the spot to meet the strategy. The negotiator who takes a chance while negotiating a treaty is selecting a new tactic to meet the strategy. Tactical performances can be quite complex.

Case/Systems Analysis Problems   Systems analysis problems require learners to understand complex, multifaceted situations. What makes these problems difficult to solve is that it is not always clear what the problem is. Because defining the problem space is more ambiguous, these problems are more ill-structured. These are commonly found in professional contexts. Systems analysis problems require the learner to articulate the nature of the problem and the different perspectives that impact the problem before suggesting solutions (Jonassen, 1997). Their solutions rely on an analysis of contextual factors. Solving business problems, including planning production, are common case problems. Deciding production levels, for instance, requires balancing human resources, technologies, inventory, and sales (Jonassen, Prevish, Christy, & Stavrulaki, 1999). Classical systems analysis problems also exist in politics, ecology, sociology, and most other social sciences. Their solutions typically require knowledge of several fields of study. Learners must also learn to argue for and justify their solutions.

Design Problems   One of the most ill-structured kinds of problems is designing something. Whether it be an electronic circuit, a house, or any other product or system, designing requires applying a great deal of domain knowledge with a lot of strategic knowledge resulting in an original design. Instructional design is a classic example of ill-structured problem solving. Despite our allegiance to design models, given any instructional design problem, there are an infinite number of possible solutions to that problem. And, despite claims to the contrary, there is not a sufficient research base to support any model in diverse settings. It is rarely clear to inexperienced designers which model is most appropriate. Nor are the criteria for the best solution always obvious, so skills in argumentation and justification help designers to rationalize their designs. Although designers always hope for the best solution, the best solution is seldom ever known. In addition to being ill-structured, most design problems are complex, requiring the designer to balance many needs and constraints in the design. The importance of design problems cannot be diminished. Most professionals get paid for designing things (products, systems, etc.), not for taking examinations. More experience with design problems in formal curricula is an important goal.

Dilemmas   Dilemmas or issue-based problems are the most ill-structured and unpredictable, often because there is no solution that will ever be acceptable to a significant portion of the people affected by the problem. The continuing crisis in the Middle East is a prime example of a dilemma problem. Usually there are many valuable perspectives on the situation (military, political, social, ethical, etc.); however, none is able to offer a generally acceptable solution to the crisis. The situation is so complex and unpredictable that no best solution can ever be known. That does not mean that there are not any solutions that can be attempted with variable degrees of success; however, none will ever meet the needs of the majority of people or escape the prospects of catastrophe. Dilemmas are often complex, social situations with conflicting perspectives, and they are usually the most vexing of problems.

Summary   The purpose for describing these kinds of problem solving was not for you to memorize them. Rather, we wanted to demonstrate to you the range and complexity of problem solving as an activity. You may have inferred, as we have, that the most interesting problems come from the nonschool world. We fervently believe that whenever possible, those nonschool problems should be used as the purpose for learning in schools. That is, rather than studying content as prescribed by the curriculum (content that has little meaning to students because they have no explicit, let alone implicit, purpose for studying it), classrooms should import problems from the real world and work on solving them in the classroom. No one expects classrooms to solve those problems, though you never know.

Where do you as a teacher find such problems? Abandoning curricular content is scary without some focus. So, if you try problem-based instruction, where do you get the problems? Problems are everywhere. Your school is full of problems, as is your community. Pick up any daily newspaper, and the front pages contain information about numerous local, regional, national, and international problems. At a local level, questions abound, like where should the new school be built? How can we improve the performance of the football team? How can we get the city council to pass a needed referendum? These problems, when investigated, may have the most meaning for students. However, there are also numerous global problems. The Union of International Associations (www.uia.org) maintains a database of over 26,000 problems that plague the world. If they do not comprise a sufficient curriculum, then you have way too much time on your hands.

The point is simple: problem solving is more interesting than memorizing. When trying to solve a problem, students assume ownership of the problem and often expend far more effort in understanding the content surrounding that problem than they would without such a purpose. That is, they are conceptually engaged (Dole & Sinatra, 1998). The purpose of this book is to show you how technologies can be used to help students learn meaningfully through problem solving. This book cannot teach you how to use technology to solve all of these kinds of problems. Why? Because we do not yet know how to do that, and even if we did, it would require a monstrously large book.

PROBLEM SOLVING WITH TECHNOLOGY

We do believe that technologies can play very important roles in helping learners to solve problems. But first, you must identify problems and challenge your students to solve them. If students accept the challenge, then technologies described in this book will help them to seek information needed to solve the problem, model the system or domain in which the problem occurs, make decisions about how to solve these problems, and design different technology-enhanced representations of those systems. We will briefly describe these kinds of problem-solving activities. Throughout the remainder of the book, we will analyze the different learning activities that we recommend in terms of the kinds of problem-solving processes engaged, along with the kinds of meaningful learning processes (described in chapter 1) engaged.

Information Searching

Too many educators tacitly equate information searching with learning. They believe that if students are busily searching for information online, they will naturally make sense of what they find. To that end, many teachers provide WebQuests to guide the students' searching through the morass of information on the World Wide Web. When students complete the information quests, teachers believe that they have learned. We do not agree, nor do others (Fidel et al., 1999; Schacter, Chung, & Dorr, 1998) whose research has found that when students search for predetermined answers and copy them down, they are not comprehending or reflecting on the meaning of what they have found. Their intention is to complete the assignment—to find the one answer that the teacher is looking for. This searching for the "right" answer results in fast clicking with no possibility for learning. Simply asking students to find information on the Web will probably not result in learning.

Yet, information searching is essential to meaning making and problem solving. In order to learn from information being sought, students must have an intention to find information that will help them to solve a problem. They must have a purpose other than fulfilling the requirements of an assignment. Intentional information searching requires at least a four-step process: (a) plan; (b) use strategies to search the Web; (c) evaluate; and (d) triangulate sources (Jonassen & Colaric, 2001).

In planning a search, students are required to identify what they need to know. First, students should articulate their intentions and verbalize what they are looking for, as well as *why* that information is needed. This thought-process activates knowledge that the learner already has and clarifies for the learner the dissonance that exists. Next, the learner must develop a conscious and intentional search strategy in order to locate information sources that may be useful. Selection of search terms can be a difficult process. It will be necessary for you, the teacher, to model the process of asking questions such as who, where, when, and what in order to identify search terms that are associated with the problem. These terms can then be developed into a search string that would be appropriate to use in a search engine.

When Web sites are located, the information contained in them must be evaluated. That evaluation process should engage the learner in two separate aspects of evaluation—relevancy and credibility. First, is the information on the site related to the problem? Does it contribute to the intention of the search? That is, does the site contain information that pertains to the learner's expressed intention? Does it provide an explanation, examples, alternative perspectives, or other pieces of information that the learner can use to construct their own knowledge?

Second, it is necessary that learners evaluate the credibility of the information. Evaluation of credibility usually involves two processes—evaluating the source of the information and evaluating the treatment of the subject. The teacher can model for the students the process of dissecting a Web site and should provide guiding questions to help students identify what to look for. In fact, the use of guiding questions to prime students to evaluate information more closely has been shown to be effective in children as young as 5. Examples of questions to evaluate the source of the information include:

- Does the site author have authority in that field?
- If the site is published by an organization, is it one you recognize?
- Does the organization have a vested interest or bias concerning the information presented?
- Is the site owner affiliated with an organization (such as an educational institution or government agency) that has authority in the stated subject area?
- Is it clear when the site was developed and last updated?
- Is a bibliography or resource list included?
- Are the references used in the bibliography credible?

Examples of questions to evaluate the treatment of the subject include:

- Is the content factual or opinion?
- Does it follow a logical presentation of sequence?

- Is the intended audience clear?
- Are there any gaps in logic or is there missing information that is relevant to the subject?
- Are there political or ideological biases?
- Is this primarily an advertising or marketing site?
- Is the language used inflammatory or extreme?
- Is the text well written? Are there misspellings or is poor grammar used?

In asking the learner to evaluate for relevancy and credibility, you are asking him or her to engage in reflective thinking about what is really needed and what is missing. You are also asking the student to question the authority of the documents and to become more information literate by critically evaluating sources of information. A final step in this process is to triangulate the search—identify at least two other sources that verify the information found.

Problem solving almost always requires information searching. Problem solvers must understand the problem area well enough to be able to generate solution alternatives. However, information searching does not necessarily imply problem solving. In fact, most technology-enhanced information does not even result in comprehension, let alone problem solving. Why? Because students are not fulfilling their information needs. They are satisfying the teacher's requirement. Stated differently, information searching is a necessary but not a sufficient requirement for problem solving. In order to understand a problem, students must construct some kind of model of the problem.

Modeling Tasks or Content

Understanding is difficult to assess. How do you know when a student understands something? How do you know if he or she really understands it? It is never clear, but we do know that in order to really understand something, people construct a mental model of that thing. Mental models are mental representations that include different kinds of knowledge about a domain or phenomenon, such as visual-spatial, structural, and even metaphorical. A good mental model allows someone to "see the problem" in such a way that his or her model of the phenomena can be tested.

Constructing mental models of a phenomenon or a domain can be facilitated by building technology-enhanced models of the same. Building models of real-world phenomena is at the heart of scientific thinking and requires diverse mental activities such as planning, data collecting, collaborating and accessing information, data visualizing, modeling, and reporting (Soloway, Krajcik, & Finkel, 1995). Different classes of software exist for building your models of phenomena. In *Computers as Mindtools for Schools: Engaging Critical Thinking*, Jonassen (2000a), describes several classes of tools for modeling one's knowledge, including databases, semantic networking, spreadsheets, expert systems, system modeling tools, hypermedia, visualization tools, and microworlds. Chapter 8 in this book describes one of the more popular of those tools, semantic networking or concept mapping. Each tool enables learners to construct different kinds of models of what they know.

A complete mental model might be thought of as the combination of all of those kinds of models. Modeling is critical to understanding. Experts, those who know the best, represent what they know in multiple ways. Using technologies to help students to represent what they are learning will definitely lead to greater understanding. We also know that the most important part of the problem-solving process is representing the problem space. These tools can be used to help students create models of problems in order to more effectively solve them.

Decision Making

Everyday life is full of decisions. Some are easy (what shall we have for dinner this evening?) and others are quite complex (which health plan should I select to provide maximum benefits to my entire family?). Decision making is both a kind of problem and a process in more complex kinds of problem solving. Deciding which kind of car to buy is an example of a decision-making problem. Getting the maximum functionality or ego gratification for all drivers while maintaining a budget can be a vexing example of a decision problem. Simple decisions with a single solution and a limited number of choices are more likely to be solved through some form of rational analysis. More complex kinds of problem solving, like diagnosing a medical case, involves many decisions as part of the problem-solving process (which test should I order? what manner should I take with the patient? etc.). Those decisions require that the problem solver make multiple decisions under risk and uncertainty.

Decision-making problems typically involve selecting a single option from a set of alternatives based on a set of criteria. Decision makers must choose from a set of alternatives, each of which has one or more consequences. Mullen and Roth (1991) describe decision making as a process that includes problem recognition and values analysis (changing the present course of one's life for opportunity or to avoid detriment); generating alternative choices (gathering information about choices); evaluating choices (identifying best choice or satisfying some external criteria by analyzing cost and benefits of outcomes); and committing to the choice while ignoring effort already expended.

Technologies can also aid in decision making. As described in the previous section, technologies can be used to model decision situations. Those models can be used to test predictions about the outcomes of different choices. Technologies can also be used in gathering and representing different perspectives about the decision. Chapter 4 describes a number of synchronous and asynchronous technologies for soliciting input about decisions. Those perspectives can also be represented using technology-enhanced decision-making aids. So, decision making often represents a distinct problem and frequently is part of other problem-solving processes.

Designing

Design problems are usually among the most complex and ill-structured kinds of problems that we ever encounter. Why are they so ill-structured? Because for most design problems, we are uncertain what the goals are, let alone the solution. An architect knows, for instance, that she is designing a house. But there are an infinite number of designs for houses. So, the designer must expend a great deal of effort in identifying what the problem is. Designers do that by identifying constraints in the design. A house, for example, must accommodate a certain number of people, meet budgetary constraints, have a certain feel, and meet various local code requirements. Whether it be a house, an electronic circuit, a new menu item for a restaurant, a musical composition, an essay, or any other product or system, designing requires applying knowledge from multiple domains. Most design problems cannot be solved using knowledge from a single domain.

Another reason why design problems are so ill-structured is that there is limited or delayed feedback from the world. When feedback is provided, the answers tend to be neither right nor wrong, only better or worse. Success is determined only by the acceptance of the product that is designed. The customers either like it or they don't, and often they are unable to articulate why.

Every technology included in this book can engage students in design problem solving. Whether the students are creating a video or designing a Web page or multimedia program, they are necessarily engaged in design. Students will be required to accomplish information searching, modeling, and decision making in order to design technology productions. Although design problems are the most ill-structured and often the most complex kinds of problems, they are also the most engaging. When students are designing and producing their multimedia and Web pages, for instance, they have ownership of the process and product as well as the ideas contained therein. Ownership is the key to constructivism. Ownership usually entails commitment, pride, and satisfaction. Those are desirable outcomes from any learning experience.

THINGS TO THINK ABOUT

If you would like to reflect on the ideas presented in this chapter, consider your responses to the following questions.

What do you know the most about? That is, what topic or skills might you consider yourself to be an expert on? What is your mental model of that topic? How many ways do you know about that topic? Can you see examples of it? Can you predict what will happen if you make changes in that model?

REFERENCES

Dole, J. A. & Sinatra, G. M. (1998). Reconceptualizing change in the cognitive construction of knowledge. *Educational Psychologist, 33*(213), 109–128.

Fidel, R., Davies, R. K., Douglass, M. H., Kohlder, J. K., Hopkins, C. J., Kushner, E. J., et al. (1999). A visit to the information mall: Web searching behavior of high school students. *Journal of the American Society for Information Science, 50*(1), 24–37.

Jonassen, D. H. (1997). Instructional design model for well-structured and ill-structured problem-solving learning outcomes. *Educational*

Technology: Research and Development 45(1), 65–95.

Jonassen, D. H. (2000a). *Computers as mindtools for schools: Engaging critical thinking.* Upper Saddle River, NJ: Prentice Hall.

Jonassen, D. H. (2000b). Toward a design theory of problem solving. *Educational Technology: Research & Development, 48*(4), 63–85.

Jonassen, D. H. (in press). Designing instruction for story problems. *Educational Technology: Research & Development.*

Jonassen, D. H., & Colaric, S. (2001). Information landfills contain knowledge; searching equals learning; hyperlinking is good instruction; and other myths about learning from the Internet. *Computers in Schools, 17*(3/4), Part I, 159–170.

Jonassen, D., Prevish, T., Christy, D., & Stavrulaki, E. (1999). Learning to solve problems on the Web: Aggregate planning in a business management course. *Distance Education: An International Journal, 20*(1), 49–63.

McCloskey, M., Caramaza, A., & Basili, A. (1985). Cognitive mechanisms in number processing and calculation: Evidence from dyscalculia. *Brain and Cognition, 4,* 171–196.

Mullen, J. D., & Roth, B. M. (1991). *Decision-making: Its logic and practice.* Savage, MD: Rowman & Littlefield.

Schacter, J., Chung, G. K. W. K., & Dorr, A. (1998). Children's Internet searching on complex problems: Performance and process analyses. *Journal of the American Society for Information Science, 49,* 840–850.

Learning From the Internet: Information to Knowledge Through Inquiry

In *The Power of the Internet for Learning,* a report of the Web-Based Education Commission to the president and Congress of the United States (2000), Senator Bob Kerrey and Representative Johnny Isakson say,

> The Internet is a powerful new means of communication. It is global, it is fast, and it is growing rapidly. Reaching to the far corners of the earth, the Internet is making the world at once smaller and more connected, transmitting information at nearly real-time speed. An estimated 377 million people are currently using the Internet, only half of whom are in the United States. The World Wide Web is bringing rapid and radical change into our lives—from the wonderfully beneficial to the terrifyingly difficult. (p. i)

What kinds of change will the World Wide Web (WWW) cause in education? While the Internet is certainly a great source of information and holds the power to connect people around the world, its incredible potential as a learning environment to support constructive learning is often underutilized.

The Internet can immerse students in stimulating, challenging, motivating, vibrant learning environments that provide a context in which computer literacy develops, not as a goal but as a requirement in order to achieve much higher goals. As President George W. Bush (2001) states in his education plan, "The Administration believes schools should use technology as a tool to improve academic achievement, and that using the latest technology in the classroom should not be an end unto itself." We believe that technology can help students develop both academically and personally. The skills and attributes of successful professionals in the future (what Costa and Kallick [2000] call "habits of mind") include, but are not limited to, creativity, problem solving, global awareness, respectful skepticism, cooperation, responsibility, independence, self-discipline, ethics, systems thinking, and (of course) conventional and technological literacy.

Scardamalia and Bereiter (1999) argue that although the purpose of schools is to support learning, most schools could not be characterized as true learning organizations from an organizational standpoint. In considering how schools could be reformed, they ask, "What kind of education will best prepare students for life in a knowledge society? Typical answers to this question list characteristics that such education should foster: flexibility, creativity, problem-solving ability, technological literacy, information-finding skills, and above all a lifelong readiness to learn."

In *Getting America's Students Ready for the 21st Century,* an unnamed high school student succinctly described the real power of technologies:

> Exposure to computers has changed the type of student I am and my methods for attacking problems. I now gain a far better understanding of the topics I pursue, and discover links and connections between them. (1996, p. 20)

We believe that the Internet, if used to engage learners in meaningful learning, has the potential to transform education.

WHAT IS THE INTERNET?

The Internet is a worldwide *network of networks* composed of thousands of smaller regional networks connecting millions of users in more than 90 nations around the globe. These regional networks are composed of still smaller networks that serve institutions, businesses, and individuals who connect their computers to the regional networks via modems and telephone lines. To gain access to the Internet, you need to connect your computer to a network that is part of the Internet, or contact an *access provider* that will allow you to connect to its network for a fee.

The computers on the Internet fall into two main categories: *servers* and *clients*. Servers are computers that offer information to users who access the information using their *client* machines. It's sort of like a high-speed, universal, electronic library system, in which requests from patrons are quickly answered. The servers are like the libraries, and the clients are like the library patrons. Here's how it works.

Each computer on the Internet has a *name*, which may be thought of as an address that uniquely identifies it. Each segment of information made available to the public has a *Universal Resource Locator* (URL), which functions like an address and includes the address of the server on which it is located. You (and the millions of other Internet users) request a certain piece of information by sending a request that contains the address of the desired information to the appropriate server. The server then sends an electronic copy of the information to your computer's address, where *browser* software (such as Netscape or Internet Explorer) displays it for you. People talk about the Internet as if they were *going to* an address, using analogies such as *surfing* from one place to another. In reality, the information comes to you.

As more and more Web pages are published, there is an increasing demand for unique name identification. In 2000, the first new top-level domain types (other than country codes) since 1988 were added: .aero, .biz, .coop, .info, .museum, and .name. See the Internet Corporation for Assigned Names and Numbers (http://www.icann.org/) for complete listings of all domain and country codes. Here is a list of other common domain and country codes:

Code	Country	Code	Type
.au	Australia	.com	Commercial
.ca	Canada	.edu	Educational
.ch	Switzerland	.gov	Governmental
.de	Germany	.int	International
.dk	Denmark	.mil	Military
.es	Spain	.net	Internet resource
.fr	France	.org	Nonprofit organization
.il	Israel	.k12	Public school
.it	Italy		
.jp	Japan		
.mx	Mexico		
.nz	New Zealand		

Code	Country
.pl	Poland
.ru	Russia
.tr	Turkey
.uk	United Kingdom
.us	United States
.va	Vatican

What's on the Internet and How Is It Managed?

Most people are less interested in the Internet than they are in the resources and opportunities made available by it. In its early days, the Internet allowed users to send and access text documents only. In 1993, the first widely adopted browser with a graphical interface (Mosaic) was created. Now, in addition to delivery of images, the Internet is being used to deliver animations, sounds, music, telephone calls, and video. Technological advances have flung open the doors to opportunities unimaginable just a few years ago. Streaming audio and video offer not only linked files, but also access to real-time media delivery.

Access to the Internet usually means access to electronic mail, information resources, electronic conversations in the form of asynchronous bulletin boards and synchronous chat or videoconferencing, and the ability to transfer files from computer to computer and from person to person. These capabilities are being used to inform, to teach, to sell, to connect people, and more.

Think of the WWW as the sum of all documents stored using a multimedia format (hypertext transfer protocol, or HTTP) and made accessible via the Internet. Just as nobody owns the Internet, nobody owns the WWW. Because nobody owns the Internet, there is no single governing body that controls what happens on it or to it. Hundreds of thousands of people around the world make information they create and harvest available to the computer users of the world from their homes, workplaces, and schools.

The Web's vast archive of information in text, image, sound, and video formats and its ability to provide links that tie related information together (no matter where in the world it is stored) have captured the attention of educators, and the millions of people (potential consumers) who use the Internet have captured the imagination of businesses. Both the resources and the people the Internet brings to the learning enterprise excite educators who seek to provide stimulating learning environments to their students. The connection of millions of people (thinkers, as opposed to consumers) in a real-time environment has opened fantastic potential for human communication and exploration. And, when combined with a vast array of information at the student's fingertips, the possibilities for exploration and growth seem almost limitless.

What's New With the Internet?

In a national report of the Web-Based Education Committee (2000), several technology trends were noted. Table 3.1 represents the direction in which Internet technology is moving.

Table 3.1 Internet Technology Trends

Moving from:	Moving to:
Narrowband	Broadband
Plain, single mode (e.g., text or speech)	Multimodal rich connectivity
Tethered (wired) access	Untethered (wireless) access
Users adapting to the technology	The technology adapting to the user

Internet technology is becoming faster, multifaceted, and more user-friendly. Let's take a look at some recent developments.

Increased Access, Bandwidth, and Multimedia Classroom access to the Internet has increased dramatically since 1994 when only 35% of public elementary and secondary schools and 3% of public school classrooms had access to the Internet. By 1999, 95% of schools and 63% of classrooms had access to the Internet, an increase of 60%. On average, this provides one instructional computer with an Internet connection for every nine students (Williams, 2000). In 2001, the market research firm Quality Education Data reported that 97% of public schools in the United States now have Internet connectivity, 84% of public school classrooms are online, and 90% of teachers use the Internet as a teaching resource.

Much of what can be done through the Internet has been dependent on the speed of transmission. One of the most exciting advances in the Internet's evolution is the increase in bandwidth available with cable modems, Asynchronous Digital Subscriber Line (ADSL) telephone lines, wireless connections, and Internet2. Picture a narrow water pipe allowing a trickle of water. Now imagine that pipe expanded so that the trickle becomes a torrent. Increased bandwidth capability enables larger quantities of data to be moved more smoothly and rapidly from servers to users. In the past, multimedia files such as audio and video have often been choppy as parts of the files (data packets) were dropped because data outstripped the capability of transmission speed. The speedier data flow enabled by faster connections allows seamless streaming audio and video.

Streaming multimedia is now integrated in browser software as helper applications (plug-ins) such as RealPlayer and Windows Media Player that automatically play multimedia files when they are encountered. These helper applications enable features such as Scholastic's Teacher Radio (http://teacher.scholastic.com/teacherradio/index.htm), a weekly audio magazine. Teacher Radio features News Zone Radio, hosted by kids and facilitating global connections. For instance, on International Kid-to-Kid News, five Senegalese students discussed issues in their country including pollution, kidnapping, water conservation, and peace.

Videoconferences: Virtually Being There   Recent advances in computer and telecommunications technologies include compressed video systems that support Internet-based videoconferencing. Using a computer, camera, microphone, and speaker, people can communicate in affordable two-way connections. Because an Internet-based connection shares or competes for bandwidth with other Internet data, users on slow networks may encounter delays resulting in jerky video and audio clipping. However, many schools, libraries, and other institutions are experiencing better results with Internet Protocol (IP) videoconferencing as high-bandwidth networks are developed.

H. 323 is a standard that specifies the components, protocols, and procedures that provide multimedia communication services—real-time audio, video, and data communications—over packet networks, including IP-based networks (http://www.iec.org/online/tutorials/h323/). Whereas videoconferencing with H. 323 provides high-quality data transmission using equipment based on H. 323 protocol, even less expensive webcams are becoming widely used on the Internet. These small video recorders attached to a computer can provide live video of weather conditions, animal habitats, and student-to-student interactions.

For example, the Cornell Lab of Ornithology provides live video cameras coupled with Internet technology that allow students to observe and interpret the nesting behaviors of cavity-nesting birds and promote understanding of their breeding biology. Pictures are taken periodically (approximately once a minute during daylight hours) and uploaded to a server where they are accessible through their Web site. Figure 3.1 shows an example of an owl sitting in her nestbox (http://birds.cornell.edu/birdhouse/nestboxcam/).

For a listing of hundreds of webcams arranged by category, visit EarthCam (http://www.earthcam.com). See chapter 5 for more information about videoconferencing.

Florida
Barn Owl Cam
(Tyto alba)

The Barn Owls are at it again! On December 18th, our cam host in Florida discovered another active nest! The female is currently sitting on EIGHT eggs!

View Winter 2001-02 Barn Owl archives

Automatically updating pop-up window

Figure 3.1   Barn Owl Nesting (Photo courtesy of Cornell Lab of Ornithology)

Internet2   The Internet that we know and use was developed by a partnership among government, industry, and academia. The e-mail and WWW that we enjoy today were originally developed to allow collaboration among researchers. Internet2 is a similar collaborative initiative, established in 1997, that is using increased bandwidth as it develops advanced network applications and technologies that will become the Internet of tomorrow. Among the advanced technologies enabled by Internet2 are exciting possibilities such as virtual laboratories, multicasting of streaming video, high-fidelity videoconferencing, and digital libraries with high-quality, on-demand delivery of multimedia information. One of the main goals of Internet2 is widely transferring these new applications of technology to the education community.

You can find out more about Internet2 on the Internet2 Web sites at http://www.internet2.edu/ and http://apps.internet2.edu/, where examples of Internet2 applications are showcased. Past showcases of Internet2 projects included teleimmersion with a live distributed musical and live HDTV presentation.

Wireless and Human-Centric Computing   Until recently, wires, cables, and computer size have placed limits on using the Internet. Computers needed to be hard-wired to Internet connections through telephone lines or Ethernet. Implementing wireless communication through radiowave, infrared, microwave, and 3G (third generation) reduces cost and requires less space than traditional wired communication technology. It also removes the physical constraints of being place-bound. Wireless users are no longer tethered in one place by cables and connections.

Apple's AirPort is an example of a wireless local area network (LAN) that uses radio frequencies to communicate between AirPort-enabled computers and a school's existing network. An AirPort Base Station connected directly to an Ethernet network allows computers with an AirPort card to access the network from up to 150 feet away from the base station. High-speed file sharing between computers is also possible (http://www.apple.com/airport/).

Wireless networks enable students and teachers to access the school network and Internet anywhere in the building without being "plugged in." Imagine a classroom of students, each with a laptop computer that is connected to the Internet via a wireless network. As the teacher projects the National Geographics' Xpeditions Web site on a Smartboard, students follow on their personal computers and explore different areas in small groups. Students can bookmark Web sites, take notes, write reports, and create multimedia presentations on their personal computers. They can walk down the hall to the media center with a laptop, find print resources, and access the Internet again.

In the future, we can expect designers to continue shrinking the size of wireless technology and offering wearable devices. Wireless technology will combine the functionality of what is now separated into several devices such as cellular phones and personal digital assistants (PDA).

While graphing calculators are becoming widely used, the potential of alternate devices such as Palm and Handspring Visor handhelds may enable children to engage in flexible learning environments that permeate their daily lives (Inkpen, 1999). These inexpensive, miniaturized devices are the size of a pocket calculator. While teachers are finding handhelds useful for administrative tasks such as gradebooks and attendance, their potential as a learning tool is in its infancy. An example of handheld use is Edge Lab (Exploring Dynamic Groupware Environments) who designed Geney, a collaborative problem-solving application to help children explore genetics concepts. The Geney application, designed for handheld computers, is downloaded by students. The downloaded Zwiki, who are creatures from faraway stars, "live" on the handhelds and need help to return home. Students must share knowledge and collaborate to successfully create the traits and special creature that will enable their return (http://geney.juxta.com/).

A "what-if" feature is now being used with Geney, combining multiple interconnected devices to form a larger, shared workspace. Children collaborate in producing a fish with a particular set of characteristics by exchanging fish with their friends through the handheld's infrared port. Hypothesizing, synthesizing information, and engaging in rich social interactions are among the benefits researchers are finding from Geney's use (Danesh, Inkpen, Lau, Shu, & Booth, 2001).

The low cost and portability of these Wireless Internet Learning Devices (WILDs) offer exciting possibilities. These devices enable ubiquitous use of technology rather than technology being used intermittently as an add-on (Soloway, et al., 2001). Many attributes mentioned earlier that are needed for success in a knowledge society can be fostered through the creative use of handheld WILDs.

Increase in Distance Learning The proliferation of online learning requires a "paradigm shift in bedrock views on teaching and learning" (Hopper, 2001, p. 36). When we think of schools, most of us imagine a brick and mortar building with rooms of children usually segregated by age-imposed grade levels. The resources contained in that space largely determine the curriculum and learning opportunities. The Internet has opened the schoolroom doors for many students, expanding their learning opportunities by enabling them to take courses not otherwise offered and to pursue other interests while still in high school.

Although no more than 5% of high school distance-learning students take classes solely online, 44% of school districts provide distance learning through online and television technologies, an increase from 35% in 1996–1997 (McCafferty, 2001). For those students who need flexibility, the Internet is providing a new means for learning. In small school districts, access to advanced courses is often minimal. Tom Layton, founder of the Eugene, Oregon based Cyberschool, said, "Our goal was to provide courses for rural students who otherwise wouldn't be able to take them." Additionally, students who move frequently or have extended absences due to illness find this alternative education environment beneficial (DeVera, 2001).

SO WHAT? WHAT SHOULD WE DO WITH THE INTERNET AND THE WEB?

Education (and more specifically, developmental education) has evolved as the result of technology. Beginning with the hunting and gathering age, through the agrarian age, and then into the industrial age, expert elders taught and developed their apprentices using oral communication such as storytelling and recitation. With the invention of technologies like writing 5,000 years ago and the printing press 500 years ago, these elders were able to use these technologies to collect and organize data bits of their knowledge and convert it into printed information, making it available to growing numbers of apprentices who were the emerging literate. Thus education shifted as a result of technology toward teaching the novice how to develop knowledge from information—knowledge development resulting from thinking while reading, from debating what has been read, from coming to group understanding, and from expressing individual understanding through speaking and writing (Caverly, 2000).

What will we do with the power offered us by the Web and the Internet? Will it be the blackboard of the future or will we use it to move beyond blackboards? If it is impossible to transfer knowledge from one person's mind to another's (as we argued in chapter 1), then the blackboard metaphor breaks down. If the act of exploring and making discoveries in a context rich with challenges results in meaningful learning and the development of cognitive strategies that will serve the learner throughout life, then we need a newer, more powerful metaphor than the blackboard. Perhaps a more useful metaphor for envisioning the Internet is as an agent to connect people—to other people, to information, to ideas, and to learning opportunities that support knowledge creation.

The Internet may be no more than an electronic worksheet if the old prescriptive model of learning is plugged in to this new technology. Yet the Internet is a tool with the potential to transform traditional teacher-directed instruction into powerful, student-led, inquiry-based learning. The Internet expands opportunities for learning with a wide variety of resources and people, providing multiple perspectives, access to diverse cultures, access to experts, and access to information.

Current evidence points to the need for teachers' professional development in using the Internet as a learning tool. Riley (1998, February 17), in his Fifth Annual State of American Education speech, said, "And there is not a moment to be lost in making sure that America's teachers are up to speed and really know how to integrate technology into their lesson plans. We really ought to be past the time when many students know more about computers than some of their teachers."

But are we past that time? NetDay (2001), a national education technology nonprofit, reports that although more than 8 out of 10 teachers (84%) believed that the quality of education is improved by computers and access to the Internet, two-thirds of those teachers agreed the Internet is not well integrated into their classrooms. Almost half of the teachers believed the Internet has become an important tool for teaching over the last 2 years, yet across every demographic group of teachers, half or more use the Internet at school for less than 30 minutes a day. While teachers are aware of many uses for the Internet, most say that it has not changed the way they teach. Rather, the Internet is mainly seen as having potential as a research tool. This finding parallels statistics from Quality Education Data (2001), which indicate that 96% of students who use the Internet weekly use it for research. According to NetDay, these findings suggest that helping teachers learn how to move beyond basic research functions is a critical component in maximizing use of the Internet.

Researching With the Internet

In the following sections we will explore many ways the Internet can be used to encourage compelling, meaningful learning. Collaborative problem- and project-based learning activities do, however, often begin with online research as a first step. The important thing to remember is that research is just a step—a means to a bigger end. Unless there is an intentional outcome, researching is a meaningless activity. Unfortunately, research often "ends with the harvesting of the data, rather than extending into the next stage of the process. While a Web hunt for close-ended questions from a Web site might technically be a form of research, it lacks the value of an active learning experience that can result if the information gathered is applied" (Kelly, 2000).

With the concept of "research as first step" firmly in mind, let's consider what it takes to become competent in using the Internet for information searches.

Searching for Information   Using the Internet as the vast online library that it is requires dual skills. Like a two-sided coin, effective information gleaning from the Internet combines expertise in searching for information and then evaluating the worth of that information.

Finding the information one needs on the Internet can be extremely challenging because of the millions of Web pages that are available. Among the concerns about the WWW as a learning tool is that there are so many interesting topics to explore and it is so easy to explore that students are often off-task, following links that take them away from, rather than toward, their learning goal.

Along with the technical skill of conducting an effective search, learners also need to develop awareness and self-regulatory skills in order to make the Internet a tool for effective learning. As they navigate the Internet, they must also be thinking about the information they encounter and how it relates to their existing knowledge. Understanding requires thinking. Browsing does not necessarily cause thinking.

A self-regulated learner who keeps his or her information-seeking goals in mind and makes good decisions can find the WWW an essential information resource during intentional learning. That is, the educational secret to the Internet is intentionality. When students say, "I am looking for information to help me answer a question/build my own knowledge base/evaluate someone else's ideas/etc.," then they will likely learn from the experience.

Intentionality and focus are enhanced when a group of learners is committed to the same goals. They regulate each other's performance. So, when learners have an information need and they articulate that need in some coherent way, there is a high likelihood that they will benefit from searching the Web.

How can we support students in conducting intentional searches with the metacognition that keeps them focused and productive? Equipping students with the skills to search effectively is the first step in using the Internet as a source of information. One strategy for effective searching is understanding the different types of search tools that are available, their differences, how they work, and when a specific type is appropriate.

We can divide search tools into two broad categories: search engines and directories. Search engines and directories are both databases of Web sites, but they are constructed differently. Search engines such as Google, Northern Light, and Lycos use programs called robots (also known as spiders or crawlers) that travel the Internet, cataloging Web pages for search engine databases.

Directories, such as Yahoo, are databases that use a hierarchical structure. This structure is familiar to most people because the groupings are by category, much like the subject sections in a bookstore. So if you are interested in finding information on the aurora borealis you would follow the path through the subject categories: Science, Astronomy, and Northern Lights. From here you can connect to a number of Web sites that will show you what auroras look like from space and on Earth, explain how they are created, and show you where they can be found. Directories are an easy place to find information when you are looking on the Web because people review the sites on them and group the sites into appropriate categories.

In order for a Web page to be listed in a directory, the page developer submits a request to the directory along with suggestions as to which category it should be located in. The people working at the directory then examine the page and decide whether to include the page as a link from their directory and where it belongs. This takes quite a bit of time and effort, so only a small fraction of the available sites on the Web are listed with each directory. To find obscure information or all the possible sites covering a subject, you need a more in-depth search. For this you need a search engine.

There are many search engines available on the Web, often using different methods of organizing and searching. Each search tool has specific features that may be best suited for particular information needs. The ePALS Web site (http://www.epals.com) offers an extensive listing of recommended search tools for specific needs such as refining a keyword search, finding biographical information, locating primary sources, and accessing multimedia files.

Each robot operates differently—some search all the text in a Web page, some just the heading and first few paragraphs, others include the hidden code of the page in the information they collect. Each one also searches at different speeds. Although Web page authors can submit their page to the search engines, most pages are added to the database by the robot following links from other pages that it already knows about; therefore, the Web sites listed with each search engine may be different.

Each search engine operates differently in reference to how a search term can be entered, whether Boolean logic or other advanced search capabilities are supported, and the different truncation symbols that may be used. Methods of ranking relevancy can also vary. In addition, search engines change their structure and capabilities, often without notice, so it is difficult to know whether the search you performed one day will still be supported the next.

If the term "aurora" were typed into a search engine you may find information on the aurora borealis returned, but you are also likely to get advertisements for the Aurora automobile or the Hotel Aurora in Italy. Robots work by matching strings of letters together—there is no human review of the Web sites to separate cars from constellations.

A subset of search engines are meta-search engines. We can think of these powerful tools as a search engine clearinghouse. When a search is conducted in a meta-search engine such as Dogpile, IxQuick, or Metacrawler, it is sent to a number of search engines and the results from these multiple search engines are returned.

Most search engines include links with directions on advanced search techniques for that particular tool. Lycos also provides a help page with advanced search filters, frequently asked questions about searching, and advice on understanding search results.

Evaluating Information   Once information has been located, what next? Anyone who has access to a server can create and post Web pages. So how do we determine what is or is not accurate? Knowing whether a Web site is reputable and contains accurate information is the second essential step in using the Internet as a source of information.

"Neophytes in the high-tech world often *mistake downloading for thinking*" (Healy, 1998, p. 251). Students, often with teachers' and parents' blessings, construct their own representations by appropriating information and graphics from other Web sites without evaluating the viability of the ideas. There are no Internet police. Anyone can put anything on an Internet server (propaganda, pornography, and perjury), and they often do. Commercial sites are increasing at a faster rate than other types of sites. Organizations committed to hatred are finding new voice on the Internet. Students are the most likely victims. It is vital that students learn how to discriminate fact from fiction, information from opinion, and reality from fantasy. Before your students download anything, they should become Info-Tectives (Healy, 1998, pp. 252–253) by asking:

1. Who provided this information? Why?

2. Is someone trying to sell us a product or point of view?

3. What kind of site did it come from (com = commercial, gov = government, edu = educational institution, org = nonprofit organization)? How might the source affect the accuracy? Can we believe everything that comes from the government or an educational institution?

4. What biases are likely held by the providers?

5. If quotes or data are provided, are they properly referenced?

6. How can we validate the information provided? Can we check the sources?

7. Does the information represent theory or evidence, fact from fiction, etc.? How do we distinguish between these?

8. How do the visuals, sound, or animation influence how we interpret the information? Do visuals and text convey the same meaning?

Students should also ask:

1. Is the author a known expert? If not, is the page linked from a credible source with whom the author is affiliated? Can you find authoritative sources that cite the author?

2. Are the author's credentials listed? Is contact information included?

3. When was the Web site published? Is there a publication date or a last updated entry? Is the information on the Web site current?

Learning these critical viewing skills should be mandatory for any students using the Internet to collect information. Tammy Payton's Evaluation Rubrics for Web sites are specifically designed as an aid for primary, intermediate, and secondary students (http://www.siec.k12.in.us/west/edu/evaltr.htm). Another resource for developing evaluation skills is Joyce Valenza's Evaluating Web Pages: A WebQuest (http://mciunix.mciu.k12.pa.us/~spjvweb/evalwebteach.html). This was designed for 9th- through 12th-grade students to meet information and technology literacy standards across content areas. Student teams examine Web sites through the filter roles of specialists in Content, Authority/Credibility, Bias/Purpose, and Usability/Design. Through a class discussion, teachers can help students understand critical evaluation skills.

Many schools, concerned about students encountering offensive or objectionable material on the Web, employ Internet filtering software that screens for certain words or phrases and blocks access to that site. Unfortunately, filtering software does not consider context when deciding whether a word such as "breast" is considered objectionable. Therefore, a student researching breast cancer would find many legitimate Web sites unavailable. Two avenues of thought exist about the usefulness and appropriateness of installing filtering software in schools. Some people reason that "The Internet, while offering valuable information, contains dangerous and inappropriate material from which students must be protected. Filtering software will prevent them from exposure to objectionable web sites." Those holding the opposite viewpoint realize that students will not be shielded forever and believe that they should be taught what to do when they inadvertently run across offensive Web sites. They also see an opportunity to teach effective search skills that will increase the odds of obtaining useful, legitimate sites.

As your students visit Web sites that have been identified, they also need to evaluate whether the information that they find there supports their purpose. That is, does the site contain the information that they need to fulfill their intention? Are there any ideas at the site that can be used to answer the questions they are seeking? This type of reflective thinking allows the learner to reevaluate what he or she really needs and what is missing. If the learner thinks the original search worked, then satisfaction is attained and the searching stops. Otherwise, the learner can narrow the search by adding additional terms, expand the search by removing some of the terms, or simply scratch the original search and start over.

INTERNET LEARNING ACTIVITIES

In chapter 1, we argued that technologies could help us engage learners in active, constructive, intentional, authentic, and cooperative learning. This chapter will illustrate how the Internet can facilitate that. Increasingly, Internet learning activities are becoming collaborative ventures, connecting students and/or researchers across not only this country, but the entire world. Some of the following illustrations are also appropriate examples for the following chapter because they involve communities of learners.

Inquiry-Oriented Cooperative Learning

The educational value of Internet-based activities varies widely, from scavenger hunts that promote minimal learning to activities that require students to seek, analyze, evaluate, and apply information in the process of transforming that information into knowledge. Constructivist uses of the Internet allow students to define goals, exercise autonomy in determining purposes, and create artifacts that demonstrate learning. The Internet offers opportunities for learners to work together as they investigate. Cooperative learning may occur as small groups work together in the physical classroom and can involve collaboration that spans the Internet to include students in other schools across town or around the world.

The crucial link to effective, educationally valid use of the Internet is the development and intentional articulation of the intended learning goals. Aligning those goals with inquiry-based learning activities is a powerful combination.

Questioning is central to learning and growing. An unquestioning mind is one condemned to "feeding" on the ideas and solutions of others. An unquestioning mind may have little defense against the data smog so typical of life in this Information Age. An unquestioning mind is like a sloop without a rudder. Questions enable us to make changes in life, to invent new and better ways of doing things. In all too many cases, the questioning process has been reduced and oversimplified to a search for prepackaged answers. Artificial intelligence abounds. Questions are intended to provoke thought and inspire reflection, but all too often the process is shortcircuited by the simple answer, the quick truth or the appealing placebo. (McKenzie, 2001; see also http://fno.org/nov99/techquest.html)

WebQuests   The Internet searching and evaluation skills discussed in this chapter are essential for students' independent research. At times, however, teachers may wish to save time and ensure that students access appropriate Web sites by preselecting Web sites. The key to student learning lies in the constructivist design of activities that incorporate these Web sites. Since Bernie Dodge developed the WebQuest model in 1995, WebQuests have become a popular tool for teachers. A WebQuest is an inquiry-oriented activity in which teachers choose Web resources for students to use as information sources in activities designed to support analysis, evaluation, and synthesis of information. For teachers just beginning to use the Internet as a learning tool, WebQuests may be a good starting place because they provide a clearly defined structure and their design and use is well supported. Teachers may create their own WebQuests or use one of the many WebQuests that are already available on the Internet. There is an abundance of existing WebQuests with a wide range of quality, and, as with any instructional material, critical evaluation by the teacher is essential. Used thoughtfully, they can support constructivist learning; however, teachers may fall into the trap of using WebQuests as a prescribed roadmap for students to follow, supporting only superficial learning goals.

Dodge offers an overview of the types of tasks students may engage in during a WebQuest. This taxonomy of WebQuests lists 12 types of tasks: retelling, compilation, mystery, journalistic, design, creative product, consensus building, persuasion, self-knowledge, judgment, analytical, and scientific. Short-term WebQuests include knowledge acquisition and integration among their goals (Dodge, 1997) while long-term WebQuests are more suited for extending and refining knowledge. A short-term (knowledge acquisition) WebQuest might serve as the first step in a more cognitively stimulating activity, whereas a long-term WebQuest could stand alone as students analyze information, transform it, and create an original product.

An example from Pacific Bell's Knowledge Network Explorer Web site is "Look Who's Footing the Bill: An Introductory WebQuest on Democracy and the National Debt" (http://www.kn.pacbell.com/wired/democracy/debtquest.html). This WebQuest begins by saying, "Probably you! That's who's going to foot the bill. At least you will in the future because the United States' national debt stands at over 5 trillion dollars (that's a five with, uh . . . 12 zeroes after it?)." WebQuests are best designed with an introduction that engages students. Another common attribute of WebQuests is the assumption of roles. Students often work in small groups, with each student adding a different perspective through the various roles. In "Look Who's Footing the Bill" a Number Cruncher helps explain the meaning behind numbers such as 5 trillion. Other roles include the Fact Checker, who helps the group differentiate fact from opinion, the Growth Advocate, who advocates that a large national debt may be good, and the Budget Balancer, who presents the opposite viewpoint that debt is bad.

The "Democracy and the National Debt" WebQuest provides links to resources that help students understand the issues such as interactive Budget Simulators, a National Debt clock, and online articles. For example, the Budget Simulator uses Java programming that allows students to adjust the amount of money allocated to U.S.

federal government departments and programs, manipulating data and analyzing the resulting changes. After forming an opinion about the federal deficit based on the information they have gathered, students must communicate their stance to their congressional representatives. The main goal of the WebQuest is that students develop a well-reasoned opinion, communicate that, and get feedback from an actual representative. This authentic activity gives students the opportunity to practice the democratic process as they move toward adulthood.

eMINTS Teachers and WebQuests

Michelle Gilmer is a teacher in the eMINTS (enhancing Missouri's Instructional Networked Teaching Strategies) program, an integral part of a statewide effort to upgrade Missouri's classrooms in the 21st century by combining cutting-edge technology with first-class teaching. eMINTS classrooms are equipped with a high-speed Internet connection, multimedia teacher work station, productivity software, SMART Board, high-lumen projector, a computer for every two students, digital camera, printer, and related peripherals—such as video-conferencing equipment.

Many beginning eMINTS teachers were low-level technology users and their high-tech classrooms could be overwhelming. Where to begin? eMINTS turned to WebQuests as an easy-to-follow starting place, bringing Bernie Dodge, the originator of WebQuests, to assist with training.

Michelle Gilmer developed a short-term WebQuest for her 4th-grade class at Southeast Elementary School in Sikeston, Missouri. "The Circle of Life" is a science WebQuest designed to correspond with the school district's science objectives and with state standards. Students are introduced to the idea of nature's cycles through the words of Black Elk, an Oglala Sioux Holy Man. The questions they are to consider are: Is there a "Circle of Life"? Does every living thing depend on other living and nonliving things?

Working in teams of three, students use the Internet to research three broad areas. Students take on the roles of botanist, zoologist, and rotologist (a teacher-created word defined as studying decomposition!). After researching links provided for each area, taking notes, and citing references, the group convenes to discuss their findings and to determine the interdependency among them.

Next, when conclusions are reached about the interdependence of Earth's organisms, students represent their understanding by creating a Circle of Life mural. Howard Gardner (1991, 2000) argues that our traditional thinking of intelligence is narrowly focused on logico-mathematical intelligence, ignoring the wide range of creativity that lies in other intelligences. Learning activities that present alternate ways to represent knowledge support learners whose strengths lie in areas other than the linguistic mode that is commonly encouraged and valued. The Circle of Life provides an opportunity for artistic intelligence to be expressed. To further individualize, students may be offered the choice of representing their knowledge through writing and presenting a play, creating a dance, or composing a song that illustrates nature's cycles.

Student-Created WebQuests   Engaging in a well-designed teacher-created WebQuest can be a terrific learning experience, but student-created WebQuests can be of even greater value. Students in two Chemistry 1 Advanced Placements classes brainstormed the topic "Nuclear Issues in the 21st Century" and identified a problem (Peterson & Koeck, 2001). After teacher-led brainstorming, responses were categorized to meet the teacher's instructional objectives. Student teams chose a category to develop, with the final WebQuest being a compilation of the categories.

To develop the WebQuest, students first evaluated existing WebQuests to understand the structure. They were introduced to the GAP model (Caverly, 2000, in Peterson & Koeck) of

- **G**athering information
- **A**rranging information into meaningful formats
- Using technology tools to **P**resent that new knowledge to others

Searching for and critically analyzing information were seen as especially valuable for science students in developing inductive thinking. As teams decided what to include in their portion of the WebQuest, they engaged in further critical thinking as individuals presented and defended the information they had found. When consensus was reached, teams used Inspiration software to create concept maps of their section. Each team had one person with Web development skills whose responsibility was creating the actual Web file for the WebQuest. When the WebQuest was completed, these students presented it to university faculty and preservice teachers. This type of authentic project, whereby students actually create a WebQuest rather than simply participate in one, raises the WebQuest concept to a new level. The cognitive and social skills required to construct WebQuests offer a motivating, deep learning experience. Students made interdisciplinary connections and were challenged intellectually. At the same time, they gained experience with technology and presentation skills—and had fun!

Thematic Web Collections   Teachers (and students) who are interested in developing WebQuests may be overwhelmed by the thought of searching out and compiling the Web sites they require. Web collections may be useful in developing a WebQuest or other activity that is designed for constructivist learning. E-themes and TrackStar are two collections of Web sites that are organized thematically.

- E-themes (http://emints.more.net/ethemes/resources)
- TrackStar (http://trackstar.hprtec.org/)

Learning Processes   For students engaging in a WebQuest, its design will influence their level of learning. Some WebQuests are essentially online worksheets with little educational value. Good WebQuests incorporate cooperative learning, consideration of multiple perspectives, analysis and synthesis of information, and creation of original products that demonstrate knowledge gained. Students creating WebQuests apply skills in formulating questions and ideas, designing the WebQuest's structure, and seeking and evaluating information. The

Table 3.2 WebQuest Task Comparison: Developing Versus Doing (Courtesy of Cynthia L. Peterson & Deborah C. Koeck)

Tasks for Developing a WebQuest	Tasks for Learning from a WebQuest
Define a problem	Respond to a problem
Develop questions	Respond to questions
Search for and evaluate resources	Evaluate information within pre-selected resources
Design a site with an audience in mind	
Work on a team for project creation	Navigate within a site
Synthesize information	Work on a team for problem solution
Apply logical thinking	Synthesize information
Consider and accept multiple possible solutions	Apply logical thinking
	Arrive at a possible solution to the problem

cooperative aspect of most WebQuests requires students to work as collaborators, presenting information they find and defending its value. As team members, they learn the benefit of pooling individual efforts and how to reach consensus. As producers, they are reflective in considering their goals and the audience for whom they are designing the WebQuest—an experience that puts them on the other side as a developer rather than a consumer of instructional material.

You will recall that earlier we said intentionality and focus are enhanced when a group of learners are committed to the same goals and that they regulate each other's performance. The common goals of a WebQuest can serve to focus students on their information needs, the learning task, and the specific product or outcome they are to achieve. They see that this joint knowledge building can result in an end product that is much richer, more complex, and of higher quality than what any one individual would create.

Problem-Solving Processes Do WebQuests engage problem solving? That depends. The most caustic view of WebQuests is that they are nothing more than electronic worksheets that serve only the purpose of filling time. It is likely that some are. Others do engage problem solving, however, the kind of problem solving is difficult to predict without seeing the WebQuest.

Student-produced WebQuests, on the other hand, definitely engage problem solving. Developing a WebQuest requires a lot of purposeful information searching to fulfill a task that is designed by the students. Producing the WebQuest calls on a great many design skills, such as those engaged by producing multimedia (described in chapter 6). From designing the task, the activities, the interface, and the procedures, designing a WebQuest is a very constructivist activity that also requires a lot of decision making. We believe that student-produced WebQuests are more valuable and constructive than learning from a preexisting WebQuest.

Teacher Roles   The teacher is a critical link in the value of WebQuests (and any classroom activity). Clearly, WebQuests that promote critical thinking require careful design. While teachers may find many suitable WebQuests to use with students, developing an original WebQuest can provide a very individualized, class-specific learning experience. Identifying and defining the learning goals is the first step in developing a WebQuest. Teachers wishing to design their own will need to be proficient in the same search and evaluation skills we want students to possess. It is helpful for teachers to be familiar with existing WebQuests because comparisons can point out the vast differences in quality. Developing a WebQuest that will engage students in complex thinking and creation of original products that demonstrate knowledge synthesized from multiple areas is the goal.

Much of a teacher's work comes during the WebQuest development process, as student teams should be able to work fairly independently on many WebQuests. After a WebQuest is developed, the teacher's role is to serve as guide and resource for students as they work.

Assessing Learning   Because WebQuests are typically completed by cooperative groups, teachers must decide whether to assess individual work and effort, group work, or a combination. Depending on the WebQuest outcome, it may be difficult to separate student work for individual assessment of a team project. Teachers who want to assess individuals' work should choose or create WebQuests with a product or process outcome that specifies clear divisions of labor.

Rubrics are one of the six basic building blocks of a WebQuest and a rubric template is available on the WebQuest site. Teachers may evaluate the quality of students' questions, how effective they were in locating information, the dynamics, effort, and cohesiveness of group members, and the thoughtfulness and complexity of a resulting product that demonstrates what students have learned.

INFORMATION TO KNOWLEDGE: SCIENTIFIC INQUIRY AND EXPERIMENTATION

The major premise of this chapter is that the Internet is a tool for facilitating knowledge exploration by learners. Although the Internet contains a wealth of information, it is little more than a virtual depository unless that information is transformed into knowledge through meaningful, reflective, active learning activities. Sending students on scavenger hunts or providing them with collections of Web sites does little to promote learning unless students are searching as a means to meaningful outcomes. When information is purposefully manipulated and reconstructed in authentic, meaningful learning tasks, the Internet becomes a powerful educational tool.

While some of the activities in this section, such as field trips, can be potentially little more than superficial observation for students, building in complex learning goals strengthens the value of Internet-based learning. Exploration is most effective when learners articulate a clear purpose for their explorations—to find information to solve a problem, resolve an argument, construct an interpretation, and so on.

If the Internet is to be more than an electronic baby-sitter, learners must articulate an educational purpose for using it. The Internet can be used as a tool to develop critical thinking skills as well as provide access to a variety of information and human resources. Riel (2000) argues, "The challenge of the knowledge-centered dimension of learning is to balance knowledge construction activities with activities that help students develop the suite of mental tools needed for this task." While Internet use with older students may be easily envisioned, it is sometimes more difficult to imagine ways that younger students can benefit from it. The following purposeful activities show how the Internet can be effectively used with a range of learners.

Distributed Data Collection

Several fine examples of Internet use can be found in Sandy Callahan's kindergarten class at St. Francis Xavier School in Jefferson City, Missouri. Through the Journey North Web site (http://www.learner.org/jnorth/), these students have participated in nationwide data collection and analysis, not only building an understanding of the natural world, but also experiencing the power of collaborative effort. The first project we will examine is the monarch migration to Mexico. During the fall, Mrs. Callahan's class began learning about monarch butterflies and their life cycle. After registering to participate, Mrs. Callahan received an e-mail from Journey North alerting the class that monarchs had been sighted in Indiana and Illinois. The students accessed Journey North's Web site to watch the map of migration in progress and began to wait for monarchs to arrive in central Missouri, making predictions about their arrival time. When monarchs were sighted, students made a count and used the online "Field Notes" to record and report their observations. Journey North added their data to the aggregated data from other classrooms across the country. The students kept a classroom map, coloring in states as the monarchs moved through them, and learning about climate and geography as they plotted the monarchs' path.

Mrs. Callahan's class also participated in a project to track spring's progress across the Northern Hemisphere. The Tulip project is one of several "Signs of Spring" activities. During fall 2000, Mrs. Callahan's kindergartners planted one of the 190 tulip gardens that were established across the Northern Hemisphere, using the detailed planting instructions on Journey North's Web site to ensure consistency among gardens. The students learned important elements of scientific experimentation such as controlling variables as they took part in this project. The class registered with Journey North's official Tulip Garden Registry and began watching for the first signs of tulips in the spring. All participating classes are listed so that partner schools may be chosen for data exchanges. Again, the Journey North Web site plotted sites on a map as tulips emerged across the continent. Participants also reported when the first blooms occurred, providing a snapshot of spring's arrival from south to north.

For Mrs. Callahan's kindergartners, this project led to research about plants, seeds, bulbs, dormancy, and climate as well as scientific experimentation. Projects like these allow students to be part of a greater community of learners and to contribute as part of a community of scientists. Internet technology enables the implementation of data collection distributed across wide areas and allows students to see the results of their efforts. The activities offered by Journey North are appropriate for a wide range of learners, because they can be extended and adapted as needed. The Web site includes challenge questions, related activities and resources, and an "Ask the Expert" feature. Critical thinking is encouraged in question formation and scaffolds guide students in thinking about generating questions that only an expert could ask. Thus, learners are challenged to be independent, self-guided information seekers who make measured decisions about the sources they choose to support knowledge building.

Each February, Mrs. Callahan's class also participates in Project Groundhog, sponsored by STEM~Net, Canada's SchoolNet GrassRoots Program, and Spiderwise (http://www.stemnet.nf.ca/Groundhog/). Project Groundhog is designed to introduce young learners to the possibilities of telecommunications technology through a meaningful, curriculum-based inquiry. Following registration, students send weekly weather reports to the Project Groundhog Web site. The importance of consistency in data collection is discussed and a Fahrenheit to Celsius conversion tool assists data reporting.

Mrs. Callahan finds that partnering in collaborative projects results in students who are excited about learning, reflect on their learning, generate thoughtful questions, and make connections between scientific concepts and real-life experiences. She is also benefiting, as she comments, "I have grown and changed the way I teach. It's no longer boring. It energizes you."

Another example of partnerships in scientific learning comes from the National Science Foundation's Center for Biological Timing. Geneticists, molecular biologists, endocrinologists, and statisticians from Brandeis University, Rockefeller University, Northwestern University, and the University of Virginia collaborated with students in the Biological Timing Online Science Experiment (http://www.cbt.virginia.edu/Olh/exp.html). This three-year project involving hamsters allowed students to view webcams for real-time experimental results as they were collected. Data tables and actograms were posted on the Web site and questions were posed to the students. Students also had the opportunity to post questions to the scientists and engage in dialogue about scientific experimentation. They not only learned about hamster behaviors, but also had firsthand experience with participating in and discussing scientific method.

Project Neptune (http://www.neptune.washington.edu/) is working to establish a network of underwater observatories in the northeastern Pacific Ocean. Two thousand miles of fiber-optic cable will provide power and communications to scientific instruments for researchers and classrooms in a long-term study. Project Feeder Watch (http://birds.cornell.edu/PEW/), from the Cornell Lab of Ornithology, is a collaborative project that involves collecting data about birds frequenting feeders and sending it to scientists to assist in their tracking broad-scale movements of winter bird populations and long-term trends in bird distribution and abundance. These are just a few of the many opportunities for students to become part of a larger scientific research community, participating in meaningful, real-life learning.

Open-Ended, Student-Directed Research Projects

In open-ended and student-directed research projects, students harvest the Internet's vast information bank to learn about topics, generally in order to produce some original work using their new knowledge. *Open-ended* refers to the fact that the students are encouraged to learn as much as they can about the topic, rather than simply to find answers to questions posed by the teacher. Good teachers use these projects to help students develop strategies to determine what information is important—to develop their own set of questions. *Student-directed* implies that the students are in charge, making key decisions about search strategies, about which sites the search returns look most promising, about what to collect, about when to initiate conversations with information providers, and so on.

Student-created WebQuests are one example of a project where students can take the lead in selecting and researching a topic of their choice. Another example is Mrs. Morris's 5th-grade class at Warner Elementary School in Wilmington, Delaware, who created a Web site to disseminate information about horseshoe crabs and their importance. These students looked no further than their own Delaware Bay to find an interesting, personally relevant issue to research. Delaware Bay has more horseshoe crabs than anywhere in the world, but the students learned that their numbers may be declining due to overharvesting. To educate themselves, students began reading about horseshoe crabs and raising and observing them. They also interviewed marine biologists and other knowledgeable experts. The Web site they produced contains a wealth of information about horseshoe crabs, including pictures, animations, and a video clip. The students developed horseshoe crab games, activities, and a quiz. Their viewpoints section describes several different perspectives of people who might be interested in the fate of horseshoe crabs. Among them are a fisherman, ornithologist, property owner, and doctor. Visitors to the Web site are asked to think about the issues and vote for the perspective they most agree with, providing students with user feedback and another source of data (http://www.k12.de.us/warner/introhsc.html).

An amazing number of Web sites are available to support students' diverse interests. The Web-based Inquiry Science Environment (WISE) is a free online science learning environment for students in grades 4–12. This Web site, supported by the National Science Foundation, offers a learning environment for students to examine real-world evidence and analyze current scientific controversies. Free teacher registration generates a student registration code that identifies a class, allows students to register, and creates a class account on WISE. Teachers may create original projects, copy and use existing projects, and access management tools for student assessment and feedback. WISE can be a good starting place for generating ideas and sparking areas of interest for students.

An example of a WISE project is "The Next Big Shake," in which students critically examine earthquake predictions made by others, and predict when they think the next big earthquake will occur. Using evidence they find on the Web that illustrates earthquakes' effects on buildings and other structures, students then evaluate the safety of their own school during an earthquake. Finally, they assess how much the area in which they live risks damage from an earthquake.

Teachers who used WISE projects with students report that it increases classroom interaction, reveals science as it is in the real world, and offers exciting resources that motivate kids to learn. One teacher said, ". . . students who were unmotivated at first demonstrated a tremendous amount of knowledge on the subject matter as they presented their evidence for the debate." Another teacher thought that WISE helped her students with critical thinking skills, causing them to ask, 'Does this make sense?'—instead of kids tending to swallow everything and saying, 'Oh, there. It's all true.' I liked how [the project] seemed to intrigue them, and I heard some great questions from the kids [that] wouldn't have come up if they had been reading a textbook." (http://wise.berkeley.edu/pages/what_teachers_say.php)

Another Web site that supports scientific inquiry is Global Lab, an inquiry-based interdisciplinary science course for students in grades 7–9 (http://globallab.terc.edu/). Students identify a local "study site" to conduct environmental science investigations. Like the Delaware Bay horseshoe crab study, students are more likely to be engaged because they are making their own decisions about what to study and their investigation involves local environmental issues of importance to them. An online workspace allows students to upload their own data and download data collected by other Global Lab schools and to share and discuss findings with students participating at other schools.

ThinkQuest (http://www.thinkquest.org/) offers several programs designed to advance education through the use of technology. Student teams research science, mathematics, literature, social sciences, or arts topics and publish their research as educational Web sites. ThinkQuest competitions, such as the International Challenge, involve international collaboration among students and teacher coaches as teams research, communicate online, and manage a project resulting in a published Web site.

While the examples cited above were predominantly scientific in nature, opportunities abound in other subjects as well. Students often use the Internet to collect input for and to distribute magazines, to survey citizens of the world on social issues, and to do all sorts of research. A useful tool in collecting data is the Zoomerang survey tool (http://www.zoomerang.com/) that supports the design, implementation, and interpretation of online surveys. The goal in all of these projects is to give students an opportunity to *do*, rather than just hear about the subject of study. That is the key to active learning strategies. When learning experiences are situated in real-world contexts, as is the case in problem-based or case-based scenarios, learning, retention, and transfer to other situations are enhanced.

Learning Processes   Conducting scientific research is among the most complete intellectual activities that learners can pursue. In defining research problems,
seeking evidence using the Internet as well as observing their own studies, and
then communicating their results via the Internet engages active, constructive,
and intentional learning. Researchers are active because they manipulate environments and observe the results of their manipulations. They are constructive
because they are required to articulate the nature of scientific problems, while
reflecting on their importance. In order to conduct research, learners must regulate their own performance as well as the activities of that which they are observing. Most of the problems that these students are investigating are authentic. They
are complex without a certain answer, and they definitely emerge from the real
world. Finally, in order to accomplish most of these activities, students must cooperate with each other in defining and carrying out research topics. Reporting their
results via the Internet requires a final and important level of reflection about
what they have observed and discovered.

Problem-Solving Processes   The scientific process is not something to memorize, but rather a way of life, a way of viewing the world. When scientists do not
understand something, they seek to understand why by gathering information,
conjecturing, and building theories. These student-directed research projects
employ the scientific process, which requires a lot of problem solving. These students must perform a good deal of information searching. More importantly, they
use the information that they have collected to construct models of the information that they have collected. This model building is the hallmark of a good scientist, because they use those models to state hypotheses about the information they
have collected. Hypotheses require a theory or model to be tested. Last, but not
least, these students are engaged in design problem solving when they construct
their Web sites. Designing multimedia Web sites is described in greater detail in
chapter 6.

Teacher Roles   In order to support this kind of learning, teachers must be able
to function in these ways. Assuming that the teacher is able, his or her primary
role will be as coach, prompting the students to consider alternative ideas or
views and suggesting appropriate ways of looking at the world and additional
ways of operationalizing (e.g., how to find variables and measure them). In some
of these projects, the teacher initiated the study, suggesting topics. That may be a
useful way to start, but students should assume control of the topics and the
issues being investigated. That way, they will have greater ownership of their
learning and the products of it. Teachers can also provide tools that scaffold the
different tasks involved in the investigation. They may teach students how to use
spreadsheets to tabulate data, how to use Web authoring packages, and so on.

Assessing Learning   Assessing these kinds of learning activities should focus
on the investigation itself and the reporting of the results of those investigations.
You should think about how well the students articulated the issues and con-

ducted the investigation and then how well they communicated it to others. Questions such as these provide assessment criteria:

- How relevant was the topic to the course of study? Did it address issues relevant to your course?
- Were all of the issues identified? Were there redundant issues? How important were the issues to the topic being studied?
- Were the issues carefully articulated? Were variables identified that adequately and accurately described the issues?
- Did students carefully observe and describe these variables?
- Were student investigations of the issues thorough? Did they uncover all of the important issues? Were multiple views and perspective provided?
- Did students accurately draw conclusions from their observations?
- Did students communicate their results in easily interpretable ways? Were there adequate graphical representations? Was their writing clear?
- Did students develop independent research skills that could be used in other settings?

WEB PUBLISHING

In a White paper for the U.S. Department of Education Secretary's Conference on Educational Technology (2000), Riel wrote:

> With the growing informational and human resources on the Internet, a student, with access, can find a wide range of materials on almost any topic. If students have more latitude, in both the topic and resources selected, it is more likely that they will be able to create original knowledge products. More important than choice is an audience that is interested in the outcome of their research, development, or insights. Research has demonstrated that authentic tasks with real audiences have resulted in increased learning, stronger writing, and longer retention of learning and even increased performance on standardized tests of writing. But more than test score results, students engaged in building knowledge products for others develop a sense of purpose and value. They contribute to their community.

A central aspect of research is sharing findings with others. Publishing requires the ability to analyze information and potential audiences and design a product that communicates one's knowledge. Web publishing can also provide a means for students to disseminate their original, creative writing. While many schools have Web sites with space for individual classrooms, even teachers without access to a school server can incorporate Web publishing. Web sites such as Scholastic (http://teacher.scholastic.com/resources/) and TeacherWeb (http://TeacherWeb.com/) provide free Web space and support through Web publishing templates.

Publishing Research

Michelle Gilmer's 4th-grade class at Southeast Elementary School in Sikeston, Missouri, studied the human body as part of the science curriculum. With a partner, they first explored a WebQuest on circulatory, respiratory, and digestive systems. Students then participated in "The Human Body: A Special Report." They were grouped into small teams as reporters for the Southeast Elementary News Team to produce a special report on the human body. Using Web and print resources, each team researched a system, wrote a report, created a script and PowerPoint background, and then as news anchors reported "on the air." Mrs. Gilmer videotaped the presentations and posted them to the class Web site as 15-second mpeg files.

Mrs. Gilmer's class also researched the solar system. Small groups chose a planet to research and used Internet resources to find information. Using a class template, each group created a report that was published to the Student Showcase on the class Web site.

Mrs. Gilmer sees several benefits in student publishing. For students, knowing that their reports will be distributed to a potentially worldwide audience provides an incentive to do their best work. Posting work to the Web allows parents to see that students are using computers for much more than game playing. She also thinks that it reinforces the idea that anyone can post a Web page, making her students more critical evaluators of the Web sites they encounter and very conscientious about the accuracy of the information they publish.

The students take pride in their publications and view them as important work. Among their responses when asked about their publishing is, "It helps other kids with the computer and Internet learn about real facts. It is important to help other kids learn." This student's concept of school has expanded to include not only her role as a learner, but also as a teacher—a partner in a larger enterprise of learners. The teachers in this school nurture that perception, as Mrs. Gilmer reports, "One of my fellow 4th grade teachers even used my students' planet Web pages to help her students research the planets." Overall, Mrs. Gilmer believes that Internet publishing helps students "feel a sense of pride, accomplishment . . . that they are helping others to learn by putting their work on the Internet." (http://www.sikeston.k12.mo.us/mgilmer/)

Another class demonstrated similar peer assistance through Web publishing. At Rosa Parks Elementary School in Lexington, Kentucky, fifth graders created content-rich Web sites as part of a ThinkQuest Junior competition (http://www.techlearning.com/db_area/archives/WCE/archives/brandt.htm). The four 5th-grade classrooms each focused on one content area: math, science, social studies, or literature. Mrs. Bowen's class created a Web site designed to increase students' math knowledge. This collaborative project was entirely student-directed, with the fifth graders organizing content and designing Web pages based on their decisions. Students continually analyzed and reflected on the best way to communicate effectively to an authentic audience. As they focused on their goal—a kid-created Web site for kids—the students' sense of ownership and expertise grew. They evaluated other Web sites to use as information sources, created animated graphics, and learned new software applications to support their Web page development. Parents and teachers became partners in reviewing and providing feedback on the work.

The students' "Hungry for Math" Web site (http://library.thinkquest.org/J002328F/) explains fractions and how to perform basic mathematical operations manipulating them. Students offer a glossary, quiz, and games using fractions. Recipes such as Fraction Pretzels and Scones require the use of fractions in real-life tasks.

The Gold Star Academy of Frederick Douglass Elementary School in Philadelphia, Pennsylvania, used Web publishing to share science knowledge. Students experienced a seashore ecosystem by traveling to Island Beach State Park in Seaside Park, New Jersey. In preparation, they investigated the nonliving parts of an ecosystem—soil, rocks, and water. One second grader described preparation and predictions for a decomposition experiment. "We put holes in the bag. Then we put soil and water in the bag. We put dead leaves and red worms in the bag. In five weeks there will be gases in the bag and the leaves will be gone." Students periodically observed the bag with a magnifying glass and reported results. Armed with knowledge they built from investigating soil and rocks collected from around their school and neighborhoods, they next collected samples at the beach, using their prior learning to test and study what they collected. Gold Star Academy students published their observations, hypotheses, experiments, and results on the Web. They included photographs of their trip and drawings of what they saw. Other classes are invited to experience the seashore ecosystem through the Web site and explore further through the ocean-related links provided (http://sln.fi.edu/oceans/oceans2.html).

International Schools CyberFair (http://www.gsn.org/cf/), part of the Global SchoolNet Foundation, is an authentic learning program where students conduct research about their local communities and publish their findings on the World Wide Web. The purpose of the CyberFair Web site is to promote sharing and unity among participants. The research categories encourage a wide variety of topics including local leaders, businesses, community organizations, historical landmarks, environment, music, art, and local specialties.

Another publishing project sponsored by the Global SchoolNet Foundation is the Newsday Project. Cooperating student correspondents research and report news, students write articles, and classrooms develop their own newspapers. Many other collaborative projects can be found on The Global Schoolhouse Web site, which was founded by the Global SchoolNet Foundation through the efforts of a group of teachers over a decade ago (http://www.gsh.org/about.htm). With no budget and minimal support, they set out to create an educational information infrastructure starting at the grass-roots level—with teachers. A grant from the National Science Foundation in 1992 increased their momentum, and now corporate sponsors help them cover costs of this valuable service to teachers and their students. More discussion of the Global Schoolhouse appears in chapter 4.

Publishing Original Ideas and Thoughts

Online publishing may also be used to communicate original ideas and share thoughts through poetry, art, and other writing. Web sites in this category are examples of building communities around a purpose. Although they are presented in the Web Publishing section, they could as easily fit into the next chapter.

In Flemington, New Jersey, students at Hunterdon Central Regional High School publish an online literary magazine called Electric Soup (http://homer.hcrhs.k12.nj.us/esoup/index.html). A "Community of Writers" section invites submissions from students around the country. This creative Web site uses graphics and animation to present an online publication rich in multimedia. Anyone can submit a piece to Electric Soup—young writers are encouraged, and international submissions are translated into English. An art and photography section allows students to express themselves visually. Hunterdon students conduct and publish interviews with professionals in various fields. A special International Edition of Electric Soup was published during the summer of 2000. This joint effort between Dianye Middle School in Beijing, China, and Hunterdon features poetry and photographs from Chinese students (http://homer.hcrhs.k12.nj.us/china/poetry/).

"A Vision" is an international online literary magazine for ages 13 and up whose purpose is to highlight the commonalities between teenagers around the world despite their differences in culture, ethnicity, race, and language. Through art and creative writing, teenagers can share their thoughts, dreams, and ideas with one another, recognizing their similarities. "A Vision" is part of the iEARN Web site whose projects will be further explored in chapter 4 (http://www.iearn.org/projects/avision.html).

Learning Processes   Like multimedia and hypermedia construction, Web site construction is first and foremost constructive (constructionist, to use Papert's [1990] term). In constructing Web sites, students are developing multimedia views of the ideas that they are representing. Web site construction also involves a lot of intentional learning. Our research with hypermedia construction showed that learners reflect a lot on their designs, making sure that they are desirable and interesting to other students. Finally, Web site construction normally is complex enough that it requires collaboration among a group of learners. Students will naturally break up into research, authoring, and design teams in order to complete projects. In producing the content for Web sites, students engage in academic skills (reading, writing, revising, interviewing, editing), technical skills, and social skills (discussing, leading, listening, sharing, working cooperatively).

Publishing to a potentially worldwide audience encourages students to strive for excellence in their work and to see themselves as a critical influence in others' education as well as in their own.

Problem-Solving Processes   Web publishing is design problem solving. As explicated in chapter 6, designing hypermedia Web pages engages all of the other forms of problem solving, information searching, decision making, and modeling and requires cognitive processes such as planning and decision making, accessing, transforming, and translating information into knowledge, evaluating the knowledge base, and revising the knowledge base from the feedback. These skills are the building blocks of problem solving.

Teacher Roles　Teachers tend to be less prescriptive when students are constructing personal Web pages, but our experience has shown that when students construct topical Web pages, it is not uncommon for teachers to play a larger role. However, we suggest that teachers pass this role on to students whenever possible. Suppose, for example, that a 6th-grade class studying the states in the United States and the Canadian provinces decided to make Web pages and then use each other's pages to learn. The teacher might want the pages produced by each group of students to have similar components (e.g., commerce, population density, etc.) so that students can make comparisons and learn important concepts and principles. Instead of assigning these components, generate a discussion in which the group lists important components. The process of thinking about what is important is a valuable learning experience, and they might come up with additional useful categories. Don't stifle creativity.

Encourage groups to talk to each other and to create links as appropriate. The Web's ability to support links from one page to another (anywhere in the world) can be a great stimulus to cause students to see relationships they would otherwise have missed, and to explore areas they would have otherwise bypassed.

Encourage students to make numerous links to other student-generated work and to work of others out there. Encourage students to contact people who have developed sites to which they are linking. These contacts are often very welcome, and often lead to new friendships and productive learning experiences.

Assessing Learning　Evaluating Web sites can be done analytically or holistically. More often than not, holistic evaluation better reflects student creativity, which is the hallmark of any design project. Merely viewing most Web sites is sufficient for realizing how much effort, how much creativity, and how much mental effort students have committed. If you are looking for some criteria, you might want to try these:

- How is the Web site organized? How complex is that organization? How appropriate is that organization for describing the content of the Web site? Are there adequate links for accessing different parts of the site?
- What auditory and visual resources were used in the site? How did those resources complement, explain, or illustrate the ideas being conveyed?
- How descriptive were the hyperlinks to different parts of the Web site? Did they describe the information that was being accessed?
- How accurate is the information represented?
- Are all important information sources represented in the Web site?

As you evaluate more Web sites, more criteria should become obvious to you.

EXPANDING HORIZONS: VIRTUAL TRAVEL

Field trips have long provided an opportunity to extend and enhance learning through observations and experiences with real-life situations and locations. However, these trips are limited by logistics such as cost, time requirements, and proximity to students. The Internet has opened new vistas as students now have access to places and experiences they might otherwise never encounter. Online field trips can, however, be of little value unless students travel well equipped with intentional goals for learning.

There are two main categories of virtual travel: virtual field trips and online expeditions. Field trips generally consist of students using Web sites to virtually visit locations such as museums or other countries. Online expeditions typically involve students sharing in a trip that an explorer or researcher is taking to investigate a scientific issue or historical location. Virtual travel can provide students around the world the opportunity to explore other cultures, local people, geography, culture, the foods, sights, and sounds of the places they visit.

Virtual Field Trips

The Exploratorium in San Francisco hosts an online museum with an incredible range of experiences in science, art, and human perception. Many brick and mortar museums are hands-on environments where children can experiment and learn through active involvement. Obviously, although many real-life experiences cannot be replicated online, the Exploratorium makes extensive use of Shockwave technology to deliver interactive learning opportunities. Interactive exhibits offer categories of Seeing, Mind, Life Science, Matter/World, and Hearing. Children can experiment with sound by playing a keyboard, reaction time by hitting a baseball, and memory by playing the interactive game Droodle. In other areas of the Web site, students can build a scale model of the solar system and use an online calculator to determine dimensions, distances, and speed. Whereas an actual field trip to San Francisco to visit the Exploratorium is impossible for most classes, they can gain valuable learning experiences through the online version (http://www.exploratorium.edu/).

Other online museums to explore are the Louvre Museum in Paris (http://www.louvre.fr/louvrea.htm), the Smithsonian Institution (http://www.si.edu/), and the Museum of Science and Industry (http://www.si.edu/). The Franklin Institute leads students through an online exploration of the heart (http://sln.fi.edu/biosci/heart.html).

The Scholastic Web site offers "Immigration: Stories of Yesterday and Today," a project that lets students relive the immigration experience in many ways. They can explore Ellis Island through an interactive 3-D tour, listen to audio stories shared by immigrants, and watch video clips. A follow-up oral history scrapbook leads students through the steps of locating, interviewing, and publishing oral histories. The scrapbook contains immigrant stories that students have created (http://teacher.scholastic.com/immigrat/index.htm). "Who Lives in

America?" depicts the history of immigration through charts, graphs, and tables and includes classroom activities involving data collection, research, and analysis.

At the Field Trips site (http://www.field-trips.org/), annotated field trips developed by subject experts take students to some of the best Web sites on each trip subject. This field-trip Web site has several interesting features. First, specific focus field trips cover a single topic such as salt marshes or volcanoes. The field trips' design is such that navigation is easy and students are unlikely to get lost. A narration frame provides a space for teacher directions, instructions, or narration about the Web site visited and additional teacher resources are included.

Let's look at the "Bread Baking Field Trip" (http://www.field-trips. org/sci/bake/index.htm). This field trip about bread baking utilizes Internet resources to introduce the principles, tools, and techniques of bread making. It is designed for elementary school children in grades 4–6 but is appropriate for students of many ages and incorporates reading, math, science, and history. Beginning with information about wheat, the field trip continues to Rocky Mountain Milling near Denver, Colorado, where a series of photographs and text describe the process of milling from receiving grain shipments to grinding, packing, and storing the flour. Students learn about yeast, sourdough starters, and other bread ingredients. The next step is a Web page with a bread recipe, followed by another with step-by-step directions, tips, and photographs to help students easily make the best bread possible. The field trip ends with the history of bread, facts, superstitions, and traditions surrounding bread. A Teacher's Page contains extending activities incorporating language arts, science, and math.

Kim Foley, creator of the Field Trips site, points out that although real and virtual field trips have differences, they also have many common features, as illustrated in Table 3.3 on page 62.

Online Expeditions

Unlike virtual field trips, online expeditions typically involve students sharing in a trip that is actually being taken by real-life participants. Often these explorers are researchers. Student participants usually experience the expedition through a Web site, where frequent accounts of the real-life trip are recorded. In addition to free online expeditions, subscription sites are available. Although these sites require a payment for participation, they do offer greater involvement by allowing students to directly communicate with the explorers. Some subscription sites use student input to influence expedition team members' activities. Many sites archive past expeditions with journal entries, photographs, and other resources that can be used in the classroom.

The Global Schoolhouse has no direct expedition offerings, but does provide links to a number of online expeditions as well as advice for teachers considering this type of learning activity. They suggest researching the location before the expedition begins, formulating questions, identifying areas of interest to learn about, exploring an archived expedition, and deciding students' roles and respon-

Table 3.3   Similarities and Differences in Virtual and Real-Life Field Trips (Courtesy of Kim Foley)

Similarities

- Both real and virtual field trips are group activities where kids interact with each other.
- Both real and virtual field trips involve active, not passive learning.
- Both real and virtual field trips take the student mentally out of the classroom and into a new and different learning environment.

Differences

- Virtual field trips can be repeated over and over again.
- Virtual field trips give students more room to move at their own pace and explore things to their own depth.
- Virtual field trips can take you to places you would not otherwise go.
- Virtual field trips lack the sensory experience of a real field trip.
- Virtual field trips are safe and free of hazards.
- Virtual field trips can tap into more expert resources on a single topic.

---

sibilities as they take part in the expedition (http://www.globalschoolhouse. org/expeditions/).

   National Geographic's Explorers Hall (http://www.nationalgeographic. com/explorer/) offers several expedition opportunities. In "Congo Trek: A Journey Through the Heart of Central Africa" (http://www.nationalgeographic. com/congotrek/), Wildlife Conservation Society biologist J. Michael Fay shares his hike 1,200 miles across central Africa over a 15-month period. He and his team recorded the plants and animals they encountered along the Congo River basin to create an account of how the African forest ecosystem was before human civilization arrived. Trek Viewer is a small window that can be dragged across the map of the Congo. When locations in the window are clicked, a separate frame loads Fay's field notes and links to audio, video, and environmental descriptions. Another tool, Congo Trek 360°, allows mouse navigation around a 360° image. Clicking on animals and objects provides videos, audio, and accounts of life in extreme Africa. Related classroom ideas are offered, such as having students conduct their own transect count of plants and animals within a given subdivided area around their school or neighborhood.

   SitesALIVE! is a subscription Web site that connects classrooms with other students who are taking part in learning adventures throughout the world. Land-based field schools are located in Australia, Mexico, Costa Rica, and Turks and Caicos Islands. Class Afloat Live! visits locations such as Panama, Ecuador, Chile, Argentina, South Africa, Brazil, the United States, and Canada. One group of 49 students and 15 crew members are sailing on a tall ship for a yearlong voyage around the world. Participants can e-mail questions or post comments to bulletin boards and send letters and class projects by snail (that is, regular) mail to the land sites and ship ports of call. While subscribers have opportunities for greater interactivity, a free trial allows anyone to view student and faculty pictures and biographies, tour the ships and field sites through photos and video, and follow daily highlights. One participant said, "sitesALIVE! is a great way to become part of a global community. Our world is shrinking and this forces students to learn how to communicate with all parts of the world." (http://www.sitesalive.com/)

Classroom Connect's Quest Channel offers several online expeditions. Amazon Quest took students through the Amazon River basin to explore the biodiversity of its rainforests, assess the state of the region's most urgent issues, and act to conserve its flora, fauna, and cultures. One of the explorers' main purposes was to tell the story of this unique place and to put together a proclamation to the government to create the Amarakaeri Communal Reserve as a way of protecting the area and providing a reserve for local people. Each day during the 25-day Quest, team members posted updates to the Amazon Quest Web site. Daily video clips were also uploaded. Through video, students met a man who lives off the natural resources in the Amazon region, saw butterflies, learned about a turtle conservation program run by kids, and visited communities such as Pucallpa, Peru. The Web site lets users experience a 12-hour period in Sepahua, a cultural crossroads located where the Río Sepahua meets the Río Urubamba, by rolling over the hours of the day.

An interesting feature of Quests is the partnership of the expedition team and collaborating classrooms. The expedition team solicits input from the students and uses it to determine some of their actions. For example, in Amazon Quest, participants are asked to help decide the course of the trip as researchers travel down the Río Azul. They are given the choice of paddling quickly downstream to maximize the time available to talk with residents living on the river about their feelings regarding the proposed reserve or taking a slow trip to more closely observe wildlife. The students' choice of the slow trip is represented in a graph on the Web site and students' other trip ideas are posted. The researchers, directed by students, took the slow trip. Students were also asked to make decisions about the best way to explore the issues around logging in the Amazon rainforest and how the team should spend their time studying the Camisea pipeline project.

A Teacher's Lounge provided related standards-based curriculum, assessment rubrics, a newsletter, and teacher discussion forums for communicating with other Quest participants. Students could e-mail questions to the expedition team and to more than 30 experts in biology, archeology, and other areas. The Student Gallery and Student Discussion forum were other components of the Quest's Community section. Classroom Connect has also offered MayaQuest, AustraliaQuest, IslandQuest, AmericaQuest, AsiaQuest, GalapagosQuest, and AfricaQuest (http://quest.classroom.com/). The Creative Connections Project (http://www.ccph.com/projects.html) offers trips to the Amazon rainforest, Africa, and the Arctic. It is also a subscription service, but each trip offers three to four levels of participation, with corresponding rates.

Learning Processes   The real-world experiences that students can have by engaging in virtual travel enable them to explore places and ideas that might not be available to them otherwise. The interactions that many online expeditions offer give students a chance to do more than simply observe another person's journey. Instead, they are active participants who can question explorers, discuss experiences as they occur, and in some cases, influence the course of the expedition by active decision making. Students analyze data that is reported, and make predictions and/or conclusions about what the data indicate in authentic contexts. Exposure to new places with their accompanying biodiversity and culture can stimulate imaginations and provide a rich opportunity for students to make connections between their existing knowledge of the world and the new ideas they are encountering.

As noted previously, unplanned virtual travel can mean students are mindlessly visiting Web sites, often doing little more than simply browsing the site. As with a physical field trip (and any trip!), being well prepared usually results in a more successful journey. Students who journey with no advance thought will probably engage in some unintentional learning; however, without intentional goals, the learning potential is largely unrealized. As with the information searches discussed earlier in the chapter, students must not merely encounter information but should think about what they are finding and how it relates to what they already know. Only through this process of manipulating and transforming information will stray bits of interesting trivia become connected in a meaningful construction of knowledge.

Problem-Solving Processes   Although students may not be engaged in the actual planning of the expeditions, they can vicariously engage in online planning. Planning any kind of activity is replete with decision-making problems. Decision-making problems, in turn, require a lot of information-searching problem solving.

Teacher Roles   The more a teacher allows students to be the drivers on virtual trips, the more successful the trips are likely to be. This does not imply a lack of involvement on the teacher's part. Rather, the teacher should be a partner in the journey—much like a hired tour guide who is available to assist a traveler when needed by answering questions, providing resources, and gently guiding visitors toward areas, or "not-to-be-missed" landmarks that the guide is aware are important. Teachers should also serve as "travel agents" who help with trip details such as setting up the tour, suggesting things that will make the trip more valuable for the travelers, and doing whatever possible to enhance the trip so visitors will want to embark on another journey.

Assessing Learning   One criterion for evaluating online field trips and expeditions is whether children are motivated to learn more about the topic after engaging in virtual travel (Schrock, 1998). Students should be involved in the process of deciding where to travel, what to do and see, and how to represent what they have learned from their journey. Teachers can assess the quality of learning from online travel by asking students to keep a journal log, to reflect on events during the travel, and to explain their decisions regarding choices made during an expedition. Assessment can also include evaluation of student projects that demonstrate understanding of scientific or environmental issues that are part of an online expedition. Student-created WebQuests are one method for analyzing experiences and information, then transforming that knowledge into a concrete product that demonstrates learning.

CONCLUSIONS

The U.S. Department of Education's 1996 report *Getting America's Students Ready for the 21st Century* included a section titled "Characteristics of Successful Technology-rich Schools." That section summarizes a host of research on the effectiveness of technology in schools, and then describes the characteristics shared by the most impressive sites. The following is a summary of the research:

> We know that successful technology-rich schools generate impressive results for students, including improved achievement; higher test scores; improved student attitude, enthusiasm, and engagement; richer classroom content; and improved student retention and job placement rates. Of the hundreds of studies that show positive benefits from the use of technology, two are worth noting for their comprehensiveness. The first, a U.S. Department of Education-funded study of nine technology-rich schools, concluded that the use of technology resulted in educational gains for all students regardless of age, race, parental income, or other characteristics. The second, a 10-year study supported by Apple Computer, Inc., concluded that students provided with technology-rich learning environments "continued to perform well on standardized tests but were also developing a variety of competencies not usually measured. Students explored and represented information dynamically and in many forms; became socially aware and more confident; communicated effectively about complex processes; became independent learners and self-starters; knew their areas of expertise and shared that expertise spontaneously." Moreover, research that demonstrates the effective use of technology is borne out in many successful schools across the nation. (p. 22)

Pay close attention to the last few lines of that paragraph. Many of the major benefits reveal themselves in ways that are not generally measured. The real benefit of students learning with technologies are in higher order skills and understanding of complex processes. This should come as no surprise if the technologies are used in the ways described in this chapter—to engage students in important, challenging work, and to cause them to discuss this work with others and to think deeply about it themselves.

The report identifies four "key features" these successful schools have in common:

- concentrated, conscious, and explicit planning among school leaders, families, and students to create "learner-centered" environments

- the goals and challenging standards for student achievement are clearly articulated
- restructuring of the school to support the learner-centered environment and achievement of standards (such as redesigned classrooms and buildings, changes in the use of time, new methods of delivering curriculum, better partnerships among teachers, administrators, parents, and students)
- near universal access to computer technology—at least one computer for every five students (pp. 22–23, 25)

There are real benefits to be harvested by putting today's networked computer technologies in the hands of students, especially when students are asked to use those technologies in ways that are active, constructive, collaborative, intentional, complex, contextual, conversational, and reflective. Do some active, reflective, complex, constructive, and perhaps even collaborative thinking *of your own*, and you'll see many opportunities to enhance the learning environment you create for your students. Rogers (1999) said, "The true power of what we do in our classrooms depends less on technology, and more on what we do with the technology we have."

THINGS TO THINK ABOUT

If you would like to reflect on the ideas presented in this chapter, then articulate your responses to the following questions and compare them with others' responses.

1. Why is the Internet far more than the "blackboard of the future"? What does the blackboard imply that limits our conception of the Internet?

2. Why is the concept of technology literacy so limiting? Should we study technologies? If so, how? Have you ever taken a course in washing machine literacy? Why is it unnecessary?

3. The Internet is the connection of thousands of networks. Can you think of an analogy for this agglomeration?

4. Is the Internet hardware, documents, or people? Is it the computers, the programs, and multimedia documents that people store and make available on it, or is it the people who contribute the ideas? Or is the Internet "only minds"?

5. With the evolution of the global schoolhouse, will physical schoolhouses disappear in the future? What evidence can you provide to support your prediction?

6. In the virtual school, students have classmates all over the world. What draws them together? How can that attraction be used to restructure the ways that physical schools operate?

7. Many educators worry about the impact of students' interactions with the world outside the school as they survey other students and the commu-

nity at large. Are there dangers? What are the educators really worried about?

8 In chapter 5, we suggest that students make videos about themselves. How are student home pages different from student videos? Which is better able to depict the individual?

9 Research has shown that browsing without a purpose probably will not result in learning. Yet thousands of hobby-oriented sites exist. Do individuals learn from exploring their hobbies? If so, what lessons are there for curriculum design?

10 What kinds of tools might be helpful to support student surveys using the Internet?

11 Groupware is becoming more powerful, enabling individuals to share and collaboratively work on text, graphics, sounds, video, or any other kind of file. How will software like this affect the educational process?

12 If you could select a mentor to teach you what you would like to know, who would it be? What would you like to know from him or her? How could the Internet be used to foster that relationship?

13 How can virtual field trips be better than real ones? How are they limited?

REFERENCES

Bush, G. W. (2001). *Enhancing education through technology. No child left behind.* Retrieved from http://www.ed.gov/inits/nclb/partx.html

Caverly, D. C. (2000). Technology and the "Knowledge Age." In D. B. Lundell & J. L. Higbee (Eds.), *Proceedings of the First Intentional Meeting on Future Directions in Developmental Education* (pp. 34–36). Minneapolis: University of Minnesota, General College and The Center for Research on Developmental Education and Urban Literacy. http://www.gen.umn.edu/research/crdeul

Costa, A., & Kallick, B. (2000). *Habits of mind: A developmental series.* Alexandria, VA: Association for Supervision and Curriculum Development.

Danesh, A., Inkpen, K. M., Lau, F., Shu, K., & Booth, K. S. (2001, April). *Geney: Designing a collaborative activity for the Palm hand-held computer.* In Proceedings of CHI, Conference on Human Factors in Computing Systems. Seattle, Washington.

DeVera, C. (2001, June 10). Online to graduate. *Columbia Daily Tribune.* Retrieved from http://archive.showmenews.com/2001/jun/20010610news002.asp

Dodge, B. (1997). *WebQuest taskonomy: A taxonomy of tasks.* Retrieved from http://edweb.sdsu.edu/webquest/taskonomy.html

Gardner, H. (1991). *The unschooled mind: How children think and how schools should teach.* New York: Basic Books.

Gardner, H. (2000). *Intelligence reframed: Multiple intelligences for the 21st century.* New York: Basic Books.

Healy, J. (1998). *Failure to connect: How computers affect our childrens' minds—and what we can do about it.* New York: Touchstone Books.

Hopper, K. (2001). Is the Internet a classroom? *TechTrends 45*(5), 35–43.

Inkpen, K. M. (1999). Designing hand-held technologies for kids. *Personal Technologies Journal, 3* (1&2), 81–89.

Kelly, D. (2000, October) Online research skills for students. *Classroom Connect, 7*(2), 3–4.

McCafferty, D. (2001). The net: A new tool for skipping school. *USAWEEKEND* magazine.

Retrieved from http://www.usaweekend.com/ 01_issues/010610/010610cyberschool. html

McKenzie, J. (2001). *Beyond technology: Questioning, research and the information literate school community*. FNO Press. Retrieved from http://fno. org/beyondtech.html

NetDay. (2001, March 29). *84% of teachers say Internet improves quality of education* press release Retrieved from http://www.netday.org/ news_survey.htm

Papert, S. (1990). Introduction by Seymour Papert. In I. Harel (Ed.), *Constructionist learning*. Boston: MIT Laboratory.

Peterson, C. L., & Koeck, D. C. (2001). When students create their own Webquests. *Learning & Leading with Technology 29* 1.

Quality Education Data. (2001). *Internet in U.S. public schools: Usage and trends 2001–2002*. Retrieved January 12, 2002, from http://www.qeddata. com/October_pr.htm

Riel, M. (2000). New designs for connected teaching and learning. White paper for U.S. Department of Education Secretary's Conference on Educational Technology. Retrieved from http:// www.gse.uci.edu/mriel/whitepaper/learn1. html

Riley, R. (1998, February 17). *Education first: Building America's future*. The Fifth Annual State of American Education speech. Seattle, Washington. Retrieved from http://www.ed.gov/Speeches/ 980217.htm

Rogers, A. (1999). *The origins of a global learning network*. Retrieved from http://gsh.lightspan. com/teach/articles/feb99_article.htm

Schrock, K. (1998). *Kathy Schrock's guide for educators: Evaluation of virtual tours*. Retrieved from ht.com/schrockguide/evaltour.html

Scardamalia, M., & Bereiter, C. (1999). Schools as knowledge-building organizations. In D. Keating & C. Hertzman (Eds.), *Today's children, tomorrow's society: The developmental health and wealth of nations* (pp. 274–289). New York: Guilford. Retrieved from http://csile.oise. utoronto.ca/abstracts/ciar-understanding.html

Soloway, E., Norris, C., Blumenfeld, P., Fishman, B., Krajcik, J., & Marx, R. (2001, June). Log on education: Hand-held devices are ready-at-hand. *Communications of the ACM, 44*(6), 15–20.

U.S. Department of Education. (1996). *Getting America's students ready for the 21st century: Meeting the technology literacy challenge*. Washington, DC: U.S. Department of Education.

Web-Based Education Commission. (2000). *The power of the Internet for learning: Moving from promise to practice*. Washington, DC: U.S. Department of Education.

Williams, C. (2000). *Internet access in public schools: 1994–1999* (NCES 2000–086). Washington, DC: National Center for Educational Statistics, U.S. Department of Education. Retrieved from http://nces.ed.gov/

Building Technology-Supported Learning Communities on the Internet

FORMING COMMUNITIES

Margaret Riel (1991) tells a story about a 4-year-old in her mother's office.

> The mother, wanting to involve her daughter in her work, realizes the daughter has never heard modem noises, and begins explaining:
>
> "You see these words on the screen. Well, this little modem takes those words and turns them into sounds. They go on the telephone lines just like someone talking, and a computer on the other end is going to get them. Then that computer will send them to other computers. So my message will be sent all over the world!"
>
> The child looked up from her coloring and said, "Oh, like a talking drum."
> The mother, dumbfounded, finally asked, "A talking drum?"
> "You know, like a talking drum." The mother thought some more, and then she remembered that not long ago, an African storyteller had visited her daughter's preschool and shown the class an African drum. When villagers wanted to get a message out to neighbors about a festival or a market, they would use the drum, and the message would be sent from village to village.

The point of the story is that although modems and networks are relatively new, people have always found ways to communicate with each other in order to support community goals and activities; they have overcome obstacles and used considerable ingenuity in doing so. If working and learning together in communities is so natural, why do schools individualize learning and make its outcomes competitive among students?

Years ago, John Dewey commented on the dangers of a complex society that relies on schools and classrooms to convey essential knowledge and tools to its youth:

> As societies become more complex in structure and resources, the need for formal teaching and learning increases. As formal teaching and training grows, there's a danger of creating an undesirable split between the experience gained in direct association and what is acquired in school. This danger was never greater than at the present time on account of the rapid growth of the last few centuries, of knowledge and technical modes of skill. (Cited in Riel, 1991)

The schism between real-world experience and school learning is a serious concern. As we have tried to illustrate throughout this book, technologies of various kinds can serve as bridges between schools and students' outside experiences, if they are used in the right way within a supportive context. Technologies can support learning communities by providing communications vehicles to all learners.

The notion of community is used in a variety of ways. Increasingly, our notion of community is expanding to become a more global concept. The Internet enables community to move beyond geographical boundaries and provides a vehicle for people around the world to interact and learn together. We will discuss several key variations on the concept of community.

Discourse Communities

People are social creatures who like to talk with each other. Generally, they talk about common interests—sports, gardening, cars, dancing, video games—whatever objects and activities engage them. Whenever they can, people talk face to face about their interests. When they must reach beyond their neighborhood to find others who share their interests, or to expand their discourse community, people talk to each other at a distance through newsletters, magazines, and television shows. If you examine the magazine counter in your supermarket, you will find discourse communities focused on everything from brides to monster trucks. Cable television supports discourse networks on sports, cooking, and shopping. Computer networks have evolved to support discourse communities through different forms of computer conferences. For instance, thousands of bulletin boards, Usenet and Netnews services, and chat rooms support special-interest discussion groups oriented to a wide range of topics, from computer games to sexual deviancies. More than 500 different organized Usenet groups discuss computer issues alone. More than 10,000 other groups support conversations on topics as diverse as baseball, poetry, model railroading, abortion, gun control, and religion. Thousands of chat rooms and multiuser dungeons (MUDs) connect millions of users who converse daily about their lives, their dreams, and their inadequacies. One-to-one communication is widely occurring through Internet Relay Chat, commonly known as instant messaging. The number of active and interactive discourse communities has expanded exponentially with the growth of telecommunications. These communities can now stay in constant contact about their interests.

Communities of Practice

In the real world, when people need to learn something, they usually do not remove themselves from their normal situations and force themselves into sterile rooms to listen to lectures on formal principles about what they are doing. Rather, they tend to form work groups (practice communities), assign roles, teach and support each other, and develop identities that are defined by the roles they play in support of the group. Kathryn Fulton and Margaret Riel (1999) state, "A community of practice is a group of people who share a common interest in a topic or area, a particular way of talking about their phenomena, tools and sense-making approaches for building their collaborative knowledge with a sense of common collective tasks." In other words, learning results naturally from becoming a participating member of a community of practice. You cannot do your job without learning about the skills, the knowledge, and the social context that surrounds that job because the context, to a large degree, defines the nature of the job. How many times have you heard the phrase, "the way we do it here"? Knowledge of the context and its customs is not only acquired by the people, but it also becomes part of their identity, which is part of the social fabric of the community, so that "learning, thinking, and knowing are relations among people engaged in activity" (Lave, 1991, p. 67).

Knowledge-Building Communities

Scardamalia and Bereiter (1996) argue that schools inhibit, rather than support, knowledge building by (1) focusing on individual students' abilities and learning; (2) requiring only demonstrable knowledge, activities, and skills as evidence of learning; and (3) teacher-hoarding wisdom and expertise. Students' knowledge tends to be devalued or ignored, except as evidenced by their understanding of the curriculum. What students know and believe is unimportant. Or is it? Should student knowledge not be the focus of schools, and should not schools support student knowledge-building? The goal of knowledge-building communities is to support students to "actively and strategically pursue learning as a goal"—that is, intentional learning (Scardamalia, Bereiter, & Lamon, 1994, p. 201). Learning, especially intentional learning by students, is a byproduct of schoolwork. To support intentional learning among students, Scardamalia and Bereiter have developed environments where students produce their own knowledge databases in their own knowledge-building community (Computer-Supported Intentional Learning Environments or CSILEs, and Knowledge Forum, described later in the chapter). Thus, student knowledge can be "objectified, represented in an overt form so that it [can] be evaluated, examined for gaps and inadequacies, added to, revised, and reformulated" (p. 201). When students own the knowledge, rather than the teacher or the textbook, they become committed to building knowledge, rather than merely receiving and reprocessing it. Knowledge building becomes a social activity, not a solitary one of retention and regurgitation. Technology plays a key role in knowledge-building communities by providing a medium for storing, organizing, and reformulating the ideas that are contributed by each community member. Although these knowledge-building technology environments treat knowledge as a commodity, to the community of students it represents the synthesis of their thinking, something they own and for which they can be proud. In this sense, we believe, the goal of schools should be to foster knowledge-building communities.

Learning Communities

Classrooms and schools can be communities of learners, although they often are not. Why? A community is a social organization of people who share knowledge, values, and goals. Classrooms typically are not communities, because students are disconnected or are competing with one another. The students do not share common learning goals or interests. Within classrooms there are social communities or cliques, but their purpose is not to learn together or from one another. Rather, those cliques seek to socially reinforce their own identities by excluding others. Learning communities emerge when students share common interests. Telecommunications connect learners within the same class or around the world in order to pursue some common learning objectives. The Journey North activities, described in chapter 3, represent a scientific learning agenda that kids around the country can share. The Internet supports Netnews and Usenet groups that share common goals and interests. Learning communities emerge when learners work together toward their common goals. Many of the projects in this chapter constitute learning communities. They can be fostered by having the participants conduct research (reading, studying, viewing, consulting experts) and share information in the pursuit of a meaningful, consequential task (Harris, 1998). Many of these learning communities support reflection on the knowledge constructed and the processes used to construct it by the learners.

The concepts of discourse community, community of practice, knowledge-building community, and learning community overlap considerably. Their common belief is that rather than forcing students to conform to prepackaged instructional requirements, emphasis should be placed on the social and cognitive contributions of a group of learners to each other, with students collaborating and supporting each other toward commonly accepted learning goals. Learning and knowledge-building communities depend heavily on both student and teacher buy-in, responsibility, and continuing motivation, as well as a rich collection of information and learning resources to support them. We believe that learning communities can be an important vehicle for reforming schools. In this chapter, we show how technology can support learning communities. We then develop and illustrate the concepts of discourse and knowledge-building communities and suggest ways of nurturing a sense of community within classrooms and beyond.

SUPPORTIVE TECHNOLOGIES

Chapter 3 introduced you to the various technologies available through the Internet. In this section, we review both the underlying technologies and related activities and programs that allow learning communities to take shape.

The technological breakthrough that has afforded these learning communities is the Internet and networking technologies. The Internet, particularly the World Wide Web (WWW), has become more than a source for retrieving archived information; it has become the medium that connects scattered people and resources together. Why? In many ways, the Internet's strength lies in its decentralized nature.

As we saw in chapter 3, the Internet is the ultimate distributed network, linking users and institutions together, allowing interactions of all kinds to occur. The Internet can become the communications vehicle that both liberates and ties learners together, including students and teachers, into coherent learning communities. The Internet can be part of the glue that keeps people connected—talking with each other, noticing and appreciating differences, working out divergent views, and serving as role models and audiences for one another. The education future portended by the Internet, therefore, is not isolated and targeted to individuals. Rather, it is a community-centered future that accommodates each person through the workings of the larger community of learners.

At the core of learning communities is the cultivation of a certain quality of relationship among teachers and students. Learning communities are united by a common cause of mutual support and by shared values and experiences. Communities may originate from assignment (e.g., typical K–12 classrooms) or through self-selection (Netnews groups or chat rooms on the Internet). Learning communities provide a means for learning within an atmosphere of trust, support, common goals, and respect for diversity. They make use of various technologies— machines, products, information sources, even language itself—to accomplish their goals. Learning communities existed long before networking technologies came into being, but the potential scale of adoption expands with the technologies available.

Modern network technologies hold a key advantage that early visionaries did not enjoy: Students and teachers can more easily escape the confines of the closed classroom and open things up to include elements of the outside world— other classes, students, teachers, and experts; other information, projects, and media. As Riel (1996) noted:

> We send children to school to give them the opportunity to move beyond the constraints of family and friends to open to them a vast range of possible futures. However the classroom in today's society, by its very nature, is constraining. It isolates both students and teachers from many experiences that will help them to understand the past, develop skills for building a future, and to prepare for their role as citizens. . . . If it once took the whole village to raise a child, then can we expect a succession of isolated teachers to give students all the skills they need to [be] productive members of society? (Riel, 1996; text reordered)

Students can be introduced to much more of the "world out there" through communications and multimedia technologies.

The Cognition and Technology Group at Vanderbilt (1994) developed a list of core values and principles for learning communities, presented in Table 4.1. The Peabody Perspective contributes to our discussion in two ways. First, it articulates in greater detail the instructional-design foundations on which learning communities rest. Careful attention to the design of projects and curriculum is something inherited from the fields of instructional design and cognitive psychology. Second, the Peabody Perspective places learning communities within the school and community context, addressing issues such as assessment, support from the larger community, and management. This larger perspective further underscores the huge task of developing and maintaining learning communities, and the many systemic factors that must be incorporated into successful efforts.

Online Communication (Telecommunications)

Communication in an online forum is different from, and in several important ways better than, face-to-face communication and other technology-based forms (like telephone conversations and videoconferencing). It is true that an online discussion doesn't have the richness or, to use a computer metaphor, the "bandwidth" of a face-to-face conversation. We lose important communication cues such as body language, tone of voice, accents, dialects, pace, pauses, and other

Table 4.1 The Peabody Perspective on Learning Communities (Cognition and Technology Group at Vanderbilt, 1994)

1. Curriculum and Instruction
   - Emphasizes active, problem-focused teaching and learning
   - Integrates subject areas
   - Emphasizes varied instructional strategies, depending on student needs
   - Relies on heterogeneous, collaborative student groups/teams
   - Focuses on project-based activities, while also giving attention to the development of key concepts and skills

2. Assessment
   - Focuses on thinking and communicating as well as on concepts and skills
   - Is authentic
   - Informs instruction
   - Gives schools the flexibility to respond to the uniqueness of the population they serve, while still being held accountable to state and national goals and standards

3. Professional Development and School Organization
   - Provides meaningful opportunities for education to learn and improve
   - Redefines "professionals as isolated experts" to "professionals as collaborators and facilitators of learning"
   - Keeps decision making open and responsive to parent, student, and community input

4. Community Connections
   - Keeps parents involved in their children's education
   - Creates shared responsibility for children and cooperative efforts to provide resources and support for learning
   - Ensures adequate and coordinated health and social services for children
   - Fosters a concern for the common good

5. Technology
   - Supports all areas of the learning community—learning, assessment, management, professional development, and community connectedness

important cues to meaning. Although this may be limiting, it may also be helpful, as authors must take more care to see that they are communicating clearly.

Paraphrasing a television commercial run by a major telecommunications vendor, on the Internet there is no race, no gender, no age, no infirmities—only minds: people talking to people.

Online communications are often *asynchronous* (not in real time), making them different in important ways. Howard Gardner (1991, 2000) has proposed a Theory of Multiple Intelligences, which suggests that intelligence is not a single capacity, but rather a series of distinct capabilities. He suggests that rather than asking, "How smart are you?" we should ask, "How are you smart?" Some people, Gardner believes, are high in *verbal intelligence*. They are often verbally deft and capable of carrying out stimulating conversations. They tend to do well in traditional school environments. This does not mean they are the best thinkers or communicators. Other people want more time to consider an idea and formulate their responses. Rather than speaking extemporaneously, they are often minimal contributors to real-time conversations—the conversation is off to other topics before they have developed their ideas and ways to share them.

When given a chance to think and then speak, as is the case in several forms of online conversation, these people experience a new freedom and level of participation. They can be heard clearly, and the power of their responses is often impressive. When combined with the removal of biases, as already described, it becomes easy to imagine why a number of strong friendships (some crossing international borders and generations) and even romances have begun on the Internet.

Table 4.2 on page 77 shows how communication technologies—primarily e-mail, conferencing, and the Web—facilitate a variety of learning activities, particularly those requiring collaboration and group effort. Moreover, technologies useful for individual or one-on-one interactions are subsumed and appropriated by collaborating groups, resulting in a fairly powerful set of tools available to groups and communities.

Forms of Online Communication Communication takes a variety of forms online, including simple browsing of Web pages, e-mail, use of listservs, electronic bulletin boards and Netnews groups, online chats, videoconferencing, and MUDs. After a quick overview of these forms of online communication, we'll see how they are used to promote meaningful learning.

Electronic Mail. Electronic mail (e-mail) allows the sender to transmit a message, almost instantly, to an individual or a group of individuals. With most e-mail programs, the transmitted message can include *attachments* that might contain complex documents, images, sounds, or even brief videos. The receiver of a piece of electronic mail can easily respond, forward the message to other users, and efficiently save the message in an electronic form.

The power of e-mail comes from its speed and its broadcasting capabilities. A print letter carried by postal services (*snail mail*) might take days to go in one direction, but electronic exchanges often complete two or three cycles in a matter of minutes. Sending e-mail to 20 people can be as easy as sending to one person. Another big difference is in cost. E-mail (when the computers and network connections are already in place) is virtually free.

Listservs. Listservs are a variation of e-mail. When users interested in a particular topic *subscribe* to a listserv on some topic, they begin to receive messages from the other members of the list. To get a message to all of the list's subscribers, a user sends a single copy of the note to the list, and the computer that hosts the list sends a copy to all subscribers. The sender generally does not even know *how many* users there are, let alone who they are.

Lists often have hundreds of subscribers, and listserv participation sometimes results in e-mail inboxes choked with messages. For this reason, some lists

Table 4.2   Learning Activities Facilitated by Different Levels of Computer Networking Technologies (Adapted from Paulson, 1996)

Communication Level	Description	Enabling Technologies	Learning Activities
One-alone	Individuals can access information resources stored on the World Wide Web. These resources can also be used by groups.	Online databases and journals Software libraries Tutorials and job aids Other Web resources	Independent inquiry Research and writing Browsing
One-to-one	Individuals can communicate to other individuals using e-mail, and can arrange for individual learning experiences such as internships or independent studies.	E-mail Chatting technologies using text, audio, and/or video	Apprenticeships and internships E-mail posts, private consultations One-on-one chats
One-to-many	Individuals can broadcast information to entire groups; information can also be "published" at Web sites to allow others access.	Distribution lists Web pages as a source of text and multimedia displays Web pages as links to outside resources	Lectures and symposiums Publishing results of research and inquiry activities Convenient access and dissemination of resources
Many-to-many	Groups of people can engage in open communication, through various discussion and activity forums, both real-time and asynchronously.	Listservs Chat and conferencing technologies MUD and MOO systems	Debates Discussion and support groups Group exercises and projects MUD and MOO learning activities

are "moderated," which means that one or more people read the message before it is copied to all members of the list, to determine whether it is worthy of distribution. For the same reason, membership on some lists is restricted. Other lists may group messages that are sent periodically in one e-mail as a "digest" instead of sending many individual messages.

Electronic Bulletin Boards.   Electronic bulletin boards, such as Netnews or Usenets, are similar in purpose to listservs. Instead of messages being sent to subscribers via e-mail, they are generally posted in a central location (on an electronic bulletin board) with a subject heading, date, time, and author's name. Users browse through the subject headings, read, and perhaps respond to messages of interest. Most responses are sent via e-mail directly to the person who posted the message, rather than being posted for all to see. It works sort of like a newspaper, in which you scan headlines, article titles, and classified ads, deciding whether to read them. If you respond, it may be to the paper itself (a letter to the editor), to an individual or organization mentioned in the article, or to the author. The software you use to look at Netnews generally keeps track of which articles you have read, and you can usually delete articles from your copy of the list of postings.

There are Netnews conversations on approximately 10,000 different topics, from trading baseball cards to discussing political science to strategies for winning at Blackjack. In fact, it is difficult to name a potentially interesting topic for which there is not an established conversation. However, teachers should be aware of two things: first, many of the conversations are not suitable for students (many are not really suitable for adults, either); and second, *flaming*, the practice of sending responses that are overly harsh, is relatively common. Students should be prepared for this before they encounter it.

Because of the storage demands created by thousands of conversations involving millions of people, Internet-access providers make only a subset of the existing Netnews conversations available. If you or your students want to be involved in conversations on a particular topic, but it does not appear available, ask your Internet provider to investigate and provide it to you.

Chats.   Chats are real-time (synchronous) exchanges among individuals who are gathered in a *virtual location*, often set up as a house, with a lobby, library, kitchen, and dining room where people go to have private conversations. This is made possible by Internet Relay Chat (IRC) software. IRC allows anyone to post a statement to the group by typing into a field and then clicking a button to submit the statement. The software adds each comment to a scrolling list. The list is sent out to participants' screens periodically, say every 20 seconds, keeping everyone informed about what has been said.

The conversations are often a bit confusing. It's rather like a cocktail party where there are several conversations going on at once. If the chat gets too busy, clusters of people can break off into another room to converse without the distraction of competing conversations. It is also possible to establish private chats, restricting entry to people who are registered to participate. Although some find this kind of communication confusing, others find it almost addictive.

Free messaging software such as ICQ (I Seek You), AOL Instant Messenger, and MSN Messenger gives users control over those they talk with through use of "buddy lists." Unless a user provides personal information to a directory, only individuals who know that user's screen name can "IM" or send instant an message to him or her. Each one-on-one conversation in this type of chat environment is contained in a small, separate screen. While this allows several private conversations, users must manage several windows and conversations at once. Based on one of the author's observations of two teenagers, managing multiple conversations in an instant messaging environment is an easily learned skill.

Videoconferencing. Low-end videoconferencing is also possible on the Internet. By connecting an inexpensive videocamera to your computer (less than $50 for black and white, less than $100 for color), you can turn your computer into a slow, but useful, videoconferencing tool (see chapter 5 for more information). If you have a fast modem—or better yet, an Ethernet connection to the Internet—you can use it to communicate with sound and rather jerky video.

More and more, applications are becoming integrated. For example, BuddyVision shareware links your webcam to AOL Instant Messenger (AIM), letting you videoconference with or send still images to your AIM friends. Applications like Microsoft NetMeeting support multipoint data conferencing, meaning that data collaboration is possible between several people at once. Users can communicate with audio and video, conference and work together using the whiteboard or shared program features.

Internet users can also connect via shareware software called CU-SeeMe to see and hear each other. To cluster more than two sites, reflector software is used. People from different locations around the world contact the reflector (video chat room), which displays their images for all to see. There is generally also a text-based option that resembles conversations described in the section on chats. These video-based chats are very stimulating to school-aged children, who love to see themselves on TV (or the computer) and who seem to get so much out of seeing the people with whom they are communicating.

Care should be taken, however, to keep the technology in a support role and not become enamored of the tool itself. Riel (1996) observes:

> Building physical space should not be confused with building community. A [listserv], a conference, or a Web page, in and of itself, does not define community. . . . It is the interactions and partnerships among and between the people who gather in these places that define a community. And these interactions will come to be perceived as "real" in the same way that we see talking on phones or listening to a president's address on television is real. These experiences do not replace face-to-face contacts, any more than phone conversation[s] replace meetings. They provide another form of social exchange that augment relationships and have real consequences.

Thus, the technologies (column 3 of Table 4.2) and the learning activities (column 4) serve an instrumental role in support of learning communities, and are not ends in themselves.

Groupware Supports. Responding largely to a global economy in which many corporations have offices distributed around the world, software developers are racing to meet a new market by providing a new line of software products known as *groupware*. These products, including LotusNotes and NetMeeting, are designed to make it easier and easier for people in different locations to work, think, and learn together.

Groupware products make it possible for people in different locations to share computer screens and documents, and use the Internet to carry audio transmissions. So, for example, suppose that we were writing this chapter together. Products such as NetMeeting would make it possible for us to make a connection through the Internet that carries our voices and lets us look at a single computer screen, leaving both our keyboards and mice active. We would be able to talk about changes, and take turns making edits—both working on the same document at the same time.

Many exchanges between collaborators are *asynchronous*, separated in time. Increasingly, collaborators are working together in *real time*, despite distance, linked by the Internet and its offspring. This will change the nature of electronic collaboration. In some ways it will be for the best, but in other ways today's asynchronous collaborations are better. In synchronous collaboration, one strong partner (faster or more vocal) can overpower other quieter participants, who if given time to produce on their own can make important contributions. And, because time differences will always be a factor between distant locations, the availability of synchronous communications might tend to limit collaboration to partners in time zones that are not too different.

USING TELECOMMUNICATIONS TO FOSTER LEARNING COMMUNITIES

Classroom learning communities may look to members for their interactions, or they may venture out and create alliances with other classes and individuals. We believe that both kinds of interaction are important. Community begins with interactions among members, but can also be strengthened and defined by its outside encounters. In this section, we consider how a number of technologies can support learning communities, both within the classroom and beyond.

So far, we have focused on the Internet infrastructure—the e-mail, discussion, and chatting capabilities afforded by the networking hardware and software. These capabilities translate into a number of strategies for teaching and learning. Judi Harris (1995, 1998, 2000) has developed a list of *activity structures* suitable for the classroom, demonstrating the variety of activities that telecommunications enables (see Table 4.3 on pages 81 and 82):

1. **Interpersonal Exchanges.** These activities give students an opportunity to interact with others from a distance. By doing so, they come to appreciate how differently people see and make sense of their world. They also have opportunities to reinforce literacy skills through extended reading and writing activities.

2. **Information Collections and Analyses.** The focus of these activities is on collaborative, distributed collection, analysis, organization, and presentation of information. Students can participate in every step of this process. Information activities may help students internalize scientific methods. They may also strengthen students' information literacy skills.

Table 4.3 Specific Activity Structures Categorized by Genre and Learning Processes. Copyright © 2000, ISTE (International Society for Technology in Education), 800.336.5191 (U.S. & Canada) or 541.302.3777 (Int'l), iste@iste.org, www.iste.org. All rights reserved.

Genre	Activity Structure	Learning Process Emphasis
Interpersonal Exchanges		
	Keypals	Longer-term, interest-driven, one-to-one written communication is based on emergent topics of conversation. Can be used to motivate students to communicate in writing.
	Global Classrooms	Longer-term, group-to-group discussion in writing of structured or semi-structured topics. Can be used to help students research and hone their assertions and arguments.
	Electronic Appearances	Short-term communication "event" with someone special by virtue of reputation and/or expertise. Good way to pique interest in a particular topic or event.
	Telementoring	Longer-term communication by writing in a mentor-protégé format. Rich possibilities for long-term professional/personal relationships/modeling.
	Question and Answer	Very short-term written communication to clarify or complete understanding of a complex topic.
	Impersonations	Variable-term written communication necessitating deep-level, actively applied understanding of a historical period or literary work. Impersonation format is usually quite motivating.
Information Collections and Analyses		
	Information Exchanges	Variable-term communication in which similar information is compared and contrasted. Especially effective when students are comparing locally generated information that differs across collection sites.
	Database Creation	Previously accumulated information is analyzed deeply enough so that it can be classified and organized for others to use to form higher-level understanding.
	Electronic Publishing	Fruits of learning efforts are formatted so that others can benefit from perusing them. Good for both learning closure and public relations.
	Telefieldtrips	People (and less frequently, animals) are shadowed while they are active so that their experiences can be vicariously perceived.

Table 4.3 Continued

Genre	Activity Structure	Learning Process Emphasis
Information Collections and Analyses		
	Pooled Data Analysis	Similar information is pooled from multiple sites so that overarching patterns can be discerned. A higher level of thinking than information exchanges.
Problem-Solving Projects		
	Information Searches	Information-searching skills are honed.
	Peer Feedback Activities	Multiple sources of feedback are provided and received so that successive drafts of student work can be prepared.
	Parallel Problem Solving	Different problem-solving strategies applied to the same challenge are compared, contrasted, and appreciated. Good for helping students realize that there are "many right answers" to a problem.
	Sequential Creations	Collaboration on a common product that occurs sequentially rather than simultaneously. Deeper-level understanding of what has been created before is necessary if the work is to continue in a consistent manner.
	Telepresent Problem Solving	Real-time brainstorming and problem-solving skills are exercised using text chat and/or videoconferencing. Good vehicle for use of previously researched information and/or prepared questions.
	Simulations	Immersion in a content-rich, individualized or collaborative context for learning produces in-depth, experiential understanding of the problem situation being explored.
	Social Action Projects	Authentic commitment to assisting others is coupled with authentic learning about a current, often global problem.

3. **Problem-Solving Projects.** These projects focus on individual, small-group, or multigroup problems. They often require higher levels of collaboration and organization between sites. Students have opportunities to learn task-management skills in addition to content objectives.

SCAFFOLDING CONVERSATIONS IN STRUCTURED COMPUTER CONFERENCES

Online communication presumes that students can communicate—that is, that they can meaningfully participate in conversations. In order to do that, they must be able to interpret messages, consider appropriate responses, and construct coherent replies. Most teachers realize that not all students can engage in cogent and coherent discourse. Why can't they? For one thing, most students have rarely been asked to contribute their opinions about topics. They have been too busy memorizing what the teachers tell them. So, it may be necessary to support students' attempts to converse. A number of online communication environments have been designed to support students' discourse skills. Several such environments are described next.

Knowledge Forum (formerly CSILE)

Over the past decade, a team of researchers, teachers, administrators, and computer scientists collaborated to create the research foundation and ensuing designs for Knowledge Forum. Knowledge Forum 3 is a second-generation product evolving from what researchers learned from its predecessor, CSILE (Computer-Supported Integrated Learning Environment). Developed by Marlene Scardamalia and Carl Bereiter of the Ontario Institute for Studies in Education, CSILEs incorporated a classroom model for student inquiry and knowledge generation. Extensive research in classrooms using this original knowledge-building environment, CSILE, has verified its effectiveness and helped inform succeeding revisions.

The primary purpose of the current version, Knowledge Forum 3, is to teach students to be knowledge producers. To meet this goal, Knowledge Forum 3 allows users to create a knowledge-building community. True knowledge-building environments enable learning that focuses on ideas and builds deeper levels of understanding. Knowledge Forum is a collaborative database that supports a shared process of knowledge building by defining problems, hypothesizing, researching, collecting information, collaborating, and analyzing. Research on knowledge-building environments suggests that the sustained inquiry in these environments results in improved scores in conceptual development as well as basic skills, and a degree of student interaction that occurs regardless of ability. Gains in student confidence and the quality of student inquiry were also reported. The Knowledge Forum system has two important features:

- A special computer program for developing a common information base, installed on a local-area network (LAN) or on a remote server accessible through the Internet.
- A systematic model of inquiry based on the scientific method and informed by current research in cognitive psychology.

Using Knowledge Forum 3, a user community creates a database where notes are stored, ideas are connected, and knowledge is produced. The design of Knowledge Forum's structured environment facilitates these processes. Users connect to their databases either through the Knowledge Forum Client, an application stored on their computer, or via a browser using the WWW. While the Client and the browser both connect to the same database and display the information visually, their displays and features are different, providing flexibility. Figure 4.1 illustrates the differences between the Client and Web browser interfaces.

In Knowledge Forum, students are expected to be contributors. The knowledge-building process requires them to formulate questions, define their own learning goals, acquire and build a knowledge base, and collaborate with one another. Throughout this process, information sharing occurs due to Knowledge Forum's inherent structure. Students are cued to the thinking strategies that "expert learners" demonstrate through built-in scaffolds. Students contribute public notes, use an annotation feature to refine and extend others' ideas, and cite the work of their peers (see Figure 4.2). Engaging in these activities helps students develop the learning strategies used by expert learners.

Learning is not a byproduct of Knowledge Forum activities; it is a direct goal. Students are encouraged to make school more meaningful by being mindful and goal-directed in their pursuit of learning objectives. Like scientists, Knowledge Forum participants approach a problem, develop hypotheses or theories about the problem, then seek to confirm, modify, or discard their theories through research, observation, and interpretation. Also like scientists, participants collaborate, review each other's work, and publish their confirmed results. Knowledge Forum supports users in approaching information from multiple perspectives, building new connections from the knowledge base (see Figures 4.3 and 4.4).

The theory behind Knowledge Forum is largely embodied in the software program used for entering, archiving, and retrieving student research. For example, students must select a label for each message they send, based on a simple set of categories. A student posting an opinion is scaffolded in supporting that opinion through evidence, example, or reasoning. Examples are given in Table 4.4. To get a better feel for Knowledge Forum as a learning environment, you may wish to browse the Knowledge Forum Web site (http://www.knowledgeforum.com/).

Knowledge Forum can be applied to various subjects. Unlike many online projects, which resemble electronic field trips or online databases, Knowledge Forum is a comprehensive model for inquiry designed to help students conceptu-

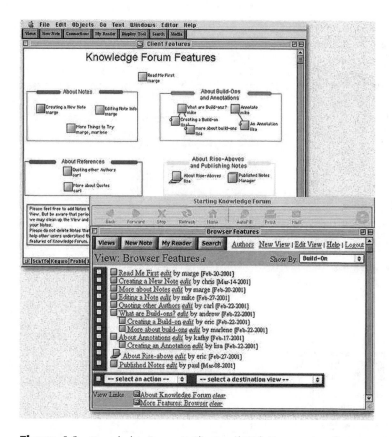

Figure 4.1 Knowledge Forum 3 Client and Web Browser Interfaces
(Photo courtesy of Knowledge Forum®)

alize and research a problem area. As such, it is more easily adopted within contained classrooms (relying less on outside Web access) and more demanding (requiring students to follow strict rules of reasoning and inquiry). Also in contrast to many online projects, considerable research has been conducted on CSILE and Knowledge Forum, consistently demonstrating positive effects on learning (Scardamalia, Bereiter, & Lamon, 1994).

CaMILE and Swiki

A second example of scaffolded conversations is provided by a program called CaMILE. Developed at the EduTech Institute at the Georgia Institute of Technology, the basis of CaMILE is a collaborative NoteBase where students post notes associated with group discussions. Each added note is a response to a note that someone else has contributed to the discussion. Students enter a Comment note (bottom window of Figure 4.5) into an ongoing discussion (top window of

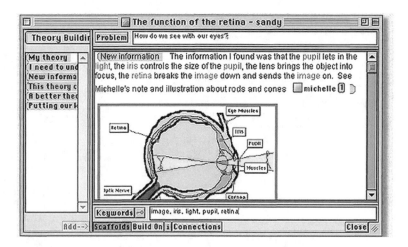

Figure 4.2   Idea Representation Through a Knowledge Forum Note (Photo courtesy of Knowledge Forum®)

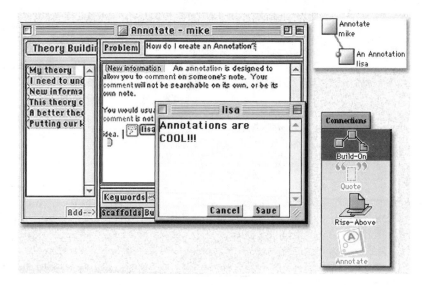

Figure 4.3   Multiple Perspective Views of the Knowledge Base (Photo courtesy of Knowledge Forum®)

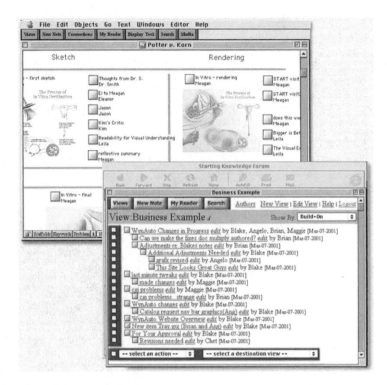

Figure 4.4   Connection and Elaboration Enabled in Knowledge Forum
(Photo courtesy of Knowledge Forum®)

Figure 4.5). In addition to the text, the student has included a QuickTime movie, as evidenced by the multimedia margin that shows links to pictures, sounds, spreadsheets, or any other kind of file. CaMILE also provides space for making suggestions (upper right) based on the Comment note. When a student reads through a discussion and wants to comment on a note, the student must specify the kind of response it is (a question, a comment, a rebuttal, an alternative—see Figure 4.6). Having to specify the response type scaffolds the development of discussion and argumentation skills.

Swikis are a development in anchored collaborative learning environments that evolved from the use of CaMILE. A Swiki is an open-source, collaborative Web site (CoWeb) space developed by Mark Guzdial and others at Georgia Tech's Graphics, Visualization, and Usability Center. Anyone given a password as part of a Swiki group can create a new page and/or edit an existing page. Users of a particular Swiki can use the Edit tool to make changes to the Web page. Files may be attached to the page and a History button displays dated edits with links to all versions. This archiving feature allows a Swiki to serve as a group memory with a collective repository of dialogue and knowledge. Swikis can be a useful tool for

Table 4.4 Example of a CSILE Discussion Note (Similar to Knowledge Forum). The various names (Problem, My Theory, etc.) are selected by students as they prepare messages. The topic is biology; keywords are biology and cell function. Adapted from Scardamalia and Bereiter (1996); used with permission.

Problem (Andrea):	How does a cell function?
My Theory (Andrea):	I think a cell functions by oxygen coming into the cell and the cell then can do its work by breathing.
My Theory (Jane):	I agree with your theory, but when the cell functions I don't think it is breathing. I think that the oxygen you're breathing in is doing it.
My Theory (Sue):	I think a cell functions by the "things" inside itself. (organelles)
I Need to Understand (Andrea):	How does the oxygen get into the cell, if the cell really does breathe oxygen?
My Theory (Sue):	I don't think that cells breathe oxygen, I just think that the cells need oxygen to do their work. But if the cells do breathe oxygen, I think there is some kind of a tube in the cell that helps the cell get the oxygen it needs.
New Information (Andrea):	I found out that the cell takes food and oxygen in through the membrane. This happens regularly. The cell then changes the food and oxygen into energy. It uses the energy to do its work.
I Need to Understand (Andrea):	How do the food and oxygen get to the cell's membrane?
My Theory (Andrea):	I think there are very small tubes that lead to each other and the food and oxygen go down those tubes and into the cell through the cell's membrane.
My Theory (Sue):	I disagree with your theory, Andrea. I think that the oxygen and food go into the cell automatically as a daily process.
I Need to Understand (Sue):	What does the oxygen do when it gets to the cell?
My Theory (Andrea):	This is what I think the oxygen does when it gets to the cell. I think that the oxygen goes into the cell through the membrane and then it goes to the nucleus where it is turned into energy.

collaborative writing. For more on Swiki, see http://pbl.cc.gatech.edu:8080/myswiki.1

Shadow netWorkspace

The development of Shadow netWorkspace (SNS) is a key project of Internet Schools, developed at the University of Missouri's Center for Technology Innovations in Education. Shadow netWorkspace provides schools with access to open-source licensed software for implementing learning communities and advanced network services. Open source means that software code is freely available to users, who may modify it as desired. SNS's goal is to build and deliver a common platform of integrated network applications that is readily available and usable by teachers and students worldwide. You can think of SNS as a Web-based operating system that enables files you create or upload and online communica-

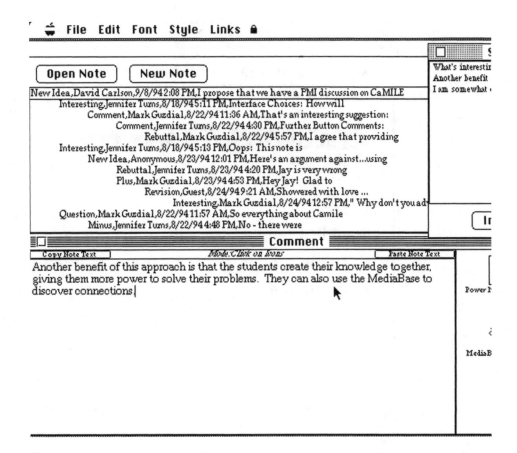

Figure 4.5 A Comment Note Added to CaMILE NoteBase. Courtesy Georgia Institute of Technology. Reprinted by permission.

tions in SNS to be accessed from a Web browser, anytime, anywhere. Based on the belief that schools should support collaboration, communication, and representation, SNS strives to create communities of learners with shared workspaces for collaboration. Discussion boards, chat, e-mail, and messenger systems facilitate communication. Built-in open source Web-based document editors and viewers allow knowledge representation.

Schools or any type of learning community can establish an intranet with networkspaces for all members and classes. The structured discussion boards in SNS provide scaffolding similar to Knowledge Forum, with built-in prompts. SNS users can form groups and the group owner is able to create response categories within discussion board threads (http://sns.internetschools.org).

Learning Processes The programs just described share a critical feature: Each provides an explicit structure for engaging in thoughtful, reasoned, written discourse. Students need to practice thinking and reasoning! Written papers require

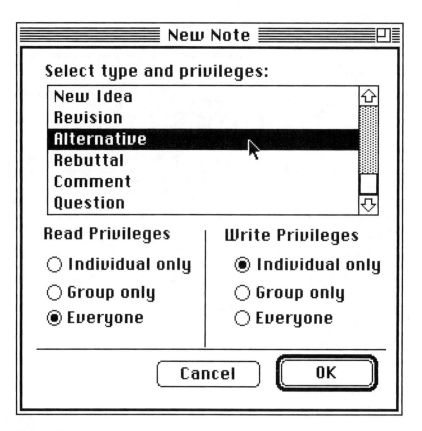

Figure 4.6   Specifying the Response Type in CaMILE. Courtesy Georgia
Institute of Technology. Reprinted by permission.

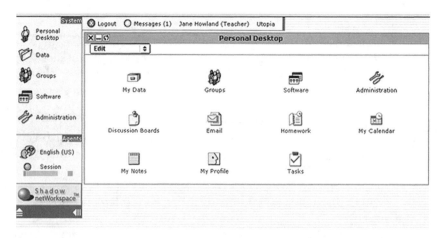

Figure 4.7   User's Personal Desktop in Shadow netWorkspace. Courtesy University
of Missouri. Reprinted by permission.

reasoning, but they tend to be one-way monologues without opportunities to respond to questions from an audience. In-class oral discussions also provide reasoning opportunities, but studies show that bright students tend to dominate class discussions, leaving many students in passive roles as observers. Programs like Knowledge Forum, CaMILE, Swiki, and SNS seek to combine the best elements of writing assignments and live discussions. The communication medium is the written word, but the interactivity is similar to class discussions. Yet the programs provide more scaffolding and support for systematic reasoning than either writing assignments or class discussions: Their imposed structure directs students to provide support for claims, to consider competing evidence or hypotheses, and to carefully respond to counterarguments or queries from classmates. The structured discourse that results can help students learn the norms and rules of systematic reasoning, which, in turn, becomes valuable in other, less-structured settings.

Problem-Solving Processes   The nature of the problem-solving activities will depend on the nature of the questions or challenges that are being provided by the teachers. However, it is safe to speculate that students are engaged in information searching in order to support the positions that they post to the forum. The purpose of the discussion in the forum frequently supports decision making. This form of collaborative decision making, using the forum to propose and promote argumentation, is a powerful method for teaching students to reason with evidence, which is the crux of decision-making activities.

Teacher Roles   As with so many constructivist methods, teachers are constantly observing student activities, with an eye for the individual student who is struggling or for the group that is stuck or engaged in dysfunctional processes. Teachers pay attention to content, reasoning, and outcomes, but also to attitudes, group chemistry, and the mutual support of team members. Teachers model both problem-solving processes as well as the kind of treatment of team members that is needed for successful team problem solving.

Another important teacher role is monitoring the discussion. Monitoring fulfills several purposes. The first, and perhaps most important, is to ensure that the discussion remains focused. When students bring in frivolous or irrelevant points, the teacher needs to point that out to the forum or at least communicate privately with the student. The teacher should also guard against flaming, where students ridicule each other's comments. Another important reason for monitoring the discussion is to collect data for assessing the quality of the discussion, both at the individual and group level.

Assessing Learning   What constitutes a positive conversation? When are students learning, and when are they not? Teachers must monitor and evaluate a group's total activity, as well as the learning of individual students. This becomes a challenge in constructivist environments meant to accommodate multiple learning goals for different students. Teachers continually make inferences about learning as they monitor and review student interactions. Teachers evaluate the total performance—not just the final outcome, but also the process students use in arriving at a conclusion. Structured computer conferences provide a rich, online record of student interaction; if needed, individual student contributions can be tracked from beginning to end. A huge amount of data is available to teachers—more than they can likely assimilate and fully use.

With such rich evaluative data available on demand, teachers must focus on the critical problems or obstacles faced by students. This is where teachers' professional judgment becomes crucial. Knowing where to focus one's attention—when demands on attention are being pulled in so many different directions—is a hallmark of the expert teacher.

To date, structured conferencing programs like Knowledge Forum have limited tools to aid learning assessment. Because of Knowledge Forum's explicitly documented nature, however, tools to aid student assessment should not be too difficult to develop. In future versions of these programs we would like to see a number of report capabilities, such as:

- Number and volume of contributions, reported by student
- Type of contributions, reported by student
- Certain kinds of response patterns (e.g., the number of comments made without a teammate's reply)

Such reports may be of some help to teachers looking for evidence concerning student use of the system and may give an idea about the learning outcomes associated with the program. Use reports are no substitute, though, for the qualitative evaluation of student learning needs and outcomes.

Learning Circles

Learning Circles support constructive learning among a small number of schools located throughout the world through highly interactive, collaborative, project-based partnerships. Developed by Margaret Riel and a team of collaborators, Learning Circles employ a "task force structure" (Riel, 1991). Like a task force, Learning Circles have a heavy work or activity orientation. Groups of classrooms, usually about eight, sign on to communicate and collaborate from a distance, following a time line to accomplish a defined task. The specific task may be any of a number of different activities, such as research, information sharing, compilation of a database, or publishing on a common subject. Riel (1996) also likens Learning Circles to local chapters of a larger organization, like scout troops affiliated with a larger council. Local troops "set their own goals and tasks but remain connected to those who work in other locations as part of a community with shared goals and values." She describes this cooperation between local and larger levels:

> In online Learning Circles, as in scout troops or in a Red Cross task force, the overall task and structure is clearly defined. There are enough examples for participants to use at every step. However, the members of the circle, troop, or task force know that they can take control and develop the ideas that arise from the participants. (Riel, 1996)

Learning Circles are often organized in support of a specific project or online activity. For example, the Web provides a number of interesting resources, such as:

- A tour of the White House
- A Web page describing and showing sacred lands of a Native American tribe
- A NASA project allowing access to space-shuttle pictures and data
- A virtual museum, with exhibits, artifacts, and descriptions

Individual students may choose to visit and browse these resources, or a teacher may incorporate them into a unit. Learning Circles may extend the usefulness of such resources by allowing collaboration and comparisons between classes on work related to the Web site. In this way, Learning Circles can augment an online resource into a deeper and more meaningful learning experience.

Learning Processes Learning Circles require high levels of collaboration and teamwork within participating classes and, to some extent, between classes. Much of the learning takes place as students participate in the virtual world of Internet resources. Other times, students complete off-line activities and report results to other members of their circle. The best Learning Circles have clear work activities specified that require planning, execution, and reporting of activities, followed by comparison and collaboration across sites.

Problem-Solving Processes Learning Circles often engage in more complex activities. Unlike forums where students are tasked with discussing issues or problems, Learning Circles often have a problem-solving purpose for their existence. That purpose may involve designing some artifact (a newspaper, Web site, or project). In order to complete any of these kinds of projects, decision-making problems almost always arise, so it is safe to speculate that Learning Circles, at the very least, engage students in decision making.

Teacher Roles The best teacher within Learning Circles keeps the project going, yet knows how to get out of the way when students are working well together. The teacher's critical role is one of attentive vigilance, with occasional support and intervention when obstacles threaten team progress. Teachers also need to maintain contact with other participating teachers, ensuring continuity and continuing attention to project goals.

Assessing Learning Learning Circles are thought to be successful when projects continue through a defined schedule and reach some kind of closure by completion of a product or compiled report. Because individual student learning will vary widely, a number of self-assessment activities may be appropriate, such as group debriefing and reflection, written reflections of lessons learned from the Learning Circle, and before-and-after comparisons of student work.

PROFESSIONAL DEVELOPMENT

Margaret Riel and Linda Polin (2001) say, "Sometimes a community is scattered and isolated. Unable to interact with each other or community cultural resources, members find it difficult to develop common practices or share values." Teacher isolation has long been an obstacle to the exchange of ideas and information in the teaching profession. The current structure of our school system makes it difficult for in-depth interaction and collaboration to occur among teachers. With the rapid growth and potential of using technology as a learning tool, teachers are especially challenged. How do we avoid continually reinventing strategies for technology use? How do we share stories and resources among ourselves? By sharing ideas and experiences of technology successes and failures, we can break the barriers of isolated classrooms and develop a culture of collective knowledge.

> Today's technological tools make it possible to teach in new ways—to do things differently or even to do entirely different things. Elsewhere . . . we build a case for the multiple forces at play today for educational reform and how these reform goals have led to a greater emphasis on collaboration and the creation of learning communities as appropriate and effective vehicles for new learning for students.
>
> These same forces offer the opportunity for new models for the professional growth of teachers. Learning communities share a way of knowing, a set of practices, and shared value of the knowledge that comes from these procedures. These learning communities, with expanded human and technological resources, bring together students, teachers, and community members in directing the course of education in new ways. (Fulton & Riel, 1999)

The Internet, while posing new challenges for teachers, may also be seen as a solution. Just as the Internet offers a vehicle to students for connecting with others and accessing information, it provides a means for teachers to continue their professional development. Teachers can become part of the four types of communities discussed in earlier sections—communities of discourse, of practice, of knowledge-building, and of learners. Accessing experts, materials, and ideas to use for teaching and learning, staying current on events, issues, and trends in education and technology, and supporting each other as friends and professionals are all facilitated with Internet resources. Information abounds, and like our students, we can learn by not just accessing that information but through actively engaging with it—transforming, analyzing, evaluating, reflecting, collaborating—all the processes we want our students to experience. The following examples are offered to open the doors to the vast community of educators around the world who are networking to support and improve their practice for learners.

One innovative community that combines these elements of learning and collegiality is "Tapped In." Tapped In describes itself as "the online workplace of an international community of education professionals. K–12 teachers and librarians, professional development staff, teacher education faculty and students, and researchers engage in professional development programs and informal collaborative activities with colleagues."

Tapped In uses Java to create an updated version of a MOO (Multiuser Object Oriented) environment. After registering with Tapped In, users receive the monthly calendar by e-mail. This calendar lists online events such as orientations to the Tapped In community, synchronous discussions with experts, and sessions targeting specific software and/or methods for technology integration. Tapped In offers virtual offices, which are private online spaces within the Web site where private conversations and meetings may be held. A unique feature is the capability of recording chats, with a transcript automatically e-mailed to the office's owner immediately after logging off.

Other Web sites supporting professional development are the Global Schoolhouse (http://www.gsn.org) and Classroom Connect's Quest Teacher Community (http://www.classroomconnect.com), where teachers can communicate with other teachers who use the Quests in their classrooms. Scholastic Teachers offers extensive professional resources that include Teacher Radio and professional discussion groups. Teachers can hear authors reading, experts offering advice and ideas, and other teachers sharing stories about their experiences on Teacher Radio. Experts moderate professional discussion groups; discussion groups for students are also available (http://teacher.scholastic.com). Teaching.com offers Mighty Mentors and TeacherTalk. TeacherTalk is a discussion forum where K–12 teachers can discuss teaching techniques, trade lesson plan ideas, and support one another. Mighty Mentors can help teachers find a mentor or mentee for a short- or long-term mentoring partnership. It enables teachers to safely mentor one another via e-mail as teachers communicate with other teachers to improve their teaching techniques, troubleshoot classroom problems, and so on.

Southwest Educational Development Laboratory's Southwest Consortium for the Improvement of Math and Science Teaching (SCIMAST) offers the Math and Science Mentoring Archives (http://www.sedl.org/scimast/archives/). These Archives contain questions and answers about resources and teaching assessment issues. Existing archive information may be searched or teachers may send questions to a mentor.

Trends in Education is hosted by the U.S. Department of Education's Office of Educational Technology (http://www.ed.gov/Technology/index.html). This site contains reports, federal technology initiatives and grant information, conferences and speeches, and the latest technology trends and plans.

Teachers who are looking for structured learning can find online courses and programs at many colleges and universities. Noncredit courses are also available on the Internet. An example is the Teacher Training Network (http://www.teachertrain.net), where classes are all instructor-led by certified teachers with weekly support and dialogue for students.

The Internet offers opportunities for professional development in many areas of a teacher's practice. The value of professional development in the use of computers and the Internet is vital in equipping teachers with knowledge and skills that will increase the odds of their students becoming more technologically capable and literate. Rowand (2000) reported that teachers with that kind of professional development were more likely to assign students various types of work involving computers or the Internet. Teachers with more than 32 hours of technology professional development were more likely to assign problem-solving activities (41%) than were teachers with no technology professional development (14%) or those with only 1 to 8 hours of professional development (24%). They made higher use of graphical presentations (31% compared with 10% and 16% for the same groups), and demonstrations or simulations (29% compared with 8% and 13% for the same groups). Clearly, it is important that teachers are active, ongoing learners in the use and applications of both new and existing technologies. Knowledgeable teachers who are confident in their use of technology will not only plan more learning experiences involving technology for their students, but those experiences will also encourage learning processes that require students to be active, constructive participants who engage in cooperative, authentic tasks with intentional goals and outcomes.

SUPPORTING GLOBAL DISCOURSE THROUGH TELECOMMUNITIES

KIDLINK

KIDLINK is a grassroots project that is intended to interconnect as many kids, aged 10–15, as possible to participate in a global dialogue. Running in annual cycles since 1990, more than 60,000 kids from 87 countries, from Antarctica to Finland, from Belarus to the Bahamas, have joined the conversation. The KIDLINK Web site is available in 20 languages. Because of language constraints, KIDLINK provides several different dialogues. Some dialogues are individual and some are between classrooms.

Before joining a dialogue, all new participants introduce themselves and answer the following questions (see Figure 4.8):

Question 1: Who am I? What is your full name? How old are you? Are you a boy or a girl? Where do you live (city, country)? What is the name of your school? What are some of your interests, your hobbies, your concerns? What else do you want others to know about yourself?

Question 2: What do I want to be when I grow up? Share your vision of what you want to be when you grow up in terms of work, education, and in general.

Question 3: How do I want the world to be better when I grow up? How would you like to improve the way we treat each other and the environment we share?

Question 4: What can I do now to make this happen? What steps can you take now to realize your personal goals and your vision of the world?

KIDLINK supports different dialogues such as KIDCAFE, KIDPROJECT, and KIDLEADER, each with several language choices. In each discussion group, a

```
Date:         Sun, 3 Feb 2002 08:58:00 -0600
Reply-To:     respmod@universe.kidlink.org
Sender:       "KIDLINK List: Answers to 4 Questions"
              <RESPONSE@LISTSERV.NODAK.EDU>
From:         respmod@universe.kidlink.org
Subject:      Alaa from Sweden


Question 1: Who am I?

Name/Age/Gender: Alaa, 13, Girl
Country: Sweden
Date: 3-Feb-2002

My name is Alaa, iam a girl and iam 13 years old.
My hobbies is to play sports, specielly, basketball, football and handball.
And i like to shop and be with my friends.

Question 2: What do I want to be when I grow up?

I would like to be a louard, when i grow up, becuse
thats the funniest job i know.

Question 3: How do I want the world to be better when I grow up?

I would like too see the would peacefull.

Question 4: What can I do now to make this happen?

You can be peacefull and not fight
with everyone.
```

Figure 4.8 Response to the Four KIDLINK Questions. Courtesy KIDLINK,
www.kidlink.org. Reprinted by permission.

table of contents lists subject lines, and messages may be sorted by author or posting date. For example, a recent list of messages included:

> *Anime fans from Japan?*
>   *   Re: Anime fans from Japan? (20 lines)
>   From: Yudai Yoneda ⟨j192151b@OCEC.NE.JP⟩
>   *   Re: Anime fans from Japan? (27 lines)
>   From: Queeno California ⟨queenocalifornia@HOTMAIL.COM⟩
> *Danilo Fazzalari for John Ellis*
>   *   Danilo Fazzalari for John Ellis (68 lines)
>   From: I.C.S. Condove ⟨ics.condove@TIN.IT⟩
>   *   Re: Danilo Fazzalari for John Ellis (124 lines)
>   From: Lynn Ellis ⟨ebay@COX.NET⟩
> *Hi Mimi*
>   *   Re: Hi Mimi (29 lines)
>   From: Sue Owen ⟨sue@OWFAM.GLOBALNET.CO.UK⟩
>   *   Re: Hi Mimi (58 lines)
>   From: Miriam Wertheimer ⟨themimsta@HOTMAIL.COM⟩
> *I want a penfriend.*
>   *   Re: I want a penfriend. (49 lines)
>   From: Chelsea French ⟨girl_0_10@HOTMAIL.COM⟩
> *I want penpals from Japan and China and even other countries!*

*   I want penpals from Japan and China and even other countries! (78 lines)
From: Hasslöskolan ⟨hassloskolan@TELIA.COM⟩
MESSAGE FOR Valentina Fontana
*   MESSAGE FOR Valentina Fontana (61 lines)
From: Bergitte Lowzow ⟨bergitte@LEVERPOSTEI.COM⟩
Please give me mail.
*   Please give me mail. (36 lines)
From: Kenta Yamanouchi ⟨j192151b@OCEC.NE.JP⟩
*   Re: Please give me mail. (20 lines)
From: Queeno California ⟨queenocalifornia@HOTMAIL.COM⟩
To Hyeon-W Bae from Marco Valletta
*   To Hyeon-W Bae from Marco Valletta (30 lines)
From: IC Mediglia ⟨ic.mediglia@TISCALINET.IT⟩
To a kind boy.
*   To a kind boy. (17 lines)
From: Bergitte Lowzow ⟨bergitte@LEVERPOSTEI.COM⟩
To boys or girls 12–15
*   To boys or girls 12–15 (17 lines)
From: Bergitte Lowzow ⟨bergitte@LEVERPOSTEI.COM⟩
aury e katia
*   aury e katia (64 lines)
From: I.C.S. Condove ⟨ics.condove@TIN.IT⟩
*   Re: aury e katia (43 lines)
From: Bergitte Lowzow ⟨bergitte@LEVERPOSTEI.COM⟩
*   Re: aury e katia (45 lines)
From: Chelsea French ⟨girl_0_10@HOTMAIL.COM⟩
for Bong-Hong Yoon
*   for Bong-Hong Yoon (81 lines)
From: I.C.S. Condove ⟨ics.condove@TIN.IT⟩
from Veronica to new keypals
*   from Veronica to new keypals (81 lines)
From: I.C.S. Condove ⟨ics.condove@TIN.IT⟩

It is obvious from the country codes in these messages that the dialogue that day was indeed global (Italy, Japan, United Kingdom, and the United States) and covered a wide variety of topics. Some dialogues are constrained by topic and language. For that reason, there are volunteer translators who facilitate communication as well as language-specific conferences. In Figure 4.9, a Swedish boy requests Japanese and Chinese penpals. Communicating with students from other countries in their native languages is one of the most constructive, authentic, and meaningful ways to study a second language that we can think of. Even if the students are communicating about their favorite stars or bands, they are still communicating, which is the purpose of learning a second language.

The Global Schoolhouse

Another major project supporting global learning communities is the Global Schoolhouse (GSH) project, which was mentioned in the previous chapter. GSH

Date:	Fri, 11 Jan 2002 12:27:21 +0100
Reply-To:	KIDLINK Individual Keypals <KIDCAFE-INDIVIDUAL@LISTSERV.NODAK.EDU>
Sender:	KIDLINK Individual Keypals <KIDCAFE-INDIVIDUAL@LISTSERV.NODAK.EDU>
From:	Hasslöskolan <hassloskolan@TELIA.COM>
Subject:	**I want penpals from Japan and China and even other countries!**
Content-Type:	multipart/alternative;

Hello everybody!

Hello!

My name is Andreas and I search for penfriends, Chinese and Japanse, please! My nickname is Anden. My interests are GIRLS, table tennis, football and street hockey. I'm intrested in China and Japan and want to learn the language. So please write to: hassloskolan@telia.com

Andreas Månsson, Hasslo School, Sweden

Figure 4.9   Swedish Boy's Request for Penpals. Courtesy KIDLINK, www.kidlink.org. Reprinted by permission.

seeks to create *telecommunities* to unite students from around the world and teach them to work cooperatively. Andres (1995) believes that the best collaborative projects require students to "measure, collect, evaluate, write, read, publish, simulate, hypothesize, compare, debate, examine, investigate, organize, share, and report." To accomplish this, teachers are encouraged to break up classes into small, collaborative teams. The teams access Internet database relevant to their project and then relate their findings to other students through the Internet. GSH encourages students to serve as "student ambassadors" by training other students and teachers and acting as reporters.

Why should classrooms join telecommunities? Andres (1995) argues that students:

- Enjoy writing more when they are able to write for a distant audience of their peers
- Enjoy communicating with schools from different geographical locations
- Are given opportunities to understand different cultures and so begin to consider global issues, in addition to local issues

Clearly, telecommunities open up vast new horizons to students, engendering a broader, more tolerant worldview for those involved. That should be an important goal of schools.

Building Understanding, Promoting Peace   As part of the University of Missouri-Columbia College of Education's Global Initiative, a partnership between Taipei Taiwan's Municipal Lan-Ya Primary School and Bryant Elementary School in Independence, Missouri, is working to develop literacy by connecting classrooms via technology for professional development and learning. Annette Martin and Angie Hathaway's 5th-grade classes are learning about Taiwan's culture and sharing with Lan-Ya students to discover differences and similarities among themselves. For example, classes collected information about what students did after school and created graphs from the data. They shared three-day itineraries with each other and learned about Christmas and Chinese New Year. All students will receive individual e-mail accounts, and school Web sites will serve as publishing space for projects. Mrs. Hathaway said,

> What I notice in my students regarding this experience is that it really sparks the kids' interest in finding out about other students their age and what they like to do. It also has given them a better sense of geography in knowing where other places are located in relationship to the U.S. The kids at our school don't get many opportunities to travel outside of the state of Missouri, much less countries around the world. This experience allows them that opportunity. They are much more aware of language, religion, and other cultural differences among each other.

The relationships begun via the Internet have flourished, with plans for 20 Lan-Ya students to visit Bryant Elementary School. What a field trip—made possible through connections enabled by the Internet (http://global.lyps.tp.edu.tw/).

The Friendship Through Education consortium is a coalition of several groups including the Global SchoolNet Foundation, iEARN, ePALS, Schools Online, and World Wise Schools (part of the Peace Corps). The Friendship Through Education Consortium is committed to creating both online and off-line interactions between youth to promote a culture of peace where all humans' rights and dignity are respected. The initial focus is on connecting links between schools in the United States and Islamic countries to "foster mutual respect and greater understanding of cultural differences." (http://www.friendshiptrougheducation.org/)

Global SchoolNet Foundation sponsors a "Kids Share Hope" message board as part of the Friendship Through Education consortium. In the month following the September 11, 2001, terrorist attacks in the United States, over 100 messages of hope and support were posted from around the world (http://groups.yahoo.com/group/KidsShareHope/). iEARN (International Education & Resource Network) hosts Feeding Minds Feeding Hunger, an international classroom for exploring the problems of hunger, malnutrition, and food insecurity (http://www.feedingminds.org/). iEARN also sponsors the Laws of Life Project (http://www.iearn.org/projects/laws.html). Youth submit essays expressing what they value most in life, describing the principles and rules that govern their lives, and sharing how those ideals were influenced and formed. Participants respond to each other, engaging in meaningful dialogue about beliefs and values and providing multiple perspectives on issues that are important to all of them.

Learning Processes   Global telecommunities bear a strong resemblance to the Learning Circles described earlier. Global groups capitalize on cultural differences as a means of broadening students' perspectives and motivating learning. The new ideas and experiences that are encountered when students interact with peers in other countries and cultures can expand thinking and shape mental models that become more complex. Students may reflect on their experience as world citizens and broaden their understanding of how others live. Studies in language, geography, current events, and culture can be augmented through these groups.

Problem-Solving Processes   In these international forums, problem solving is seldom the purpose. Students often engage in information searching; however, learning how to communicate with others in their native language constitutes a powerful form of design problem solving. Constructing ideas in a second language requires designing, to some degree.

Teacher Roles   Teachers are challenged to ensure that global communications go beyond chatting and socializing, but have a specific direction. This is done as the project is negotiated and defined. Teachers may need to monitor interactions to help students stay on task; however, students need a certain amount of slack to explore and become acquainted with different cultures and lifestyles.

Assessing Learning   A key learning outcome of global interactions has to be increased knowledge of foreign cultures, lifestyles, and languages. This can be assessed by examining products and interactions, or more directly through separate objective assessment. Other learning outcomes may be assessed using methods discussed in the cases provided.

MUDs and MOOs

New forms of Internet-based multiuser environments known as MUDs and MOOs are engaging learners in high-level conversations that support personal reflection. According to a MUD users group (http://webnet.mednet.gu.se/computer/internet-services.txt):

> [T]hese are multiuser, text-based, virtual reality games . . . A MUD (Multiuser Dungeon) is a computer program that users can log into and explore. Each user takes control of a computerized persona/avatar/incarnation/character. You can walk around, chat with other characters, explore dangerous monster-infested areas, solve puzzles, and even create your very own rooms, descriptions, and items. There are an astounding number of variations on the MUD theme.

MUDs (multiuser domains) and MOOs (object-oriented MUDs) are virtual environments that you enter and participate in. Originally derived from online "Dungeons and Dragons" environments, some MUDs have an educational focus, such as MIT's MicroMUSE. Users can enter the virtual environment and travel between locations—for example, homes, museums, coffee shops, or science labs. Visitors not only interact, but, depending on their level of experience, can participate in the design and construction of the environment itself.

Currently, MUDs are text based, but advances in virtual-reality and multimedia technologies will soon result in graphic depictions of these virtual environments. A simple search of the Internet will reveal several of these environments.

Some welcome newcomers, but most are a bit difficult to understand and navigate. (Documenting their accomplishments and the interface is apparently not as stimulating as creating and using MUDs.)

To date, most of the MUDs and their offspring are primarily adventure games, with debatable educational value. Some projects, however, are specifically educational in nature. Hughes and Walters (1995; Walters & Hughes, 1995) reported very promising initial findings from their work with MariMUSE and Pueblo.

Amy Bruckerman (1998) has also found positive results from her work with MOOSE Crossing. The MOOSE Crossing MUD is a text-based, virtual-reality learning community designed at MIT by Bruckerman. The educational theory underlying MOOSE Crossing is constructionism, which states that our experiences guide our knowledge construction and that personally meaningful projects lead to better learning. Students can create objects by learning simple computer programming on MOOSE Crossing. Bruckerman says it is "an excellent way for kids 13 and under to expand creative writing skills and learn to program at the same time. Kids can create objects ranging from magic carpets to virtual pets to even a Pokémon; a world based on your imaginations. They can also build virtual rooms and cities, such as King Tut's Pyramid, the Emerald City of Oz, or Hogwarts. Kids can meet and interact with other kids from all around the world. The world of MOOSE Crossing is built by kids, for kids." Moose Crossing enables students to not only participate in learning communities, but to be involved in the actual construction of those communities (http://www.cc.gatech.edu/elc/moose-crossing/).

Bruckerman (1998) reported the following conversation among two children using MOOSE Crossing. It is evident from this conversation that as students create together, they may engage in novel roles of teaching and learning. Jack, who is familiar with MOOSE Crossing, is scaffolding Miranda's use.

Jack says, 'OK. first, create $thing called gem.'
    [Lady types "create gem" which doesn't work.]
    Miranda whispers to Jack, 'hi'
    Jack whispers to Miranda, 'hi'
    Miranda whispers to Jack, 'What's the gem going to do?'
    Lady says, 'how'
    Jack says, 'type this: CREATE $thing called gem'
    [Miranda types what Jack was proposing to check it, and then immediately recycles the gem she has made.]
    Miranda opens a hidden trash chute.
    Jack whispers to Miranda, 'I don't know yet!'
    Lady says, 'Oh, cool'
    Miranda whispers to Jack, 'how about it sparkles when someone touches it'
    Jack says, 'good!'
    Jack whispers to Miranda, 'cool!'
    Jack says, 'OK. first, create $thing called gem.'
    [Lady types "create gem" which doesn't work.]

Miranda whispers to Jack, 'hi'
Jack whispers to Miranda, 'hi'
Miranda whispers to Jack, 'What's the gem going to do?'
Lady says, 'how'
Jack says, 'type this: CREATE $thing called gem'
[Miranda types what Jack was proposing to check it, and then immediately recycles the gem she has made.]
Miranda opens a hidden trash chute.
Jack whispers to Miranda, 'I don't know yet!'
Lady says, 'Oh, cool'
Miranda whispers to Jack, 'how about it sparkles when someone touches it'
Jack says, 'good!'
Jack whispers to Miranda, 'cool!'

Learning Processes   Ironically, the low-tech nature of MUDs has become a learning asset. MUDs' text-only interface means that children must use words to communicate. Motivation is maintained by the game-like atmosphere. The practice and reinforcement of literacy skills can yield educational benefits for children participating in MUD environments. Another interesting aspect of MUDs is the ownership that students can assert over their virtual worlds. MUDs are not like game CDs; they can be codesigned and coconstructed by the users themselves, depending entirely on the users' investment in the program. The sense that worlds depend on our own construction is an important lesson for children.

Problem-Solving Processes   It is difficult to speculate about the kinds of problem solving engaged by MOOs. MOOs tend to have such broad foci that predicting the outcomes is difficult.

Teacher Roles   MUDs have primary appeal to individual users, and are not particularly well suited to whole-class participation. Dykes and Waldorf (1995) report the activities of an independent, after-school club whose members participated in MicroMUSE. MicroMUSE activities are set in a 24th-century world, in a space station called Cyberion City II, which hovers above the earth (p. 3). Students enter the environment and encounter a variety of adventures and problems to solve, depending on their level of advancement.

Dykes and Waldorf's exploratory study yielded a number of findings, including:

- Boys seemed to show more interest than girls in the activity; more boys than girls belonged to the club.
- Older children (11–14) participated more than younger children.
- Role-playing opened up interesting possibilities for exploration. Children can assume a virtual persona different from their real-world persona. One young boy, for example, wanted to assume a female identity, while another wanted to play a child from the 18th century.
- Children enjoyed opportunities to choose their own paths through the environment, with some eventually learning to construct their own rooms and environments.

Teachers making use of MUDs in the classroom will want to take steps to ensure equitable, responsible access.

Assessing Learning   Assessing the learning from MUDs could present a challenge to teachers. In current systems, students enter MUDs individually, without having to collaborate with other classmates. Teachers might be able to gauge student learning by tracking conversation, choices, or constructions. On the other hand, students may engage in game-playing without clear learning goals. This is clearly an area in need of continuing attention. As MUDs become more commonly utilized for learning purposes, improved methods of assessment are likely to be developed.

Right now MUDs have very little presence in K–12 schools. It is easy, though, to imagine a future in which MUDs evolve to become a low-end version of virtual reality with significant educational potential. Imagine, for instance, a MUD in which a student is placed on the main street in a small community in colonial America, with the option of entering stores, blacksmith shops, pubs, jails, homes, and other buildings of the period. Inside each building would be descriptions of the people and artifacts it contained. Students would make decisions and express their choices, to which the MUD's characters and objects (and other students) would react. Imagine, too, that teachers and their classes could work together to *develop* new buildings. This option (which is often provided in MUDs) could be a great incentive for research, collaboration, problem-solving, and other high-level activities.

SUPPORTING SOCIAL CO-CONSTRUCTION OF KNOWLEDGE THROUGH COLLABORATIVE COMMUNICATION

One of the criticisms of the Internet as a learning tool is that there are so many interesting topics to explore and it is so easy to explore them (they're only a click away), that students are often off-task, following links that take them away from, rather than toward their learning goal. On the other hand, the information resources made available on the Internet are unparalleled, and a self-regulated learner who keeps the goal in mind, resists temptation, and makes good decisions can find the Internet a fantastic resource during intentional learning. That intentionality is enhanced when a group of learners are committed to the same goals. They regulate each other's performance. There are a number of projects that have maintained student focus by supporting collaborative meaning making among groups of learners.

Learning Activities

While we normally think of knowledge construction as an individual process, it can become a social process by participating in learning communities. When people work together and discuss what they are doing and why, participants develop and refine cognitive strategies as well as knowledge. The Internet is a powerful medium for collaboration; the following projects show why.

The Mural Project What do a group of students from urban New York City have in common with students living in the small, rural town of Holcomb, Missouri? That is the question Sandra Stein and David Loewenstein set out to answer. Former alumni of the same college who reconnected as a result of an article in the college's alumni magazine, Stein was an assistant professor in New York and Loewenstein a professional muralist in Kansas. Together, they created a vision of an Internet-based mural project using student artists from radically different environments, living very different lives, who would collaborate to create a mural representing themselves—without ever meeting. The first step was getting the students to know each other, investigating perceptions and stereotypes about rural and city life. They began by discussing the origin of stereotypes, media's influence, and then identifying their stereotypes. Holcomb reported that the New Yorkers imagined Missourians as being "like the Beverly Hillbillies" (McCarty, 2000, p. 22) while Holcomb students thought about crime and poverty when they envisioned New York.

The students began posting images and text on the Internet to explain to each other the way they really were. Finally, they used drawing, collage, and photography to create portraits of themselves that depicted not only their physical appearance, but also their cultural backgrounds, interests, and hopes for the future. After students had gained an understanding of each other, they began designing the mural by visualizing the more than 100 images they had collected and how those images would work together to tell the story of who they were. Their iterative design process involved small groups at each location sketching, discussing, critiquing, and posting designs for students on the other end to view. At last, it was time to create the final product. Half the mural was painted in Holcomb and half in New York City—with a twist. Students in Holcomb painted the city side while New York students painted the rural images. Throughout the painting process, students continued their collaboration. Norma Crafton, the Holcomb art teacher, said, "They posted what they did every time they painted. One week they said be sure to put in a soccer ball. Our students said 'Don't forget we want a church on our side.' It's important to them that it shows their values" (p. 22). (http://www.baruch.cuny.edu/spa/community/mural/)

Resolving Complex Social Problems Life is more complex than most books or lessons make it seem. Most authors and teachers seek to simplify topics for students in order to enhance their ability to understand them. The result is often a superficial understanding of complex problems. Most social problems require multiple perspectives or viewpoints in order to understand them. In order to get students to wrestle with appropriately complex problems, teachers need to encourage exploration of those multiple perspectives. Sizer (1996) says we are focused on covering topics rather than developing a deep understanding of them. In the excerpt below, he uses the topic of *immigration* as an example:

> The function of secondary education is not so much to get students to understand the immigration question as to get them to understand how an issue such as immigration can be understood. That is, the subject matter is but an important foil for enduring intellectual habits. Sloppy work will lead to sloppy habits.
>
> Of course, even after giving major attention to the immigration issue, high school students will not become experts in this field. What they will gain, however, is a sense of the wide sweep of important influences on an issue of this sort and humility about what they now can and cannot say about the matter. From such humility—an awareness of the complexity of things and of all that one does not yet know—comes deep understanding. (p. 87)

By exploring issues such as foreign policy, the United Nations, and terrorism with peers from around the world, it becomes obvious that these issues are even more complex than they appear when they are viewed from a single nation's perspective.

The Internet is a tremendous information resource for students with good questions. Rather than automatically seeking the wisdom of the teachers, students develop information-seeking skills and gain the satisfaction of answering their own questions. Whether the question is "Why is the sky blue? or "How does a cell phone work?" the answers and the people who wrote them are probably out there.

Information Please (http://infoplease.lycos.com/)

Ask Jeeves (http://www.askjeeves.com/index.asp)

HowStuffWorks (http://www.howstuffworks.com/)

Collaborative Authorship   Another Internet project that seems to have this potential is titled *The Pigman—Chapter Sixteen*. In this project, developed by Eileen Skarecki of Columbia Middle School in New Jersey, students read the popular adolescent novel, *The Pigman*, which, in Skarecki's words "leaves the reader hanging." Her response? Have students write a final chapter, and post the submissions on the Internet for others to read and respond to.

This simple activity will cause students to think deeply about the book and about writing. It will also cause them to write with a purpose, to think critically about what they write, to read what others have produced, and to compare their own work to the work of others.

This is but one example of a reflective use of the Internet. Others might include putting students in contact with professionals or hobbyists who will help them think about their work. The Internet also offers great opportunities for peer tutoring. Consider setting up mentoring programs that pair young students with older ones. Such programs have proven to help students at both ends of the mentoring relationship.

It is worth noting that the mere prospect of placing their work on the Web for public access inspires many students to take their work more seriously and to engage in a level of reflection about their work that is otherwise rare. In addition to this new level of reflection inspired by Web publishing, it is possible to design activities that cause students to be more reflective—to think about their work and the work of others in ways that lead to academic growth.

Learning Processes

Social co-construction of meaning through conversation is primarily constructive and cooperative. When joining in conversations, individuals are required to articulate their points of view and to reflect on the perspectives provided by other participants as well as their own. Collaborative discussions are primarily conversational and, of course, cooperative in nature with individuals contributing to the discussion. What is most significant about this combination of learning processes is the level of ownership that students feel when they are in control of the discussion.

Problem-Solving Processes Social collaboration seldom occurs to support anything other than problem solving. The nature of the projects varies, but nearly all engage decision making and many engage design problems.

Teacher Roles You may begin the process by positing a question or problem, if students don't have one to begin with. Chances are that students will soon generate their own issues or topics to focus discussion on, so the primary role of teachers in this kind of activity is to monitor the discussion. You should continuously monitor the contributions of students to make sure that they are tasteful and to the point. Students who flame or needlessly criticize others' perspectives should be censured. You may also use this activity to teach students about points of argumentation—that claims should be supported by principles or well-articulated beliefs, which should be supported by evidence. Try not to intervene in the conversation unless necessary.

Assessing Learning The quality of any conversation is implicit in the level of interactivity and the nature of individual contributions. What determines these is the nature of the question or the issue. If it is something that students are interested in or committed to, then the conversation will be meaningful. Evaluating conversations is difficult; you might want to use some of these criteria:

- What were the affective goals of the project? Were they achieved?
- How many learners contributed to the project goals? What was the nature of their contribution, that is, how meaningful were student responses? Were the contributions evenly distributed among students?
- How many perspectives or views were represented? Did groups support their perspective with evidence?
- Was there consensus provided; that is, did the collaborative project reach any conclusions?

- What information sources were used? Were those sources critically chosen? Did they contribute important evidence?
- How interactive was the collaboration? Did students seek information/input from all members?

CYBERMENTORING: COMMUNICATING THROUGH THE INTERNET

As we have seen, the Internet provides many different forms of communication. E-mail, listservs, newsgroups, videoconferencing, and even MUDs can be used effectively to get students talking about what they are learning, and to enrich their thinking with input from others. Technology (in this case, the Internet) can be used to create strong relationships that have the potential to change the learner's perception of the whole learning enterprise. The Internet is first and foremost a communications medium—not a publishing medium. It was designed to facilitate communications and the exchange of information between people. The new paradigm implicit in the WWW is the ability of the Internet to foster conversations between writers and readers. Given the potential of this kind of interactive dialogue, we now see an amalgamation of various strands of educational research of the past dozen or more years. Constructivist and cooperative learning, process writing, authentic assessment, and more are all logical and natural aspects of this new medium; they are built right into the medium. Much of what educational reformers have sought to do is happening as a natural matter of course in well-designed Internet and Web-based projects.

E-mail Mentoring Program: Creating Electronic Advocates for Students at Risk

In an article titled "Using the Internet as a Tool to Reconnect Students to the Educational Process," Kathy A. Kane (1997) describes a program at Pennsylvania's Montgomery County Intermediate Unit Youth Center, a detention center designed to return problem students to the normal classroom environment. The program's goal is broader than just correcting unacceptable behavior, however. They are working to "develop students committed to lifelong learning, students who are competent, responsible, respectful, and contributing members of our society." The program "helps students to connect to their education through: a strong core curriculum that is developmentally appropriate; distance learning; use of the Internet; and online mentoring." They understand that the special circumstances of the detention center magnifies the need to engage students in meaningful learning, and they find that technology can help them meet this challenge.

The Buddy Project uses the Internet to "bring the world into the classroom, accommodate varied learning styles and paces of learning within one classroom, encourage students to become lifelong learners, develop the student's proficiency in basic technological skills needed to take their places in society, and most importantly, pique the student's curiosity and motivate the learner to seek more knowledge through continued education, by staying in school." Their students perform a variety of Internet-based activities, including creating Web pages, conducting research, publishing their work, and talking via e-mail with professionals who have agreed to serve as mentors.

The mentoring program is extensive, with mentors identified from across the country who report that they have long wanted to make a contribution, but the travel and the longer sessions required by traditional mentoring have prevented their participation. By eliminating the need to go to schools or homes on a regular basis, replacing that with a series of briefer (but more frequent) electronic contacts, a high-quality pool of mentors has emerged. Their mentors include: scientists working in the biotechnology field; chemists; an attorney for the appellate court of North Carolina; a medical doctor; a retired psychologist; a playwright/educator; a scientific advisor for a patent firm; Montgomery County Health Department directors; a university library conservator; a physicist; a sales representative for San Diego Zoo; an Australian woman who works in LaJolla, California; a scientist who works at Salk Institute in California; a Harvard law school student; and two chemists who work for the U.S. government who correspond with Spanish-speaking students in Spanish. (The Spanish-speaking students correspond with their mentors in Spanish, so that they can communicate freely, and they translate all correspondence to share with their English-speaking teachers.)

The project reports that the mentoring relationship serves students by:

- Enriching children's lives and addressing the isolation of some students from adult contact
- Providing support and advocacy, personalized attention and care; affiliation for detained students
- Fostering a spirit of success and helping move students toward their education, career, and personal goals
- Providing assistance to define goals and implement a plan to meet goals
- Improving relationships, communication, and writing skills
- Providing the student motivation, knowledge, skills, and solutions to use resources available to succeed
- Providing security of a caring relationship with a responsible adult who will listen to and respect the student's opinion
- Increasing student's regard for people of other races and cultures
- Promoting access to people of different occupational and social worlds

Benefits to the mentor are reported to include:

- Satisfaction derived from helping others
- Personal growth
- Opportunity to make a difference in the future of a young person
- Pride of being selected as a mentor

Like many teachers who understand the power of the Internet, Kane and her team use a variety of Internet-based strategies to produce an engaging school day, and these activities, too are valued:

Internet activities improve a student's education by requiring the student to think critically, analyze information, and write clearly. Using the Internet as a classroom resource instills problem-solving, discriminatory and organizational skills, and teamwork while it improves computer skills and encourages a positive attitude toward learning. Exploring the Internet and contributing original work instills confidence in the student's own ability. When students prepare work for the world to see, they seem to be more careful about spelling, punctuation, grammar, and content; be more willing to write, proofread, and rewrite; enjoy writing more; be better organized and more fluent, and state their ideas more clearly and with more conviction. The Internet is an invaluable and comprehensive classroom resource. (p. 3)

Learning Processes

While cybermentoring engages most of the forms of meaning making, the most distinctive characteristics of learning are authentic and cooperative. Cybermentors are from real-world contexts with real-world experience, that is, they are more authentic. Because of that, they are more believable. Successful mentors are collaborators, rather than teachers, as they interact with their pupils.

TECHNIQUE

- The educator who sets up an electronic mentoring program has a crucial role to play. As Kane reports, the *relationship* that is developed between the mentor and the student is the most important component in the success of a program like this. For this reason, she personally contacted each mentor and outlined the expected outcomes of the mentoring relationship. Kane required each mentor "to agree to give personalized attention and caring, to maintain a positive attitude and high expectations of the student, and to make a commitment to the student to be accessible and responsive in a timely manner."

- Student and mentor must get to know each other quickly. To achieve this purpose, Kane asked all of the Internet mentors to send a short biography through e-mail, and allowed students to read the biographies, select a mentor, and begin to correspond with the mentor. This selection process was, in itself, a valuable learning experience in disguise, because during this process students are engaged in thinking about careers, places, and the attributes of people that make them attractive and useful. Consider using student-generated home pages posted on the WWW as a way for mentors to get to know their students.

- Online mentoring can be a great strategy, but you must do your homework. Make sure that the mentors are good models for sustained contact with students, and make sure they are committed, since a mentor who takes the job lightly can be worse than none. Make sure students and mentors get to know each other quickly. Establish an understanding with students and mentors that they can contact you at any time with any type of information (good or bad). Consider requesting regular reporting, perhaps alternating this responsibility between the student and mentor. And then, step back and let the relationship grow.

Teacher Roles While student roles vary with the relationship, good mentors maintain an honest and productive conversation with their pupils. Their most important goal is to establish and maintain the student's trust. Having done that, they focus on how their experiences can relate to the students. They should function as coach and cheerleader for the student, rather than purveyor of wisdom.

FOSTERING COMMUNITY

Learning communities can be fostered through communication, attention to differences, shared culture, adaptation, dialogue, and access to information resources. Each of these facilitating features is discussed here. In this final section of this chapter, we discuss in general how to foster learning communities. We first describe the essential characteristics of communities that need to be fostered.

Communication

Imagine a classroom—perhaps a televised lecture—where the teacher sends out signals but has no means of receiving feedback from students. In such a scenario, the teacher's activities can spin wildly out of control, becoming less and less appropriate to students' needs. Students may be completely lost or completely bored, and the teacher has no way of knowing an adjustment is needed.

Communication is the key that allows people to make adjustments to each other. Feedback is given not just for correctness of answers, but in all sorts of subtle, informal ways, resulting in a feeling of inclusion and accommodation. Students come to feel, "I am being listened to, understood, and respected." Teachers can feel, "I am having some kind of effect." Effective communication among members allows the group to acquire a personality and sense of direction, while communicating the views and needs of individuals.

Attention to Differences

Like all complex adaptive systems, learning communities thrive on differences. Every group member shares some things in common with the group and holds other things unique. Most differences among group members go no further than the individual learner; however, every so often a different perspective or strategy will be found to have utility within the group as a whole. As different perspectives and strategies are routinely shared throughout the group, the powerful results of some innovations are noticed and diffused, eventually changing the practice of the entire group. Thus, differences between community members are a key to growth, leading sometimes to innovations that benefit everyone. The risk-taking, creative attitude that leads to innovation is important to the group's success.

Shared Culture

Appreciation of diversity is, however, only half the story. To move from "group" to real community, people need to feel bound together by something strong and enduring. This could be a shared goal or objective, such as passing a critical exam or producing a new product. Beyond outcomes, though, communities are fostered by a shared set of values, reflected in a local culture. "Culture" is like water to a fish. It's everything that's all around, but not noticed—how we talk, walk, listen, and participate; all the unspoken, unwritten rules that govern our behavior toward each other. Every learning community develops a local mini-culture, complete with accepted norms, practices, rituals, and language.

Teachers, as classroom leaders, are critical in setting a tone, creating expectations, and negotiating acceptable values. The teacher's influence comes through both precept and example. If a teacher occasionally belittles, ignores, or dismisses the needs of a student, then class members feel license to act that way toward each other. If a teacher is judgmental or arbitrary in asserting certain facts or knowledge to the group, then where are students to learn the rules of reasoning and support for claims? A successful conveyance of certain values—tolerance, respect, willingness to take risks, openness to change, commitment to hard work, and so on—make building communities much more feasible.

Online communities in some ways mirror classroom communities; in other ways, they have greater latitude at defining themselves. Riel (1996) noted:

> There will always be a sense of adventure and excitement associated with frontiers—they are wild and free. We can design "places," within technical and social constraints, in ways that allow us to experiment with social reality. Freedom from time and space does not automatically lead to rewarding patterns of social discourse. Online communities face the same issues of freedom of speech vs. censorship, of security and control, of private and public spaces, of inclusion and exclusion, of unity and diversity, that exist in all social organizations. It takes intense and continual social negotiation to find the best balance between absolute freedom for citizens and collective control.

As online collaboration increases, teachers will need to address these same issues over and over. But that's good, because that's the way the world really is!

Adaptation

A good teacher enters a classroom with an agenda—learning goals, planned activities, methods for assessing progress, and so on. At the same time, that teacher will be sensitive to the needs of the group. Within the first day of a new school year, a teacher may throw out the window certain planned goals and activities, realizing that the particular mix of students dictates adjustments in the plan. The teacher will adapt to the needs of the group. Similarly, students quickly learn to adapt to the style of the instructor and the norms of the group. Adaptation is the result of the change process, which we have seen is synonymous with learning—which is what education is all about.

Dialogue

What's the difference between argument and dialogue? In an argument, your job is to define a position and support it, to the point of convincing your advocate or a third party of the superiority of your position. A true conversation or dialogue is something different. You actually listen to the person across from you with the hope of learning something new. Dialogue, in the best sense, is not oppositional or confrontational; rather, it is just the opposite. Dialogue involves a willingness to *suspend* one's beliefs in favor of listening to another, to surrender and *give up* one's position if doing so serves the needs of the group. Within a community that values dialogue, reasoned arguments still have a place, but they should be conducted with mutual respect and trust toward all participants.

As you can imagine, cultivating an atmosphere of dialogue is not easily accomplished. In our culture, a willingness to surrender one's position and defer to the group seems almost un-American! Powerful forces push all of us toward a style of jousting competitiveness, flexing of muscles, posturing, and pretense. Yet these behaviors that are so easily the norm need to be tempered by the cultivated and taught values of dialogue, conversation, and commitment to the interests of the whole group.

Access to Information

Open, unrestricted access to information is the lifeblood of a democracy. In a similar way, access to multiple sources of information becomes critical for the success of a learning community. Students look to teachers as role models for reasoning more than as information dispensers; thus, students can come to respect the teacher's opinion without depending exclusively on it. Finding ways to triangulate and cross-compare evidence only serves to strengthen one's position and perspective. In many ways, the vitality of a learning community depends on the quality of the information available to it.

Some Internet critics are concerned about all the "garbage" available out there—not just the pornography, but the unreliable, unsubstantiated information. How can students be expected to weigh, evaluate, and determine the usefulness of information on the Web, much of it conflicting and inaccurate? To these critics we respond, "Welcome to the real world!" Amid the conflicting perceptions and worldviews, our students can learn only by jumping in and participating. Rather than be shielded from complexity, students need to be guided through it and taught methods and tools for managing it. Formally trained librarians, who may be tempted to eschew Web resources in favor of more respectable published outlets, need to support students in their acquiring the "information literacy" skills needed to help them evaluate information from a variety of sources, Web as well as non-Web (Walster, 1996).

Membership

Who participates in learning communities? Participants must be learners, willing to change and grow according to the goals and activities of the group. Certainly students are learners, but so are teachers. Teachers read and critique papers and projects, learning as they do so. They listen to students and learn from their interests and research. Teachers, for example, who lack technical skills with the Internet, can often be taught by the gurus in class who seem to know the answer to every question. The community thus is strengthened by its interdependencies—the teacher needs the class "techno-geeks," just as the students need the direction and support of the teacher. As St. Paul noted, "members," like hands and feet to the body, are needed parts, contributing to the healthy functioning of the whole community (1 Cor. 12). Thus, moving toward learning communities becomes a powerful staff-development exercise for teachers. Teachers should prepare to go into "high learning mode" and stay there for a while!

Outside experts can serve the role of "visiting scholar" within the learning community. While the experts' role is primarily to provide consultation and advice, the learning circle extends to include them as well. Experts should not be shocked when students ask questions that leave them at a loss; the normal flow includes having to go back to resources for answers. Experts unprepared to engage in the dialectical process of learning and teaching will prove to be of limited utility to the learning community.

Learning communities can also establish relationships with outside groups, at times forming a larger collaborating community. This is all to say that learning communities are not defined in fixed, immutable terms. Members may drift in and out, alliances may be formed with outside individuals and communities. Although they enjoy a degree of coherence, communities typically have "soft" boundaries.

Motivation

A continuing thread in the discussion is this: Learning communities depend on autonomous, responsible, motivated learners. But pull on that thread and the fabric becomes unraveled. What can we say to the teacher who says, "My students just aren't motivated for this"? Here is a catch-22 about any activities that empower students: *Doing* it can be incredibly motivating for students, but *helping* students get to the point of doing it can be a struggle. That is to say, how can students decide that they like something when they haven't seen it? And how can they come to see the advantages of an activity unless they cooperate?

This problem calls for a systemic perspective. Just as students can devolve into a loop of negative outcomes—working less at school, liking school less because they're not working, leading to even less engagement—so they can begin a loop of rewards and reinforcement—getting a taste of empowerment and ownership, leading to more engagement, which, in turn, allows further empowerment, and so on. Classes *become* communities by learning a step at a time. Granted, motivation is a key component to the success of learning communities, but striving toward learning communities is a key to motivation.

Advice to Teachers

Here are some responses to the teacher looking for ways to convert these ideas into some concrete actions in the classroom:

1. **Remember, the concept of learning communities is an ideal.** Nobody ever attains it completely. So relax; don't worry about perfection.

Movement is the thing. Which way are you and your students moving? Are you approaching community, or moving away from it?

2. **Technology, resources, and models can help.** There is nothing magic about the technology, but certain activities and expectations are feasible with access to the Internet that would have been unthinkable without it. Just as you may require that a paper be typed or word processed, with access to appropriate tools and resources, you can raise the bar and heighten your students' expectations for what can reasonably be done.

3. **It's not all or nothing.** Many of the models and technologies discussed here can be used in a variety of ways. Yes, each innovation takes work to integrate into the curriculum, but take it in small steps, observing effects and making adjustments as you go. Just as you ask your students to be thoughtful and innovative, your integration of new technologies is like a perpetual action research project of your own.

4. **Respect your own knowledge and situation.** Let's say you decide to engage in a Global Schoolhouse project. Judi Harris (1999) has a helpful model and checklist for embarking on such a project, and a Web site with links to accompanying literature and support (Table 4.5). Nonetheless, your classroom is unique. Your own learning community goes beyond whatever model was used in its inception or design. Moreover, your success in adopting any particular framework or model depends as much on local factors as on the details of the model itself. The mix of students and teachers, the available technology and facilities, the expectations of the school and the surrounding community, your insights and energy as project leader—these will account for the success of the project at least as much as the quality of the thinking that went into the model in the first place. Another way of saying this is, "The community is not its model." Some theorists may forget this sometimes, but you never should lose sight of the primacy of your own experience and expertise.

I have probably had as many network failures behind me as I do successes. It isn't easy . . . In fact the progressive education of the sixties failed, to a large extent, because people misunderstood the role of the teacher . . . as well as the problem of the technical support. . . . [T]eachers were told that they were supposed to be facilitators and that kids would learn on their own, teachers stood back and waited for things to happen. . . . People again and again think that you can put the technology in place and if you give people the communication potential, that suddenly, education is going to happen all by itself. (Riel, 1991)

We suspect that Riel's success rate has improved over the years, but her remarks remind us to contain our expectations about our students and about the innovation. Indeed, students *can* learn to work on their own, but teacher support and guidance along the way is critical to success. The U.S. Department of Education's *Teacher's Guide to International Collaboration on the Internet* is a

Table 4.5   Steps for Successful Design and Completion of Global SchoolNet Projects (Adapted from Harris, 1999)

How to Design a Successful Project

1. Design a project with specific goals, tasks, and outcomes. The more closely aligned with curriculum-based goals, the better.

2. Explore examples of similar projects.

3. Create a timeline. Set specific beginning and ending dates with deadlines for participant responses. Make a timeline that allows for lots of lead time for announcements and recruiting.

4. If possible, do a small-scale tryout with a close colleague.

5. Announce your project. Create a "call for collaboration" following a standard template, such as the NickNacks Telecollaboration Planner available online. Post your first call for collaboration six to eight weeks before the starting date. Repeat your call again two weeks before the starting date. Include in your call:
   • Goals and objectives
   • Grade levels desired
   • How many responses you would like
   • Contact person
   • Timeline and deadlines
   • Your location and complete contact information
   • Examples of the kinds of writing or data students will submit
   • What you will do with student and team submissions (teams will need some interaction or other incentives to collaborate)

6. Find and train students. You will need a cohort of responsible and trained students to help you with the project. This step becomes an essential timesaver when using technology in the classroom.

7. At the project's conclusion, follow through on sharing project results with all participants, including a hard copy of all publications, a Web-published, class-written project summary, and student-written thank-you notes. Also send the summary to your principal, PTA president, superintendent, and school board president.

8. Your leadership as teacher is critical. Riel (1991) stressed that networking technologies and Learning Circles are not magic.

---

comprehensive guide with resources, suggestions for developing and running online collaborative projects, and many more examples of online project opportunities across the curriculum (http://www.ed.gov/Technology/guide/ international/index.html).

Our central goal has been to present some key ideas, then let you as a teacher find ways to incorporate those ideas into your daily practice. With years of experience, you are smarter than we are. You know your students, your school, your community. You can adapt concepts to your own situation; in that respect, you are much smarter than any technology or textbook ever devised!

CONCLUSIONS

Are learning communities just another educational fad? We think not. Seen as complex systems, networks become the mechanisms that allow adaptation and change, and adaptation and change equate to learning. Thus, while a business organization "learns" by adapting to its environment, teachers and students learn when they respond and adapt to each other and to information resources. As we see in a variety of settings, adaptive change goes hand in hand with a certain kind of structure—not hierarchical, static, or centrally controlled, but decentralized, complex, dynamic, Web-like networks of collaborating contributors. When classes or groups of students function together like that, they become more capable of learning.

Individual community members—students and teachers—work independently as well as collaboratively. In doing so, innovations, insights, and solutions to problems are developed that are shared with the community at large. As students and teachers continue their work, the community takes on common attributes that shape its overall character and behavior.

What advantages does computer conferencing have over a good old-fashioned discussion? Why not just converse face to face, rather than talking through computers? There are several reasons one might want to participate in a computer-mediated conference. First, computer conferencing can support discussions, debates, and collaborative efforts among groups of people who are colocated or at a distance. Students do not have to be in the same place in order to converse and learn. Many classrooms are becoming virtual-communications and learning spaces located within a networked system connecting learners all over the country. Why it is necessary for students to share the same physical space with a teacher in order to listen to the teacher, ask questions, get assignments, or otherwise communicate with the teacher? The obvious answer is that computer conferencing supports long-distance collaboration among learners.

A second advantage is that computer conferencing enables learners to reflect on their ideas or responses before making them. In addition to providing opportunities to research topics and to develop arguments, conferences allow the students the opportunity to adequately present the group's position on the conference. That requires reflecting on your argument before carefully presenting it. Thinking about what you are going to say before saying it is fostered by computer conferences.

Third, and perhaps most important, different kinds of thinking can be scaffolded in computer conferences. Although in-class conversation is a powerful learning method, learners do not necessarily know how to constructively converse. Computer conferences can guide and scaffold students as they make comments, reminding them of needed support and development, and archiving past conversations for future use.

Computer conferences are not meant to replace face-to-face interactions. We have tried to show, however, that computer conferencing can support learners in unique ways as they engage in reasoned dialogue, collaborate with remote and diverse audiences, and learn to express themselves in writing. In learning communities, learners judge people by what they say, not by how they look.

THINGS TO THINK ABOUT

If you would like to reflect on the ideas presented in this chapter, then articulate your responses to the following questions and compare them with responses of others.

1. What responsibilities do teacher and students share in cultivating a learning community in the classroom? How can technology serve the goals of a learning community—and how might technology get in the way?
2. With technology-supported learning communities, students learn different things at different speeds. How can a teacher keep track of students' various learning needs and make sure everyone is progressing well?
3. Every community has "outliers"—people on the margins who don't seem to fit or who struggle to participate fully. How can a teacher draw all students into the community circle? What steps can be taken to motivate students who may be reluctant to participate?
4. Do you believe that learning by conversing in learning communities can be more effective than traditional instruction? What evidence would we need to confirm (or reject) that belief?
5. With the advent of virtual reality and enhanced graphical interfaces, language may become less important in communication, especially among learners of different languages. What would a virtual language look like? How would students use it to communicate?
6. Most scaffolded computer conferences support argumentation and collaborative problem solving. Would it be useful to develop a scaffolded conference to help students memorize facts? If so, what would it look like?

REFERENCES

Andres, Y. M. (1995). *Collaboration in the classroom and over the Internet.* Retrieved from http://gsh.lightspan.com/teach/articles/collaboration.html

Bruckerman, A. (1998). Community support for constructionist learning. *Computer Supported Cooperative Work, 7,* 47–86.

Cognition and Technology Group at Vanderbilt (1994). From visual word problems to learning communities: Changing conceptions of cognitive research. In K. McGilly (Ed.), *Classroom lessons:* *Integrating cognitive theory and classroom practice* (pp. 157–200). Cambridge, MA: MIT Press.

Fulton, K., & Riel, M. (1999). *Professional development through learning communities.* Retrieved from http://glef.org/

Gardner, H. (2000). *Intelligence reframed: Multiple intelligences for the 21st century.* New York: Basic Books.

Gardner, H., & Lazear, D. C. (1991). *Seven ways of knowing, teaching for multiple intelligences: A handbook of the techniques for expanding intelli-*

gence. Victoria, BC: Hawker Brownlow Education.

Harris, J. (1995, February). Organizing and facilitating telecollaborative projects. *The Computing Teacher*, 22(5), 66–69. Retrieved from http://www.ed.uiuc.edu/Mining/February95-TCT.html

Harris, J. (1998). *Virtual architecture: Designing and directing curriculum-based telecomputing*. Eugene, OR: International Society for Technology in Education.

Harris, J. (1999). *Project planning and direction*. Retrieved from http://ccwf.cc.utexas.edu/~jbharris/Virtual-Architecture/Designing+Directing/

Harris, J. (2000). Structuring Internet-enriched learning spaces for understanding and action. *Learning & Leading with Technology*, 28(4), Retrieved from http://www.iste.org/

Hughes, B., Walters, J. (1995, April). *Children, MUDs, and learning*. Paper presented at the meeting of the American Educational Research Association, San Francisco, CA.

International Society for Technology in Education (2000). *Specific activity structures categorized by genre and learning processes*. Retrieved from http://www.iste.org

Kane, K. A. (1997). Using the Internet as a tool to reconnect students to the educational process. *Interface* (Monthly newsletter of the Montgomery County Intermediate Unit). Available: 1605 B West Main Street, Norristown, PA 19403.

Knowledge building: A product of research. Retrieved January 12, 2002, from http://www.learn.motion.com/Research.html (See http://kf.oise.utoronto.ca/ for more information about the Knowledge Forum researchers at the University of Toronto's Ontario Institute for Studies in Education.)

Lave, J. (1991). Situating learning in communities of practice. In L. B. Resnick, J. M. Levine, & S. D. Teasley (Eds.), *Perspectives on socially shared cognition*. Washington, DC: American Psychological Association.

McCarty, J. (2000, May). Getting to know you. *Rural Missouri*, p. 22. Retrieved from http://www.baruch.cuny.edu/spa/community/mural/

NickNacks Telecollaborate! (2001). Retrieved from http://home.talkcity.com/academydr/nicknacks/NNplanner.html

OpenSource.org http://www.opensource.org/

Office of Educational Technology. (2000). *e-Learning: Putting a world-class education at the fingertips of all children*. Washington, DC: U.S. Department of Education.

Paulson, M. F. (1995, August). *The online report of pedagogical techniques for computer-mediated communication*. Retrieved from http://www.nki.no/~morten

Riel, M. (1996, January). *The Internet: A land to settle rather than an ocean to surf and a new "place" for school reform through community development*. Retrieved from http://gsh.lightspan.com/teach/articles/netasplace

Riel, M. (1991, June). *Transcribed lecture on children, learning, and computer-mediated communication*. Simon Fraser University, Vancouver, British Columbia, June 30, 1991. Retrieved from http://www.lhbe.edu.on.ca/teach2000/onramp/Riel.html

Riel, M., & Polin, L. (2001). Communities as places where learning occurs. Paper presented at AERA 2001, Seattle, WA. To appear in Barab, S. A., Kling, R., & Gray, J. (Eds.). *Designing for virtual communities in the service of learning*. Cambridge, MA: Cambridge University Press (in press). Retrieved from http://gsep.pepperdine.edu/~mriel/office/papers/Riel_&_Polin-LC.htm

Riley, R. W., Kunin, M. M., Smith, M. S., & Roberts, L. G. (1996, June). *Getting America's students ready for the 21st century: Meeting the technology literacy challenge. A report to the nation on technology and education*. Retrieved from http://www.ed.gov/Technology/Plan/NatTechPlan/

Rockman, S., & Sloan, K. R. (1995, April). *Assessing the growth: The Buddy Project evaluation, 1994–1995*. Unpublished final report. San Francisco, CA.

Rogers, A. (1994). *Keys to successful projects*. Retrieved from http://www.ed.uiuc.edu/Guidelines/Rogers.html

Rowand, C. (2000). *Teacher Use of Computers and the Internet in Public Schools* (NCES #2000-090). Washington, DC: National Center for Educational Statistics, U.S. Department of Education. Retrieved from http://nces.ed.gov/pubsearch/ pubsinfo.asp?pubid=200009

Scardamalia, M., & Bereiter, C. (1996). Adaptation and understanding: A case for new cultures of schooling. In S. Vosniadou, E. DeCorte, R. Glaser, & H. Mandl (Eds.), *International perspectives on the design of technology-supported learning environments* (149–163). Hillsdale, NJ: Lawrence Erlbaum Associates.

Scardamalia, M., Bereiter, C., & Lamon, D. (1994). The CSILE Project: Trying to bring the classroom into World 3. In K. McGilly (Ed.), *Classroom lessons: Integrating cognitive theory and classroom practice* (201–228). Cambridge, MA: MIT Press.

Sizer, T. (1996). *Horace's hope: What works for the American high school*. Boston: Houghton Mifflin.

Walster, D. (1996). Technologies for information access in library and information centers. In D. H. Jonassen (Ed.), *Handbook of research for educational communications and technology* (720–754). New York: Macmillan.

Walters, J., & Hughes, B. (1995, April). *Pueblo: A virtual learning community*. Paper presented at the meeting of the American Educational Research Association, San Francisco, CA.

Learning by Visualizing With Technology: Recording Realities With Video

BROADCAST TV (LEARNING FROM) VERSUS VIDEOGRAPHY (LEARNING WITH) TELEVISION

Television broadcasts began in the United States in the post-World War II years, quickly revolutionizing the ways that Americans entertained themselves. No longer did listeners at home have to imagine how the characters in the comedies looked. They could see them for themselves. And a country inured to attending movies in public theaters suddenly began to stay home and stare at their 9-inch television screens. As with every technological development in this century, educators immediately considered how this nascent technology could be used to teach.

Educational television (ETV) emerged in the early 1950s as several universities began offering telecourses. More often than not, these courses consisted of professors, supported with a variety of visual aids, lecturing at the cameras in much the same ways that they lectured in halls around their campuses. In the 1960s, many college courses began to be delivered exclusively by television. And for two decades, thousands of research studies compared the effectiveness of those televised courses with traditional courses. Most of the research was so poorly conducted that meaningful conclusions were impossible (Chu & Schramm, 1967; Reid & MacLennan, 1967). The remaining research showed generally that televised instruction was just about as effective as traditional—not a startling conclusion, since television teachers were teaching in front of cameras in the same ways they normally taught in front of classes.

In the 1960s and 1970s, the scope of ETV expanded with the emergence of the Public Broadcasting System (PBS). Telecourses became miniseries, which began to exploit the capabilities of the medium, focusing less on college courses and more on public information, news, and cultural programming. The PBS was responsible for many excellent programs and series that were hailed as cultural successes (e.g., *Civilization* and *Cosmos*) despite the fact they are rarely viewed by more than 5% of the population. Why has ETV, which had the potential of starting a cultural renaissance in the United States, been perceived as so successful, yet had so little effect on education? Why has television, which is the most universally common communication medium in the world, available in more than 97% of U.S. homes, (yes, the Internet is advancing, but has a long way to go) had so little effect on the ways that we learn within the educational system, yet such a profound effect on the ways that we perceive the world?

The Case for Television

Although much of the content of commercial television is deemed vapid, vulgar, and violent, television also supplies us with a rich collection of cultural, informational, and educational programming. Hundreds of instructional programs have been broadcast and thousands more are available on videocassette. Instructional and educational programming, such as *Sesame Street* and *3-2-1 Contact* from the Children's Television Workshop, employed teams of learning psychologists, educators, and television producers to design and produce the best educational programming possible. By 1980, thousands of high-quality, commercially prepared television programs were available, either broadcast via state networks or available on videocassette, to supplement classroom instruction. It was widely believed by producers and educators that these programs could not fail because they consisted of high-quality audiovisual messages that exposed students to experiences and cultures throughout the world that they could not be exposed to otherwise, brought multiple viewpoints into the classroom, and presented new content in the classroom that teachers could not possibly know. Television has provided a common ground for conversation and understanding internationally; it contributes to the fund of general knowledge and provides the closest thing we have to a democratic information medium (Wagschal, 1987).

While all of these arguments for the power of television are true, there exist implicit limitations to the effectiveness of television viewing for school learning. Two reasons for this lack of efficacy were examined in the 1970s: the way that television programs were integrated into the classroom and the ways that children viewed the television messages. In order to learn meaningfully from broadcast or videotaped instruction in classrooms, that instruction needs to be properly integrated into classroom instruction. Teachers were taught that they should preview and evaluate programs before using them; prepare students for learning from television by introducing new vocabulary, providing overviews and advance organizers; remain with students and encourage active viewing of the television program; and follow up the program by summarizing, reviewing, discussing, and evaluating the content learned by students (Jonassen, 1982). The problem was that teachers too seldom performed these integrative activities. Television became an electronic baby-sitter or substitute teacher in too many classrooms. When students realized that they would not be responsible for understanding any of the information contained in the television shows, they usually did not actively attend to the messages in the shows, repeating their well-rehearsed home-viewing habits in school. In an attempt to change those habits, educators attempted to change the passive reception of television messages by teaching children to become critical viewers of television.

During the 1970s, many educational and children's advocacy groups, such as Action for Children's Television, developed and promoted critical viewing curricula to ensure that elementary and junior high school students (especially) did not just watch television, they monitored it. While watching TV, children should be aware that TV programs and their messages are created to achieve specific results, that each person interprets programs and messages differently, that TV violence may take many forms, and that TV programs have an underlying economic purpose (National Cable Television Association, 1995). Most of these critical viewing curricula taught children how television and television production work, the components of entertainment television stories, the purpose of commercials and how to view their claims critically and become informed consumers, how their lives differed from television characters, that television violence should not be imitated, and how to get the most from television news programming—

generally, how to be critical viewers of the medium (Hefzallah, 1987). In order to take charge of TV viewing, it should become a conscious, planned-for activity, an interactive family event that should provide springboards to other learning experiences (National Cable Television Association, 1995). Potter (1976) best articulated these springboards by describing how commercial television could support the development of reading, thinking, math, and social studies skills—especially from reading television scripts and books about television, thereby developing valuable language skills. The major purpose of these critical viewing efforts was to make sure that children became aware of television's persuasiveness in terms of how much and what kinds of television they viewed, and to teach children to view commercial advertising skeptically. However, only a small minority of children have ever been exposed to these critical viewing curricula, while a majority of children continue to spend 25–30 hours per week in front of the television (more than in classrooms, and six times more than working on homework). Very few children, it seems, view television critically.

The Case Against Television

Can students learn from viewing educational television programs? What are the effects of entertainment television viewing on learning and study habits while viewing educational television programming, and does such viewing affect the abilities of students to think and learn? These have become important questions for teachers and parents in the past two decades.

The major reason that students do not successfully learn from watching televised instruction is that they are not mentally engaged by it. Salomon (1984) found that learners thought that learning from television was easier than learning from reading, so they did not try as hard when watching television programs. This "differential investment of mental effort" results in less learning from television because the effort is passive. Learning from television cannot be effective unless learners are helped to actively process television messages and think about them. We agree with this argument and must conclude that the reason television has failed to enlighten students is that viewing prerecorded television programming does not sufficiently engage learners in active, constructive, intentional, authentic, and cooperative learning (as described in chapter 1).

Salomon's research has been confirmed by a considerable amount of reading research. Beentjes and van der Vort (1988) reviewed a great deal of international research, concluding that television's negative effects had the greatest impact on advanced cognitive abilities needed for understanding, and that television:

- Displaces leisure reading
- Requires less mental effort than reading
- Reduces children's attention span and tenacity in solving problems

Ironically, these effects are greatest on socially advantaged and more intelligent children, who are heavy viewers.

Why are children not engaged by watching television? Because watching TV does not fulfill any purpose; it is not intentional. Children too often watch television to fill time or avoid more cognitively challenging activities. In order for television to foster learning, learners have to have a reason for watching it. They should be seeking answers or confirming hunches, either about themselves or about some problem that is presented on the television program.

Why is television programming not supportive of learning? Because most research and development, even with instructional television programming such as *Sesame Street*, has been conducted to make television programming more alluring. The small amount of quality research that has been conducted confirms that television viewing has three primary effects on children's learning abilities (Healy, 1990).

First, children's attention to the fast-paced auditory and image changes is fragmented, which causes attention disorders when trying to perform complex cognitive tasks, especially those that require sustained attention. This has been referred to as a lack of vigilance, meaning that children maintain a low state of alertness. The inability to pay attention by those who watch a lot of television makes it more difficult for them to stay actively focused on complex learning tasks. If material is the least bit boring, they stop paying attention unless something alerting or salient happens, as it always seems to in most commercial and many educational television programs.

Second, television viewing results in a lack of persistence. Because of the fast-paced, ever-changing nature of the image, television requires little sustained effort. So, if materials being studied are not readily understandable, heavy TV viewers tend to give up more readily.

Third, viewers become readily "glued" to the tube. That is, their brain activity slows down, causing a hypnotic, trance-like state while viewing. This form of addictive behavior is obviously not conducive to active learning. Wagschal (1987) also cites the simplicity (lowest common denominator) of most television programming, trivializing everything so that it is impossible to distinguish fact from fiction. Other critics, like Marie Winn (1980), have examined the social isolation that television viewing brings about, reducing interpersonal interactions among children, increasing irritability of children, and causing a disintegration of the family unit.

We must conclude that despite attempts to improve the ways that teachers use television and the ways that students view it, television viewing (watching television to learn lessons without a clear, cognitive purpose) is not sufficiently active or constructive enough for learners to engage in meaningful learning. Leisure television viewing habits appear to be impossible to discard when the content is educational. Also, and more perversely, heavy television viewing affects the ability of students to pay attention, stay on task, and make sense out of what they are viewing. Our solution is simple. If students are to view television, then give them a good reason for using television to find meaning (e.g., the *Jasper Woodbury* series, described later in this chapter). More effectively, let students produce video rather than watch television. Producing television programming will engage them in active, meaningful learning because they are solving design problems.

The Case for Video

The premise of this chapter (and the entire book) is that television technology is a powerful learning tool when students are critical users and producers, rather than consumers. Producing videos requires learners to be active, constructive, intentional, and cooperative—to solve numerous decision-making problems while solving design problems associated with production. Video production requires the application of a variety of research, organization, visualization, and interpretation skills, similar to those engaged by producing multimedia (see chapter 6). Producing videos engages critical and creative thinking in order to plan and produce programs. Additionally, there are a variety of social values of producing videos in schools (Valmont, 1994):

- Improving students' self-confidence by planning, producing, and sharing video productions in class
- Producing feelings of self-satisfaction
- Providing valuable feedback to students about how others perceive them
- Fostering cooperative learning while sharing ideas, planning and producing programs, and evaluating outcomes
- Providing great public relations at open houses and other school functions

As mentioned before, there are thousands of research studies on learning *from* television. However, there are relatively few studies on learning *with* video. We argue in this chapter that students will learn more by creating videos than by watching TV. We hope that this belief, and the assumptions that it rests on, will be researched more in the future.

In this chapter, we will describe a number of learning activities where television can provide meaningful learning contexts that can engage learners when they identify a purpose for viewing the program in order to find information and solve problems. However, most of the activities described in this chapter make students television producers. As producers, teachers and students need to understand a little about video production hardware, which we describe next.

VIDEO HARDWARE FOR THE CLASSROOM

Using video to engage meaningful learning requires three things: imaginative students willing to take chances, ideas for how to engage them, and some equipment. The equipment may be the easiest part, so let's briefly describe some of the hardware that you will need first. Following that, we will provide numerous ideas for engaging learners. You will have to provide the students.

In the 1960s and 1970s, producing educational television programs required teams of directors, engineers, camera operators, lighting technicians, and a host of others to run the bulky and expensive production equipment. Television programs were shot in studios, where large cameras wheeled around on hydraulic booms, sets, and thousands of watts of lights competed for space. In the control room, floor-standing videotape recorders, engineering consoles for controlling the video image, audio mixing boards, and a director's console, controlled the video image being produced. Since then, video equipment, like computers and most other hardware, has become incredibly smaller, cheaper, and more efficient. Today, an entire studio of equipment has been crammed into a single small box—the videocamera or camcorder. We will briefly describe videocameras and some auxiliary equipment that you will need to use video in the classroom.

Camcorders

Camcorders (camera-recorders) are portable electronic recording systems that are capable of recording live motion video and audio for later replay by VCRs (video-cassette recorders) or computers. Some newer models are also capable of taking still images. When they first arrived, camcorders recorded in analog format (VHS and beta) onto reel-to-reel tape and later videocassettes for replay from VCRs. These camcorders produced less than ideal quality images and the large video-cameras had to be rested on the shoulder. As technology improved, other smaller analogue formats became available such as S-VHS, Hi-8, and 8mm. These formats produced better quality images, were a fraction of the size of the original cam-corders, and enabled longer recording times than previously. In order to transfer the images from an analog camera to a computer, the computer had to be equipped with a video board that would convert the analog signals into digital.

Most camcorders today record images digitally. Rather than scanning line-by-line, light values for each pixel on the screen are registered digitally in memory.

Figure 5.1 Digital Videocameras

Recreating the image is a matter of lighting up each pixel on the screen. Most digital camcorders feature the following.

- Zoom lenses with electronic zoom controls (up to 500 times magnification) and optical zoom (up to 25 times magnification) for sharp and clear images
- LCD video screen for viewing the subject while recording, as well as playback and the editing of previously recorded material
- Videocassette recorder with record, playback, fast forward, and rewind controls, and playback through the viewfinder
- High video resolution range (200k–500k pixels per frame)
- Built-in microphone, CD quality sound (PCM stereo digital audio recording), and external microphone input jack. Some cameras have low base filters to eliminate the roar of the wind.
- Various shooting features, including time lapse (setting specific time intervals), slow motion, wide screen (16:9 format used by HDTV), remote control, self-timer, still image capture, and LP (extending the recording time of 60-minute Mini DV tapes to 90 minutes)
- Rechargeable NiCad and lithium ion batteries for shooting without electrical outlet, battery charger, and AC adapter. Most cameras also have battery indicators that show you an accurate indication of how much time remains on the battery.
- Automatic and manual video controls for adjusting exposure (how light or dark the video will be), shutter speed (number of images per second), white balance (for different sources of light, such as daylight, incandescent light, fluorescent light)
- Separate connection jacks for inputting and outputting audio, video, or for playback through regular TV. (*IEEE 1394 ports* [called FireWire by Apple and i.Link™ by Sony] for transferring videos from camcorder to the computer, *infrared connection* for sending videos to an infrared TV set via wireless infrared; *S-video output* which carries the brightness and color signals on separate lines within the same cable for better image quality; *composite video output, stereo audio jacks, analog line* which connect a TV or VCR to a digital camera to transfer video and audio from analog tapes to a digital format)
- Character generators, known as titlers, for adding titles or other text on your video; date and time stamp which records the date and time on the video; special effects (fade, dissolves, and wipes)
- *Autofocus* (allowing you to concentrate on the subject being recorded without having to worry about the quality) and *image stabilization* (minimizing the minute tremors of videoing by hand)

Recording with different camcorders will vary slightly, so we will not attempt to show you how to do these things. You should consult the manual that accompanies your digital videocamera and experiment extensively with your equipment before trying to use it for learning.

The backbone of student video productions is the camcorder; we suggest that you purchase as many videocameras as possible so that different student groups can work on projects simultaneously. Or, for important or complex video productions, different students can record the same events from different angles or perspectives.

Digital videocameras range in price from $250 to $20,000, based on their features. Very adequate cameras are available for $500–1,000. We also recommend that for every camcorder you acquire, you purchase a tripod to hold the camera steady while it is being used. The tripod also permits individuals to videotape themselves.

Projectors/Televisions

Although most camcorders are capable of playing back recorded videos in the viewfinder, viewing through the viewfinder is limited to a single individual, and the quality is not very good. Learning through video is completed when students critique and reflect on their productions, so you will need to acquire a large television set or LCD projectors for playing back student productions for the class. Projectors are preferable because they allow you to project video from a VCR, laserdisc, camcorder, or a computer. Normal television sets are able to play only "modulated" RF (radio frequency) broadcast TV signals (the kind that are transmitted from broadcast towers or received via cable). Most modern videocameras have modulators built in to enable playback on regular TV sets, which are cheaper than projectors; however, projectors are more flexible. Most projectors provide inputs to connect several devices to them, including two computer inputs (RGB1 and RGB2), one or two video inputs (composite video for VCR, component video for DVD), and an S-video input for a digital still camera or other devices. These projectors are more expensive, however. Among the most important features of projectors is their brightness, measured in lumens. Generally, having more lumens means that the projector will cost more money.

Most of the value of producing videos in schools relies on group viewing of the videos. If you are still using analog video equipment, you may want to purchase a VCR for playing back tapes in order to free up the camcorders for use elsewhere. The standard VCRs that populate most American homes are commonly available for less than $200 and are fine for replaying videotapes in the classroom.

Editors

Most video nowadays is shot "on location." The compact size of camcorders enables students to move around easily to get different shots. When all of the shooting in the various locations has been completed, you end up with a large number of disconnected scenes stored in the camera or on different disks. In order to arrange those disconnected scenes into a coherent production, those video sequences must be rearranged. With analog video, you need a video editor with at least two VCRs and two TVs or monitors to perform the edit functions.

Today, these editing functions are accomplished on multimedia computers with digital video editing software, such as iMovie. To make a video with iMovie, you need to follow the process illustrated in Figure 5.2. We will briefly explain the process.

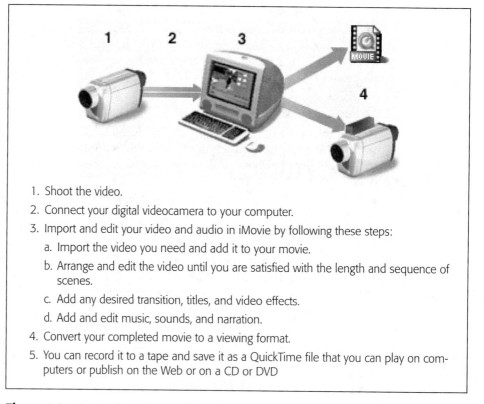

1. Shoot the video.
2. Connect your digital videocamera to your computer.
3. Import and edit your video and audio in iMovie by following these steps:
   a. Import the video you need and add it to your movie.
   b. Arrange and edit the video until you are satisfied with the length and sequence of scenes.
   c. Add any desired transition, titles, and video effects.
   d. Add and edit music, sounds, and narration.
4. Convert your completed movie to a viewing format.
5. You can record it to a tape and save it as a QuickTime file that you can play on computers or publish on the Web or on a CD or DVD

Figure 5.2 Process for Editing a Video With iMovie. Images courtesy of Apple Computer, Inc. Used with permission.

1. Connecting a Mini Digital Videocamera to Your Computer

In order to edit video with iMovie, connect the mini digital videocamera with a FireWire cable to your computer. Plug the 6-pin FireWire connector into the 6-pin FireWire port on your computer, then plug the 4-pin connector of the cable into the 4-pin port of your videocamera. Be careful not to turn on your digital videocamera before both cables are connected.

2. Importing Video

To make digital video into a movie, make sure the Movie switch is set to camera mode. After that, use the camera mode playback control to view the tape in the iMovie monitor. Then, click the Play button. When the

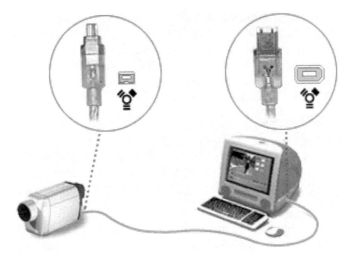

Figure 5.3 Connecting the Camcorder and Computer. Courtesy of Apple Computer Inc. Used with permission.

iMovie monitor displays the scene you want to start importing, click the Import button to begin importing. To stop importing, click the Import button again.

3. Editing Video

a. Selecting video To select a video clip, click the clip in the clip viewer or timeline viewer. If you want to select a section of a clip, select the clip, then click and drag just below the scrubber bar under the iMovie monitor. If the crop markers appear, drag them to mark the beginning and end of the selection.

b. Arranging video clips in a movie To arrange video clips in a movie, drag a clip to a position before or after another clip in the clip view. You can also change the order of video clips in the clip viewer.

c. Transitions Transitions add visual appeal through smoothing the cuts between clips. To add a transition to a clip, first click the Transition button. Then, select a transition in the Transition panel. You can modify the speed of the transition into or out of the clip using the speed slider.

If you want to change the transition direction, click an arrow to indicate the direction. After that, drag the Transition from the Transition panel to the desired location in the timeline viewer.

d. Titles A title lets you add descriptive text, such as credits, to your movie. This function covers titles, captions, credits, and subtitles. To add a title to your movie, select a title style from the list in the Titles panel, then click the Title button. After that, type the text for your title into the title fields. To speed up or slow down the titling effect, adjust the speed or pause sliders. Also, if you want to customize the text, choose a text color, a font, and the text size. Finally, drag the title from the list in the middle of the Titles panel to the clip viewer. If you want the title to appear over a clip, place it before that clip.

e. Adding video effects   You can add video effects to your movie, such as color adjustments or a sepia tone. To apply video effects to your movie, select a video effect in the Effects panel, then click the video you want to apply the effect to. Click on the Apply button when you finish adjusting the effect by using any of the sliders in the middle of the Effects panel.

f. Adding and editing audio   To bring audio into your movie, you can import video that contains audio as well and extract the audio from the video so that you can edit it separately. Use iMovie to record music from an audio CD and voice narration into the movie. Sound effects are available. You can edit audio in the following ways:

- Crop, cut, and paste it
- Reposition its place in the movie
- Mute or adjust the volume of individual clips
- Lock audio specific places in the video

4. Exporting

When your masterpiece is completed, you may want to export it so that you can share it with others. You can export it back to the camera via the camera-to-digital videotape or as a QuickTime movie in various formats.

a. Exporting to the camera   To record your movie tape, connect your mini digital videocamera to your computer using a FireWire cable. Make sure a videotape is in the camera, and you have cued it to the correct place. Then click Export Movie from the File menu. Choose Camera from the Export pop-up menu, and then click Export.

b. Saving a movie as a QuickTime file   When you want to distribute your movies electronically, convert them into QuickTime files so that you can play them on computers and put them on a Web page. To save your movie as a QuickTime file, choose Export Movie. Select QuickTime and a movie format from the "Export to" pop-up menu. After that, click the Export button, name your movie, and click Save.

Digital video editing is fast and convenient. Our experiences have shown that kids readily learn how to perform sophisticated editing. To edit on computers, you need a fairly fast computer with a lot of hard disk space and RAM. Video files on the computer require large amounts of memory to store, so an external storage device will be needed. If this kind of equipment and software are available, then digital video editing may be a desirable option.

Microphones

You may want to consider purchasing a microphone or two. All videocameras have a built-in microphone, so that whenever you record video, you are automatically recording audio as well. These microphones tend to be very sensitive, omnidirectional mics. That is, they record sounds coming from all directions. Although this is a convenient way to record ambient sounds, you may also record camera and operator sounds (breathing, talking, giggling, walking), which can be distracting to the message you wish to record. An external, omnidirectional microphone can be plugged into all videocameras, reducing the operator sounds. Moving the microphone closer to the source of the sound improves the quality of the sound. In some cases, such as an interview, you may want to use an external, unidirectional microphone (sensitive to sound from only one direction—the direction in which the microphone is pointed). A good choice here would be a lapel mike, a tiny microphone that you clip to your lapel. Decent microphones can be purchased inexpensively (less than $50). Be sure to get one with a fairly long cord.

Summary   Most of the activities described in this chapter require only a videocamera and a television monitor or projector. The more video production that you do, the more adventurous and demanding your students are likely to become, so the more equipment you will want. As money is collected from the school budgets, grants, car washes, activity fees, benefactors, or other sources, your video production facilities can be embellished.

VIDEO LEARNING ACTIVITIES

Video is, for the time being, the most familiar communication medium for school-aged students. Children are intimately familiar with the syntax and semantics of television, the ways that ideas are conceived, visualized, organized, and presented. Their knowledge of television is that it serves as a medium for entertainment, not for learning. With few exceptions, educational television is normally anathema to most students. Exceptions are the *Jasper Woodbury* and *Scientists in Action* series, which are described next. In these cases, video is used to convey an interesting problem that students are required to solve. Most of the remaining video-learning activities in this chapter describe students-as-video-producers. When students become producers of video, rather than viewers, they naturally assume more active, constructive, intentional, authentic, and cooperative roles. Television production is an example of design problem solving. Designing television programs also engages a great deal of modeling and the making of many decisions. Because of their familiarity with video, students are able to easily assume roles as directors, producers, camera operators, set designers, and actors, and they enjoy it. They construct their own understanding for ideas by representing them to others through this familiar medium. More importantly, they have ownership of the product, so it naturally has more meaning to them. The final two learning activities engage teachers in the same kinds of constructive learning experiences as the students.

Jasper and Scientists: Anchoring Instruction

Learning Activity The Cognition and Technology Group at Vanderbilt University (CTGV) has developed and tested video-based instruction that is designed to help students to reason, think, and solve problems. They engage students in these processes by creating what they call a *macro-context*, which is a reasonably complex everyday situation and story that contain a problem (Cognition and Technology Group at Vanderbilt, 1997). In solving the problem, students are required to write persuasive essays, do informal reasoning, explain how data relate to their investigation, and solve complex problems that require mathematical reasoning. These problems are different from textbook problems, which apply only the skills covered in the chapter. These problems require learners to figure out necessary subproblems, generate solutions, develop arguments and explanations to support the solutions to those subproblems, and finally to assemble those subproblems in a sequence necessary to solve the overall problem.

Most students who are successful in solving textbook problems find it difficult to solve these complex problems. The problems are embedded in an adventure story that is represented with high-quality video. In one program, Jasper Woodbury, the hero, goes fishing in the wilderness, where he comes across a wounded eagle. He uses his radio to correspond with his friends, who decide to use an ultralight aircraft to rescue the eagle. However, calculating the route requires that they consider several variables (wind direction and speed, aircraft speed, fuel capacity, location of the veterinarian, the meadow, and the gas station, etc.). The final solution requires the identification and solution of more than 20 subproblems. All of the information needed to solve these various subproblems is embedded in the video. The students need to search the video in order to find the needed information after they have determined what they need to know.

In another series, *Scientists in Action*, science learning begins with a problem, such as the *Overturned Tanker* (Goldman et al., 1996). A tanker truck, containing an unknown but obviously toxic chemical, has overturned on a highway. The tank has ruptured and the chemical is spilling into the creek. The video portrays a day-in-the-life of a hydrologist and a chemist, who are called into action following the news story about the tanker. The video ends, and students are left with the tasks of figuring out what the chemical is, how it may affect the stream, and whether it is likely to flow toward the lake or the city. Using authentic materials (topographic maps, chemical test kits, and emergency guidebooks), they have to develop a plan of action. They check their responses against the experts' when the video resumes to present more information and more problems. The purpose of the program is for the students to solve problems similar to those that real scientists would solve—ergo, scientists in action. With both sets of materials, the research conducted by CTGV has shown that students, even special-education students, can successfully solve these contextualized problems because the problems are interesting and engaging, and students' problem-solving skills transfer positively to new problems. Scientists are problem solvers. Anchored instruction causes learning to happen by presenting students with real-world problems.

The important elements of these macro-contexts are that they are video based, use a narrative format, require learners to generate the ending, embed the needed information in the story, and are complex and realistic enough to be challenging (CTGV, 1997). Video was chosen because it can convey the setting, characters, and actions in a more interesting way. Video also allows the portrayal of more complex and interconnected problems and helps learners to form their own mental models of the problem. The other very important characteristic is the story format. Stories are understood and remembered better than expository materials. Obviously, it is more engaging to the students than textbooks are. This model of instruction is known as *anchored instruction*, where the learning and thinking are anchored by a realistic, video-based problem. Anchoring learning in rich contexts is becoming an increasingly popular approach to learning in schools and universities.

Learning Processes   The primary characteristic of meaningful learning that is exemplified in anchored instruction is that it is authentic. Learners who work on meaningful, real-world tasks or simulated tasks in complex, case-based or problem-based learning contexts better understand and transfer what they learn to new situations. Seeing ideas embedded in a real-world context makes them more understandable. For instance, showing students videos of native French speakers conversing in real-world contexts throughout the school year enhanced the listening comprehension of the students in a French class (Secules, Herron & Tomasello, 1992). Student modeling of complex performances is better than student regurgitation of ideas. Anchoring instruction in authentic contexts makes learning more real.

Needless to say, students engaged in solving complex problems are active learners. They must carefully observe the video, looking for important pieces of information that they use to construct a solution. Constructing the solution requires that they continuously articulate what they know about the problem and reflect on its sufficiency for solving it. Finally, anchored instruction problems are usually solved collaboratively in groups. Cooperation requires that the group share the goal of solving the problem and discuss what they need to do in order to solve it.

Problem-Solving Processes   The primary problem-solving activities required to solve these complex problems are modeling and decision making. Students must construct models of the problem because the problems are so complex. Modeling problems is also a characteristic of expert problem solvers. Most experts will draw or construct a model of problems before attempting to solve them. Likewise, students must construct a model of the problem which they use to evaluate various solution options. When those options are fully explored, students must make a decision about the most efficient and effective solution to these complex problems. These problems, unlike most story problems in textbooks, are complex and therefore have many possible solutions. The goal of the students is to find the most efficient and effective, so decision making is a necessary part of the solution process.

Teacher Roles   In order to support solving anchored problems, the teacher functions as a coach. When students inevitably encounter difficulties in solving these complex problems, the teacher needs to prompt students for the next step by asking questions or suggesting things to think about—not by giving them the answer. If students learn that every time they encounter problems the teacher gives them the answer, they will cease to be engaged by the problem and will learn to be helpless in order to get the answer more quickly. The teacher also needs to help students to set realistic goals for themselves—that is, to identify potential steps in the solution process and to assign time, effort, and responsibility for achieving those steps. Teachers may also model problem solving by accepting another problem and showing students how they would solve it. When modeling performance, it is important not only to model the solution process but also to reflect on the reasoning used to solve each step ("This is why I did this . . . "). Generally, the teacher's role in anchored instruction should not be a direct teaching role but rather a supportive, coaching role—prompting, encouraging, and providing feedback.

Creating Your Own Macro-Contexts and Stories

Anchored instruction is especially effective in the sciences, math, and social studies; however, there is a shortage of anchored instruction problems available. One way to alleviate that shortage and also to assess learners' understanding of the kinds of problems they are solving is to have students design and produce their own problems, and embed them in their own video-based macro-contexts. Having students create their own problems is one of the clearest ways to assess whether students can transfer their learning.

Problem-Solving Processes   In order to create complex story problems, students must construct models of the problems. This is a process that we call *task analysis*. Analyzing a problem situation in order to construct a problem requires not only understanding the nature of the problem but also understanding the thinking processes that are required to solve it. This is what makes this activity so complex.

Having analyzed the nature of the problem and the problem-solving activity, students must then design a video situation that is authentic and realistic but also contains all of the information needed to solve the problem. This kind of design activity is very unconstrained. That is, there are so many kinds of scenarios that students can conceive. As a teacher, you must continue to constrain the activity based on the goals of the course. If you are teaching math, does the problem conceived by students represent good math? If social studies, are students adequately representing the social studies content? This may be one of the most challenging activities described in this book. However, challenging also implies engaging and rewarding.

Assessing Learning Understanding the concepts and principles well enough to generate a new problem is one of the most complex forms of thinking possible. In order to do this, students need to identify a problem and design a story that engages other students in solving them. In developing these stories, it is important for the students producing the macro-context to set up the problem, but not to solve it. The video should take learners to the point that they ask, "What do we do next?" Also it is important that all of the information needed to solve the problem is included somewhere in the video story, not as a litany of facts but rather as a part of the story. This is a difficult task—one that students should find challenging but very enjoyable. The problems that students create can be assessed using the following criteria:

- Is the problem representative of the kind of problem in the lesson objective?
- Is all of the information needed to solve the problem contained in the story?
- Is the story interesting enough for other students to accept?
- Can students articulate the steps needed to solve the problem?
- Can students help other students to solve the problem?

Students love to produce problems for their teachers and other students. That is a meaningful challenge that they readily become absorbed in. Anchored instruction provides a powerful model for engaging students in problem solving. Problem solving is necessarily more meaningful that memorizing information from textbooks and lectures.

Video Press Conference

In most classrooms, the teacher and the textbook are the intellectual authority. They represent the truth, and it is the students' responsibility to understand the world as they convey it. In this next video-based activity, students learn by becoming the authority for ideas being learned. What is most challenging is that they have to subject their authority to the scrutiny of their peers.

Learning Activity In most press conferences, an expert or a spokesperson makes an announcement, describes a new product or process, or explains some actions. Most of us are familiar with the press conference format through our viewing of news programs. If students are not familiar with this format, then videotape a couple of press conferences and show them to the class.

What should students conduct press conferences about? One way to make students responsible for understanding the discoveries, findings, or beliefs of experts or controversial topics is to play those experts or their representatives in a role-playing press conference. For example, in studying beginning genetics, let students play Crick and Watson, while the rest of the class asks questions about their DNA discovery, what it means, and how it works. In social studies, let students assume the role of prominent politicians, such as presidential candidates, the secretary of state, governor, mayor, or any other prominent political figure who has to defend legislation, new regulations, or plans for a new project. A quick perusal of any newspaper will provide numerous topics. As decisions are made by politicians, students can assume their roles in defending their decisions. The more controversial the topic, the more animated the conference is likely to be. In English class, let students assume the role of important literary figures or writers who have recently published a new book. They have to learn enough about the person and the work of literature to be able to discuss it. There is no subject area where a press conference cannot be used. It is especially effective in foreign language classes, since it provides another reason for students to think and communicate in the foreign language. Have students conduct the press conference in Spanish, French, German, or whatever language the students are studying. Have the student(s) being interviewed assume the role of prominent, social figures (such as an entertainment stars) from that country.

Conducting a press conference is easy. You simply need to install a podium in front of any normal classroom, and you have a useful set for a press conference. Open the press conference with a prepared, 2-minute statement from the expert in whatever language or style is appropriate (students need to study the people they are portraying intensively enough to render a meaningful portrayal). Following the opening statement, open up the conference for questions and answers.

Individual press members can identify themselves and the organization they represent, in order to add another layer of interest to the exercise. A good way to practice this questioning performance is to play "Five W's and H," where students write questions while watching a news story (Stempelski & Tomalin, 1990). The press members need to be prompted to ask *Who, What, Why, When, Where,* and *How* questions. You may want to prompt students with specific issues to construct questions about. This scenario can be adapted by asking the real people to attend class and allow students to "grill" them.

Videotaping the press conference makes it seem more real and provides an opportunity for feedback on the accuracy of the expressions. It is probably best to replay and evaluate the videotape during another class period. Delayed feedback will be more objective, and will also serve as a review of the ideas being questioned. A useful follow-up activity is to allow students to add questions after the videotape replay that they wished they would have asked during the press conference. Requiring students to think and act like someone else will require them to understand the ideas on a deeper level.

Learning Processes   The primary characteristic of meaningful learning through press conferences is that it is constructive. The students being interviewed must study and reflect on the knowledge, beliefs, and perspectives of the person being portrayed. They must construct an identity and an understanding of the person. That construction is not only cognitive but also affective. Students should also focus on the affective and stylistic characteristics of the person.

In this exercise, not every student will be active. Certainly the students being interviewed are very actively engaged. The camera crew is also actively engaged. The audience may or may not be. In order to make every student a more active participant, require all of them to have two or more questions to ask the student being interviewed.

The press conference format adds some authenticity to the project. If students review press conferences before participating in their own, they may perceive the activity as even more authentic.

Problem-Solving Processes   This activity may engage the least problem solving in this chapter. However, it is very likely that many press conferences would engage decision making, depending on the nature of the questions asked. The reporters would have to decide which question is the best (most engaging) while the expert would have to decide how to respond to the questions.

Teacher Roles   The teacher has little responsibility for this activity other than suggesting and approving topics for the press conference. The teacher should help students select roles to play, ensuring that they experience the range. The teacher may also critique or provide feedback about the scripts, making sure that the student has included most of the salient points. The teacher may also critique students' questions to be asked of the interviewee. Providing general classroom management may be the most taxing role as the students express their enthusiasm. Perhaps most consistently, the teacher should be a cheerleader, keeping the students motivated to complete their tasks.

Assessing Learning   The products of this video-based learning activity are captured and available for assessment on videotape. The teacher may assess the video for the following:

- Did the interviewee's statement accurately convey the person's point of view? Were the important elements of the position conveyed?
- Were the student's answers to questions consistent with the person's beliefs? Were they clear, incisive, and adequate?

- Was the portrayal of the character appropriate—did it capture the person's personality?
- Were the other students' questions meaningful? Were they clear, incisive, and adequate? Did the questions require the interviewee to think? Could the interviewee understand and answer the questions?
- Was the quality of the video production adequate?

Newsroom (by Lisa Bailey, Mary Bauwens, Gayle Flentge, Patty Wengert)

Perryville (Missouri) Elementary began broadcasting a daily news program to the school in February, 2000. Events of the world, the country, community, district and elementary school are shared each morning through the morning broadcast. Students and staff in the school receive the broadcast through closed-circuit television.

VIDEO TECHNIQUE

Press conferences require limited set design and camera capabilities. The set consists of a podium, commonly available in most high schools. If not available, one can be simulated by propping up a piece of plywood on top of a table in front of the classroom. Try to position the podium opposite the classroom windows—certainly never in front of the windows. Additional lights, available inexpensively at most hardware stores, or a line of fake microphones in front of the podium can add realism to the set.

For this exercise, only a single camera is required. If you are operating with only one video-camera, the camera operator should mount the camera on a tripod and position it toward the back of the audience (classroom). Most of the time, the camera will be focused on the speaker, holding a medium shot or "waist shot" (from the waist up). Leave a little (but not too much) headroom at the top of the frame. As students from the audience ask questions, the operator can zoom out a little and pan the camera right or left to include the questioner, zooming back as the speaker begins to talk. If you are using two cameras, leave one focused on the speaker and position the other in the front corner of the classroom so that the operator can shoot the questioners from the front. Those shots should be a medium or bust shot (bust to the top of the head).

We recommend using an external microphone connected to the videocamera. There is a lot of ambient noise in a classroom (coughing, shuffling, etc.), so a microphone on a stand placed directly in front of the speaker will produce much better audio, as well as add some authenticity to the scene. A second mike should be taped to a broom handle to simulate a microphone boom so that it can be pointed at the questioner. You will need another crew member to serve as the boom operator if you do this. If you use two microphones, you can use a Y-connector to plug both mikes into. Better yet, purchase a small, inexpensive (less than $50) audio mixer. Plug both mikes into it so you can control input levels for each one. See Utz (1989) for more detail.

There are two main goals emphasized in the broadcasting project. The first goal is to introduce and reinforce standards at the district, state, and national levels. When these standards are integrated into the broadcast, they are produced on a level that is interesting and entertaining to students. The second goal is to enhance communication within the elementary school. Information from anywhere in the school regarding special projects, monthly themes, and student, teacher, and classroom recognition is broadcast throughout the building. The broadcasting project is constantly revising and changing to include a variety of interesting segments and additional students, staff, and community members, as well as current events throughout our world. What is important is that the 4th-grade students provide the talent and the technical operations of the broadcast (see Figure 5.4).

Setting up a broadcasting station in a school or district requires a good deal of problem solving. The first and most burdensome problem is financing the operation. The total cost of the project can range from $2,000 to $10,000 or even more, depending on the quality of equipment and station environment. To support a broadcasting project, we looked to grants, PTO funds, building budgets, fundraisers, and local businesses. In addition to financial support, technical support is critical. During its infancy and growth, technical assistance is crucial to even a small broadcasting station.

Figure 5.4   Fourth-Grade Perryville Students Presenting the Daily News

The successful implementation and daily function of the broadcasting station is the responsibility of the students and educators involved. The role of the student includes responsibilities in front of and behind the camera. Having available time to work with the students is the key to how deeply they can become involved.

The responsibility of the educators in the project include selecting student broadcasters, writing daily scripts, incorporating special events, and creating the daily programs using the computer-editing equipment. Other responsibilities include organizing the schedule to be followed each morning and videotaping the special segments that are used for pre-taped segments.

It is important that students practice the daily scripts before the morning of the show. Students need to be punctual and dedicated to the success of the project. The student broadcasters need to speak precisely and clearly, have good posture, and proper eye contact with the audience. These are reviewed with the broadcasters prior to their appearance on the morning news show. It is also important to seek the permission of parents or guardians before a student appears as a broadcaster. The real challenge is the implementation and dedication that is taken to sustain a program at a successful and constant evolving level.

Learning Activity   Assembling a news program is a complex activity. Stories have to be identified, assigned, researched, written, and then produced. The teacher needs to work with the students to determine the scope of the stories that will be included in the program. The stories may include current events in the school or local community; local, regional, national, or international political issues and events; scientific developments, discoveries, or research conducted locally or anywhere in the world; literary or movie reviews (yes, even reviews of books of likely interest to students); health news of interest (e.g., inoculations during flu season or exercise programs); even mathematical riddles or puzzles that might interest other students. There is no reason why these stories should not be substantive; this is not a play activity. Decisions about assignments should be made by an editorial board of students, with the teacher as advisor. A useful twist on the newsroom activity is to produce the program in a foreign language being studied.

After being assigned stories, students must conduct research, preferably in teams, write the stories, locate pictures or video sequences about their stories to be included in the news program, and edit the stories. Prior to production, these stories need to be approved by the editorial board and edited to fit within time allotments. Finally, a video script is developed showing the sequence of the stories so the video producers know who the next newscaster will be.

During production of the news program, a crew of students videotapes the newscasters and their graphics. The news anchor introduces the program and the stories, with individual newscasters presenting the stories. A member of each team can assume the role of on-air talent, while the other members check the accuracy of their presentation. If the news program is broadcast live, the newscasters and camera crew must practice more extensively in order to ensure a smooth presentation. Regardless of whether the news program is live or recorded, daily or weekly, an incredible amount of thinking and learning will be invested in its production.

Learning Processes   The primary learning characteristics of the newsroom are that it is constructive, intentional, and cooperative. Students have to research information in order to construct scripts. They combine and sequence the scripts to construct a program. In order to do all of this, they must intentionally look for information to substantiate their scripts, and must develop a carefully timed and sequenced program. That process requires a great deal of self-regulation—timing program sequences, evaluating the quality of the ideas being presented, and so on. All of these activities rely on cooperation within the teams to produce the best scripts and between the announcers and the television production crew to complete the program.

Problem-Solving Processes   The primary problem-solving activities engaged by the newsroom is information searching and design. In order to provide the substance for the newscast, students must search for information to be

VIDEO TECHNIQUE

The simplest kind of set is a semicircular table or desk with a fairly neutral foreground. The anchors, of course, should sit in the middle. A mural can be drawn or painted to go behind the desk in order to add an air of authenticity.

You can produce a news show with only a single camera. If only a single camera is available, then place it in front of the semicircle. The semicircular shape allows the camera operator to pan from reporter to reporter.

Producing a news program like this can be accomplished live or delayed. A live broadcast would require a video switcher, recorder, and multiple cameras. The switcher allows the director to switch back and forth between the cameras, focusing on the reporter and the graphics camera or videotape player. If a second camera and switcher are available, the second camera can focus on the pictures or graphics that student teams have produced to illustrate their stories. The director of the program must follow the script and switch to the graphics camera whenever there is a cue in the script. See Utz (1989) for more detail.

The other production option is to shoot all of the video and edit it together, dubbing in the voices of the reporters after the video is assembled. An editor will enable you to insert video clips recorded off-air or filmed by your students on location. This can also be accomplished if you have a switcher; however, that requires a great deal more planning.

included in their stories. Using computers to search for information on the Internet, in libraries, and other sources is the first activity. Before any information is cleared for broadcast, teachers should require students to back it up, that is, verify the information with at least two or three different sources. The accuracy and objectivity of news information is essential.

Designing (writing) the stories, designing the sets, designing the script and storyboard are all examples of design activities. And like most design activities, there are many possible products that can be designed. Look at news programs on commercial television, and note how different they are in terms of format, style, substance, and so on. Similar design decisions are required when producing classroom new shows as well.

Teacher Roles   The primary roles for the teacher in the newsroom scenario are evaluator of the product and regulator of the process. The teacher should avoid directing the students but should intervene in the process if they begin to stray off course. The complexity of the process may be too much for some students, so they might need the regulation that a teacher can provide. Like the video press conference, teachers should help identify appropriate roles and function as cheerleader for the students.

Assessing Learning   We are sure that an English or journalism teacher could add meaningful criteria to our list, but these are some criteria that occur to us for assessing and evaluating the news programs that students construct:

- Is the information contained in the news stories accurate?
- Do the stories comply with standard forms for news stories: lead-in, issues, explication, and conclusion?
- How good is the writing? Is it grammatically and syntactically correct?
- Do the visuals used clarify the intent of the news stories?
- Are there meaningful connectives between the stories to tie them together?

Student Talk Shows

One of the most popular genres of commercial television, the talk show, can provide a powerful medium for student-produced videos as well. Daytime and late-night television present numerous hosts interviewing a variety of guests. It is such a common format that children naturally assume the roles of both interviewer and interviewee. Author Jerzy Kozinski experimented with videotaping children in talk-show settings and found that they naturally assumed the insouciant air of television personalities and that during interviews would divulge the most intimate secrets about their lives, even when they knew that their parents and teachers would likely see the video. We are not recommending that students be compromised or that they emulate the salacious nature of many daytime talk shows.

Rather, the talk-show format is a natural medium for getting students to converse in meaningful ways. It is important to structure the talk show so that students are discussing meaningful ideas. The following learning activity is an example of one way of doing that.

Meeting of Minds   One of the most creative educational shows ever broadcast by the PBS, in our opinion, was *A Meeting of Minds*, which was written and produced by Steve Allen. Each episode featured very improbable combinations of four guests (e.g., Ghengis Khan, Marie Antoinette, Socrates, and Charles Manson) from different historical eras in a talk-show setting, moderated by the late Steve Allen. He would provide the initial questions, and off they would go, usually culminating in passionate exchanges of ideas and beliefs. This is a rich idea for getting groups of students to reason beyond surface-level meaning about ideas. The individuals that your students portray would not have to be as diverse as Allen's in order to engage discussion. If they represented multiple perspectives on more focused historical issues, for instance, students could understand the multiple viewpoints that make up an issue. For example, students could take the role of the major players at the Pottsdam conference after World War II, or they could assume the role of popular scientists versus creationists in a discussion about evolution. Sunday news analysis programs such as this abound. Discussions could also deal with contemporary issues, and finding persons who represent divergent viewpoints (Democrats and Republicans, conservationists and developers) might make the experience more interesting. A related activity would be to construct home pages for each of the characters or pages describing the events (see chapter 6). Issues are everywhere. Again, peruse a copy of *Time*, *Newsweek*, or the daily newspaper, and issues will bubble out.

It will be necessary to select a narrator for each talk show. The narrator should be prepared to ask questions, resolve differences, and draw conclusions from the discussion. A separate team will be needed to write questions that provoke the participants and to prepare the narrator for his or her role.

Learning Processes   More than any other characteristic, the talk show is collaborative, primarily because it is founded on conversation. Forming teams to research characters, determine their responses to issues, and develop the characters will probably enhance the quality of the characters. The talk show is also very constructive, as students articulate the ideas, personality, and dialogue of the characters they are developing and reflect on the kinds of responses they would likely make on different issues. They have to know the characters much more deeply than the student writing a report on the character.

Problem-Solving Processes   Although this does not appear to be a problem-solving activity, some problem solving is required. Students must perform a lot of information searching about the characters they are portraying. This search must seek understanding of the character, not just the facts about the person's life. Students need to understand the characters they are playing in such a way that they can project how that character would respond to a question or challenge never faced in the character's life. One of the best ways of doing this is to construct a model of the person's beliefs using tools such as concept mapping tools. Modeling the organization of beliefs is a powerful way to better understand any person whom you are studying.

Teacher Roles The teacher's most vital role in this activity will be to provide encouragement and feedback to the participants when writing their scripts. The hypothetical reasoning will be new for most students who may well give up when they find there is no right or wrong answer to their constructions. Helping them to capture the character of the people they are portraying will require a delicate balance between suggestion and questioning the students about their characters.

Assessing Learning Since the learning outcomes from this activity are speculative, the criteria for evaluating them will also be somewhat speculative. They will be difficult to evaluate, not because the better responses will not be obvious, but because the criteria are not objective.

- Were the questions appropriate for the participants being portrayed? Were they likely to be able to answer them?
- Did the students accurately represent the beliefs or perspectives of the persons they were portraying?
- Did the students understand the beliefs of their characters, and were they able to convey those beliefs in impromptu comments?

Video Documentaries

Video is the tool of choice among modern storytellers and ethnographers, those social scientists who study cultures using observation, interviews, and other qualitative methods. When ethnographers visit and observe sites and interview native peoples, they often videotape the experience. The video gives them a bimodal (auditory and visual) representation of the experience, which they can study later

VIDEO TECHNIQUE

If only a single camera is available, position the actors close together in a V arrangement, with the moderator in the middle. Position the camera at the top of the V so that the operator can pan smoothly among the participants. A medium shot of individual participants or a two-shot (a medium shot including two people) is preferable. See Utz (1989) for more details.

to better convey their findings. Students can become effective ethnographers as well (see chapter 6). Ricki Goldman-Segall has developed a multimedia shell for students to collect their videos, stories, and interpretations. Her students have studied many of the First Nations cultures in British Columbia. Student storytelling and ethnography can be focused on local issues, as well. Students can create video documentaries that examine local issues or controversies. In doing so, they become more concerned and productive members of society.

Digital Storytelling (by Kate Kemker)

In digital storytelling, technology is not the focus of the activity but rather a tool used to create the story. With digital storytelling, students use their creative skills to create a storyboard on paper, use a camera to shoot their video, and finally edit their video on a computer using some type of software. Through the combination of working with visual images, text, and sound, students develop their critical thinking skills in a number of different ways that are not necessarily dependent on computer hardware. In order to create digital stories students must create a desktop movie.

In the first part of the activity (preproduction), students plan the story they will be telling. In preproduction, students research, write, and organize information about the structure of their story. It is during this portion of the activity that the majority of the work takes place, providing students with the opportunity to generate their ideas on paper before using the camera. The preproduction portion of the activity allows students to optimize their time when actually using the camcorder. An essential part of preproduction is storyboarding. The storyboard (Figure 5.5) is a document that provides students the opportunity to create a plan for their story from which they can begin filming. Storyboards can take on a number of formats combining verbal and/or graphic descriptions of screen shots. The storyboard includes specific information and the logistics for shooting the footage for the digital story.

Students should also create a checklist that includes the basic elements of a story: exposition, rising action, climax, and falling action. Students should use the checklist to evaluate their project to ensure that their story is communicating to the viewer their intended message. Sample questions could be: What is the plot? Who are the characters? Does there appear to be conflict between the characters? Is there some kind of resolution?

During the production portion of the activity, students begin to shoot their video. Before students shoot their video, it is important to prepare them with a basic knowledge of how this digital medium works. Fundamentals that the students should understand include types of camera shots, camera angles, and camera movement. Some issues in digital filming that should be addressed include: the difference between a close-up shot, a medium-range shot, and a long shot; framing a subject in the shot; camera angles not from the human eye level perspective; and creating action with the camera movement.

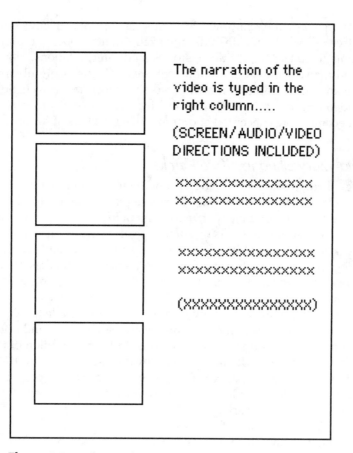

The narration of the video is typed in the right column.....

(SCREEN/AUDIO/VIDEO DIRECTIONS INCLUDED)

XXXXXXXXXXXXXXXX
XXXXXXXXXXXXXXXX

XXXXXXXXXXXXXXXXX
XXXXXXXXXXXXXXXXX

(XXXXXXXXXXXXXX)

Figure 5.5 Video Storyboard

A digital storytelling activity provides students the opportunity to work collaboratively in a variety of roles, such as director, actor, videographer, and editor. When shooting video, each student should be involved in the process. As one student uses the camera, another student should be directing the shots, other students acting, and another student should be logging the video to remember the shots taken. This type of project should lead to an understanding that each role in the production plays an important part in completing the project, and no role is more important than another. The director has the plan for how the video should be done, however she must communicate that idea effectively to the actor, the videographer, and the editor. It is a true team process.

The final stage, postproduction, is when students edit their video (described earlier). In this process, it is the role of the editor to bring to fruition what the director had envisioned for the project. In the postproduction process, students, act as editors using nonlinear editing software to create the final product (see

Figure 5.6   Students in Postproduction Editing of a Digital Story

Figure 5.6). We have used Apple iMovie as well as more powerful products like Final Cut Pro or Adobe Premiere.

At the conclusion of this activity, students should review their digital stories, as well as those done by other students. At the movie premiere, students not only take on the roles of stars, but they also act as critics to review the digital stories. A video production rubric can be used to assess students' progress based on guidelines set out for the given project. Students then write a critique for each movie, evaluating the structure, the fundamentals of digital media, and the editing.

Digital storytelling provides students with the opportunity to establish a connection between the creator and the viewer. Well-told stories can have a powerful effect on an audience, but the secret of their success is the structure of the story: how it is put together and the order in which events appear. A digital story involves the same structural components of any good story: a beginning, middle, and end. As with other types of narrative, digital storytelling also involves a sequence of events that follows characters in a particular context. Through the digital storytelling activity, students will begin to understand how all of the elements work together, and how you can manipulate video to create the effect you want for your story. Such an activity allows students to critically understand that the information they see and hear influences many of their thoughts and decisions as critical thinkers.

Personal Documentaries

A good way to get students warmed up to the process of creating documentaries is to create personal documentaries. That is, they produce a documentary about themselves. They decide the most appropriate setting, the perceptions about themselves that they want viewers to have, and the format of the personal description. Personal documentaries have taken many forms. Some students create a personal diary. Others have taken viewers on a tour of their room, while others have played musical instruments, recited poetry, or acted out different personae. The self is the most interesting topic for most kids, so this can be an engaging activity.

An extension of the personal documentary is to conduct it in a foreign language. Pelletier (1990) recommends sending out students in foreign language classes with a videocamera to tape a short tour of their room, home, classroom, or library, or create a video synopsis of some activity such as a family supper, miniature golf, bowling, or any other activity. They would be required to speak only the language they are studying. Personalizing the use of language, rather than treating it as an object to be studied, is an important component in language acquisition. So students combine new words with previously learned vocabulary in order to express more meaningful ideas. Have the students be as verbally expressive in their narrations as possible.

Pelletier also recommends that guidance be provided to students about the scope of the project. The tour should be short (3–5 minutes), focusing on a limited number of objects or phenomena. Imagine videotaping the basketball or football game and having students do the play-by-play in Spanish. You are capitalizing on the natural interests of the students. We can guarantee that vocabulary learned in this activity will be better remembered and retained than that rehearsed from a textbook.

Video documentaries should migrate outside the school into the community. The local newspaper details many local issues or controversies that students can examine. Students need to research the problems, identify the stakeholders, inter-

VIDEO TECHNIQUE

Pelletier recommends that students should not attempt to record the narration or any dialogue while videotaping the scene. That would result in choppy audio and poor-quality video. The videocamera will probably be handheld, so students should practice producing steady shots. Avoid excessive zooming in and out (a well-worn tendency among novice camera operators). Pans (side-to-side movements) should be slow and smooth. The operator should not pan while the camera is zoomed in (it accentuates the effects of the movements and will make the audience feel seasick). Shoot the scenes first, then log all of the shots, write the narration, and then dub in the audio while viewing the video in order to realize the best results. See Utz (1989) for more details.

view them, and draw some conclusions. Video is normally used to describe the problem (e.g., showing the traffic congestion, dangerous crosswalk, ecological problem) and to interview stakeholders. Like the personal, foreign language documentaries, these documentaries need to be shot out of sequence and later edited together into a coherent program.

Record Problems in Search of Solutions   As a teacher, you can identify problems or work with students to identify problems at a local or national level. Local polluters, construction of a new highway through a state forest, alleviating traffic congestion on local streets, or solving the Middle East crisis can be problems where video documentaries developed by students require them to understand the issues and ideas better. Students in an English-as-a-second-language class who produced a documentary on eating establishments on campus not only acquired significant English skills, but also developed interviewing skills and gained more confidence in the use of English (Gardner, 1994). Creating video documentaries requires students to use a complex combination of skills that leads to meaningful learning.

Learning Processes   Producing video documentaries is a meaningful learning activity incorporating active, constructive, intentional, authentic, and cooperative learning. It is authentic because students examine personally relevant topics. It is constructive because they produce a complex video program. It is perhaps more intentional than other video activities, because students must declare a specific purpose and consistently regulate their performance in its completion. Most video documentaries, other than the personal ones, require a great deal of cooperation among teams of students. Responsibility for interviewing different people, researching documents, videotaping sites, and editing the video needs to be negotiated and monitored. These activities require extensive collaboration and discussion. More than anything, video documentaries have students actively engaged in representing the personal perspectives, so there is extensive ownership (and therefore meaning) of the final product.

Problem-Solving Processes   Documentaries, like most of the other productions described in this chapter, require design skills. Designing the production requires that students make decisions about content, style, perspective, beliefs, and so on. Designing a documentary can require complex design problems presented by scripting, location shooting, and postproduction editing. Prior to designing, students must use technologies to search for information from a variety of sources. An important aspect of documentaries is objectivity, that is, the presentations of multiple perspectives and beliefs. "All Things Considered," a daily radio news broadcast by National Public Radio, can provide an excellent model for presenting these different perspectives in a professional way.

Teacher Roles   The teacher's role is primarily regulatory, making sure that topics are acceptable, stakeholders are appropriate, coverage is tasteful, and the project is not overly controversial. The teacher will also oversee the planning stage, to make sure that students are prepared when they begin shooting.

Assessing Learning   Assessing the effectiveness of video documentaries will require some research and understanding by the teacher of the issues that the students are examining:

- Was the issue or controversy clearly identified and explained?
- Were all stakeholders identified and interviewed?
- Did the video clarify the issues?
- Was the treatment biased?
- Did the sequence of the program represent a coherent argument?

Video Theater: One-Act Dramas

Learning Activity   Creating video sketches requires analyzing dialogue. An interesting learning activity for students to perform prior to writing their own plays is to provide many recipes for having them analyze both verbal and nonverbal cues and reason from short video clips (Stempelski & Tomalin, 1990). In language arts lessons, such as "Speech Bubble," students view narrative sequences and supply their own dialogue. Students are constructing meaning for what might have been said, using TV sequences as the stimulus. Students can also construct their own video sequences, rather than interpreting existing sequences.

After students become familiar with analyzing dialogues, they can produce their own. Students in any class can develop short dramatic sketches to represent ideas being studied. In history, students could write and play the roles of serfs or noblemen in medieval Europe. In science, they could create a skit reviewing the events leading up to an important discovery. In literature, performing scenes from plays would make them come alive. Have students rewrite plays using modern dialogue to help them to interpret meaning. These skits could be translated and performed in another language for foreign language classes.

Learning Processes   Producing video skits requires interpretive work, translating ideas and events into dialogue. This activity requires a very creative form of knowledge construction. Staging and producing plays also require a lot of cooperation. Cooperative learners use conversation as a means to seek out opinions and ideas from others in order to produce more creative performances.

VIDEO TECHNIQUE

Generally only a single camera is needed for this application. The preferred shot will depend on the kind of action being modeled. If you are demonstrating how to do something, then try to get an over-the-shoulder shot of the performer doing the task. Even better is to shoot the action from the point of view of the performer with only hands included in the shot (if they are appropriate). This will add realism and show the viewer just how to perform the activity.

VIDEO TECHNIQUE

A skit such as this should be carefully scripted, with the camera shots determined before you begin shooting. Multiple cameras and editing will produce much better results. If only a single camera is available, position it so that when it is zoomed all the way out, the shot will include a wide, long shot of the entire set. Start with it as an establishing shot. Know what action will occur next, so that your camera is not zoomed all the way in just as an actor takes off. If an actor is leaving the scene, do not follow him or her off stage. Let the actor walk out of the shot.

Teacher Roles   The teacher may assist students by initially acting as the director, helping to organize students' activities, and providing feedback about the dialogue, the nature of the characters, and the sets. Teachers should fade out their involvement as soon as students are able and willing to assume responsibility.

Assessing Learning   Evaluating plays is a subjective process. What pleases one person may offend another. Appreciating plays is a very personal process. We recommend checking with your drama teacher for more criteria, but here are some criteria that may be used for evaluating student-produced video skits:

- Did the play address all of the events, issues, or phenomena it was trying to depict?
- Are the characters in the performance believable, time-appropriate, and consistent with their position within the play?
- Did the setting enhance the dramatic character of the performance?
- Did the play make use of dramatic conventions?

Video Modeling and Feedback

In these final two activities, teachers can become involved in the video productions as well as, or instead of, the students. Just as video production is engaging for learners, it can also be a very engaging learning experience for teachers. The teaching materials that result can be very useful.

Learning Activity   The most obvious way to use video for teaching is to model specific performances. Video models are used frequently in teaching athletics, where skilled performers show you how to improve your golf or tennis swing. However, video modeling is useful not just for psychomotor tasks. Any kind of performance can be modeled by the teacher or other skilled performer, such as public speaking or acting for theatrical performers, empathic behavior for counselors or social workers, interpersonal communication skills for personnel workers or librarians, even thinking and research behaviors.

Teachers and students together might think about developing a study strategies video by acting out what a skilled learner would do in order to write a term paper or study for a test. Shoot the video from the point of view of the student—reading a book, looking in a catalog, searching the library stacks, turning off the television. After shooting the video, dub in the voice, using an echo chamber to make it seem like the person in the video is talking to himself or herself. Find out what skills students possess, and videotape them performing what they do best. Not only will you have a series of useful videos, but students will gain self-confidence, as well. Getting students to articulate what they should be doing is usually a good idea.

When modeling performances for students, it is important to model not only the actual performance but also the mental processes (decision making, questioning, resolving) involved with the performance. This think-aloud process can be very informative for the learners while watching the video performance, especially if the teacher conveys his or her uncertainties as well as solutions while thinking aloud.

Although providing video models of any desired performance is one of the most powerful video teaching methods available, it is maximally successful if used in conjunction with video feedback (described later). Essentially, providing video models and then videotaping the learners' performances and using those tapes as feedback is probably the most powerful use of video possible.

Learning Processes   Regardless of who the performer is, the process of modeling performance is very constructive. The performer needs to articulate the performance in the clearest possible way, which requires a great deal of reflection about the nature of their performance while they are modeling it.

Problem-Solving Processes   Students may also produce video models. When they do, they have to learn the performance to be modeled, practice it until they are skilled, and then perform it in front of a camera. That is, they need to become model performers. Another version would be to have students model some performance that they do well—playing an instrument, caring for pets, solving logic puzzles, nearly any skill.

Assessing Learning Through Video Feedback   The most powerful use of video, we believe, is to provide feedback on an individual's performance. Select virtually any meaningful performance task in schools (theatrics, foreign language usage, public speaking, performing a chemistry experiment, anything but test-taking) and assess the learners' performance by videotaping them while performing the activity. That performance can then be evaluated, and feedback about their performance can be provided to the student. Video feedback is one of the deepest, most incisive learning experiences possible. Having learners watch themselves perform provides them with an unfiltered, unbiased view of themselves. This method is often (though not often enough) used to help prepare preservice teachers for teaching. Teachers are videotaped teaching lessons to students. Reviewing the videotape, with or without a supervisory teacher to provide feedback, teaches new teachers more about teaching than all of the textbooks they have read.

In addition to providing performance feedback, video feedback affects self-perceptions (Jonassen, 1978, 1979). Viewers become more evaluative and less role-oriented in their perceptions of themselves. This experience is very powerful and should not be used with troubled individuals without proper care. Video can help learners reflect on their own performance primarily through video feedback—videotaping a performance and then viewing that performance, with or without a teacher or expert accompanying you. For instance, Orban and McLean (1990) use videocameras for self-evaluations and teacher evaluations of French-speaking ability. "Video is like a mirror in which a magician practices his tricks, a way to evaluate his performance over and over" (Taylor, 1979, p. 28). You can use video to engage constructive (articulative/reflective) learning with the following activities. A related technique for assessing individual understanding of processes and systems is the *teach-back*. The idea is simple: After teaching something to students, require them individually to teach back the ideas or processes. Students may teach the ideas back to the teacher or teach it to other novice students. Either way, it is a useful method for identifying student misconceptions or unclear mental models. These teach-backs can be videotaped and replayed later by the teacher as a form of assessment or simply as a learning activity for the students. This method capitalizes on the time-worn adage that the best way to learn something is to have to teach it. So you may want to allow students the opportunity to collect models, visuals, or conduct additional research before teaching the ideas to others. Videotaping the teach-back provides an easily assessable record of the students' understanding.

Teachers as Videographers: Creating Contexts for Learning

Students shouldn't have all of the fun. The following learning activity describes how teachers can enhance learning by producing their own instructional videos. We have argued throughout this book that learning that occurs in the context of some real-world activity is usually better understood and more readily transferred to new situations. Teachers can create those problem contexts, just like the macro-contexts described earlier in this chapter, for their students.

Learning Activity   Authentic contexts for engaging learners in problem solving can be created for any class. In mathematics, identify mathematical problems in the real world, such as the calculations and problem solving for building a house, erecting a bridge across a creek, predicting the vote from various precinct votes in the past, and so on.

VIDEO TECHNIQUE

This application requires only a single camera, which maintains a medium shot of the student-teacher, occasionally zooming out to include students' reactions to their teaching.

For language classes, teachers can take their videocameras along on vacation when visiting foreign countries. Record everyday scenes (ordering in restaurants, buying a newspaper from a newsstand, asking a police officer for directions, buying a ticket to a tourist spot). The best scenes are those in which the student has to answer the question that was posed on the tape or pose the question that was answered on the tape. These scenes can also be assembled into macro-contexts so that students have to think and act in the foreign language in order to get across the city on the Paris Metro or find a museum in Barcelona.

Science teachers can also record video experiments for use in class. Show the process of setting up the experiment and stop just before the outcome. Require the students to predict the outcome of the experiment. If these experiments can be set in real-world settings, rather than school labs, they will be much more meaningful for learners (for instance, estimating the height of a tree in the forest for a lumbering company, disposing of wastes from a local film lab, designing a lightning rod for the local courthouse).

Lawrence (1994) used video contexts for evaluating his students in physics. He showed experiments or demonstrations and asked his students to predict the outcome of the experiments and to explain any discrepancies between their predictions and the actual outcomes, which he showed after students made their predictions. "When students make their predictions, then watch what actually occurs, then make a revision, they are modeling the scientific method" (p. 17).

Social studies teachers may want to videotape a city council meeting where a controversial topic is being debated. Show students all of the perspectives and even go on location to videotape the object of discussion (e.g., expanding the waste-water treatment plant). Then allow the students to debate and resolve the issue in class and see how their solutions compare with those of the city council. The student debates may also be videotaped.

The world outside of school is full of meaningful learning experiences. Videotaping those experiences and bringing them into the classroom connects in-class learning with the real world and makes it so much more meaningful for learners. Videocameras are an easy and flexible way of bringing those experiences into the classroom.

The learning processes, problem-solving processes, teachers' roles, and assessment methods will vary so much with the nature of the problem that is videotaped that it is impossible to specify them.

Videoconferencing: Communicating Through Video

Videoconferencing   What was science fiction a couple of decades ago—full-screen viewing of people while conversing over the telephone—is now common practice in many educational institutions. Videoconferencing technology allows two or more people at different places to see and hear each other. Video signals are sent synchronously through a satellite or online over the Internet. A broadband satellite videoconferencing produces a full-motion video connection, but the equipment and transmission expense is very high.

VIDEO TECHNIQUE

All of these kinds of productions will have to be shot on location and edited together later using a video editor (described earlier). A tripod might be the last thing that you want to haul along on vacation, but it will always yield better videos. If it is too cumbersome, then practice holding the camera steady. Plan your shots to highlight the desired action. You should generally get an establishing shot—that is, a long shot of the scene establishing the context for the action. If you are asking a police officer for directions in French, then a medium or close-up shot of the asker and the officer would be appropriate. Experiments should generally include close-up shots of the apparatus. Again, avoid camera movement while zoomed in.

There are two types of videoconferencing systems available to most educational systems: group systems and personal systems. Group systems are designed for use in a broad range of environments by both groups and individuals. Group systems provide a high-quality camera, large monitor, easy keypad control, and a comprehensive selection of options. For example, Polycom's ViewStation is intended for small conference rooms. These systems use high-capacity ISDN telephone lines (special, high-capacity phone lines that cost several times as much per month to rent as a regular telephone line). They provide cameras for sending pictures of people, graphics, or video, microphones, and computers to decode and compress the video images so they fit the limited capacity of telephone lines. It has clear images at 15 frames per second (half the normal number of frames, so the picture is not quite as smooth as broadcast television). They are also small enough to sit conveniently on top of any size video monitor. These systems tend to be expensive and require three dedicated ISDN telephone lines. In the long run, however, the systems are cheaper than flying people all over the country to train them. These systems are used to provide specialized classes (e.g., advanced sciences, Latin, calculus) to rural school districts in Iowa that cannot afford specialized teachers.

Personal systems are designed for a single user. Individuals can communicate with each other whether in an office building or at home using digital telephone lines or a local computer network. In general, group systems are utilized in multimedia conference rooms and meeting rooms. Personal systems are used in private offices or at workstations. For example, Polycom's ViaVideo has a high-performance processor that enables high-quality video communications, and allows other PC applications to run effectively. It provides high-quality transmissions over the IP network. Internet-based videoconferencing requires a videocamera, microphone, speakers or headphones, sound capability, video capability, and associated software and networking components. Most multimedia computers include everything you need to use for videoconferencing except the videocamera, video software, and networking products. With less than $1,000, individuals can use high-quality videoconferencing to communicate with each other.

Videoconferencing systems have revolutionized the way that corporations conduct meetings and provide training. IBM, for instance, maintains studios in France and Germany, from which they provide training to their employees all over Europe. Videoconferencing is also revolutionizing the way that universities provide courses. It is no longer necessary for students to reside in a university town in order to attain a university degree. Distance-learning programs are being offered by most colleges and universities around the country.

Although videoconferencing sounds like the answer to many educational problems, we must report that it often is not. Videoconferencing often elicits the worst kind of education—teachers lecturing at an audience in another location. There may be some logistical advantages to videoconferenced classrooms, but there are not always learning advantages. Learners in these settings are assuming the same passive role that they always have. Can videoconferencing support meaningful learning? We think so.

Videoconferencing best supports meaningful learning by helping diverse learners to collaborate and converse with each other in order to solve problems and construct meaning. There are several ways that videoconferencing can support meaningful learning. Mainly, it can connect communities of learners.

Form Discourse Communities. Videoconferencing can support the formation of discourse communities (see chapter 4), where students with common interests can talk about, illustrate, model, or teach those interests. Most schools sponsor after-school clubs to enable students to pursue their own intellectual interests (e.g., chess, farming, photography, etc.). In schools where only a few students share a particular interest, they may be able to videoconference with students at other schools in order to share activities.

Supporting Communities of Practice. Videoconferencing can also support discussions among communities of practice (see chapter 4 for more on this). Lave (1991) sees learning not as a process of socially sharing ideas that result in internalization of knowledge by individuals, but rather as a process of becoming a member and developing an identity as a member of a sustained community of practice. As teaching and learning become less school-building-based and more distributed throughout society, people who work in the same businesses will be able to learn from each other though videoconferencing. For instance, when new hairstyles emerge, hair stylists can show others how to cut hair in that particular way.

Again, the learning processes, students' and teachers' roles, and assessment methods will vary so much with the nature of the videotaped problem that it is impossible to specify them.

CONCLUSIONS

In this chapter, we have shown how video can be used to create macro-contexts for engaging learners in complex problem solving. These videos are used not to teach, but rather to hook students into solving problems. Most of the chapter focused on the use of video as a medium for student constructions, engaging them in planning, writing, visualizing, organizing, creating, and a host of other meaningful learning activities. These video applications are but a sampling of the numerous ways that you can use video in the classroom. As you begin to use video in your teaching area, more creative ideas should occur to you. Whenever students produce their own videos, it is important that they each:

- Participate in all of the activities that are involved in shooting and producing videos
- Receive encouragement to be as creative as possible in their productions
- Use video to provide feedback on their performance
- Reflect on and analyze the ideas and skills that they have learned

THINGS TO THINK ABOUT

If you would like to reflect on the ideas presented in this chapter, then articulate your responses to the following questions and compare them with others' responses.

1. Is it ever possible to learn from television alone—that is, learn how to do something merely from watching television instruction? What meaning will it have after only watching the show? What meaning will it have after you try it yourself?
2. "Public television exists to enrich people's lives." What does that mean? In order to be enriched, what does the individual viewer have to contribute?
3. What does it mean to be a critical viewer of commercial television? What are critical viewing skills? How could you teach your students to be critical viewers?
4. Why do students think that television is easier than reading? How can you get students to invest more effort in viewing television for learning?
5. Video production is a constructionist activity; that is, students are learning by constructing an artifact. What other kinds of constructionist activities can you think of (using technologies or not)?
6. In the 1950s, the comic cop Dick Tracy wore a watch that was a picture telephone. How soon will that be a reality?
7. The producers of *Jasper Woodbury* series believed that by providing a rich, video-based story with a problem in it, learners will understand the problem better. Can you think of other ways that stories have been used to set up problems? How are they the same? How are they different?
8. After the Watergate investigation that brought down Nixon's presidency, investigative journalism increased dramatically. What kinds of issues (personal, local, regional, national) would be most likely to attract students to investigative reporting? How can you support that in your school?

9. Think of characters that your students would like to become if they were producing their own version of *Meeting of the Minds*. Why did you select them?

10. In 1997, a modern version of *Romeo and Juliet* was released as a motion-picture film. The film was a hit with youngsters, because the theme was universal but the setting was current. Can you think of other plays, stories, or books with universal themes that students would like to adapt into a modern interpretation?

11. Video feedback has been called a "mirror with a memory." Why is seeing yourself on television such a compelling and incisive experience? How do you see yourself? Why is that so powerful?

12. Do you think that technologies such as videoconferencing, which make instruction available anytime, anywhere, will eliminate the need for schools and classrooms? Why or why not?

REFERENCES

Beentjes, J., & van der Vort, T. (1988). Television's impact on children's reading skills: A review of the research. *Reading Research Quarterly, 23* (4), 389–413.

Chu, W. G., & Schramm, W. (1967). *Learning from television: What the research says.* Stanford, CA: Stanford University Institute for Communication Research. (ERIC Document Reproduction Service No. ED014900)

Cognition and Technology Group at Vanderbilt. (1997). *The Jasper project: Lessons in curriculum, instruction, assessment, and professional development.* Hillsdale, NJ: Lawrence Erlbaum Associates.

Gardner, D. (1994). Student-produced video-documentary: Hong Kong as a self-access resource. *Hong Kong Papers in Linguistics and Language Teaching, 17*, 44–53.

Goldman, S. R., Petrisino, A. J., Sherwood, R. D., Garrison, S., Hiskey, D., Bransford, J. D., et al. (1996). Anchoring science instruction in multimedia learning environments. In S. Vosniadu, E. deCorte, R. Glaser, & H. Mandl (Eds.), *International perspectives on the design of technology-supported learning environments.* Mahwah, NJ: Lawrence Erlbaum Associates.

Healy, J. M. (1990). Chaos on Sesame Street: Does this carnival of images help students read?

American Educator: The Professional Journal of the American Federation of Teachers, 14(4), 22–27.

Hefzallah, I. M. (1987). *Critical viewing of television: A book for parents and teachers.* Lanham, MI: University Press of America.

Jonassen, D. H. (1978). Video as a mediator of human behavior. *Media Message, 7*(2), 5–6.

Jonassen, D. H. (1979). Video-mediated objective self-awareness, self-perception, and locus of control. *Perceptual and Motor Skills, 48*, 255–265.

Jonassen, D. H. (1982). *Nonbook media: A self-paced instructional handbook for teachers and library media personnel.* Hamden, CT: Library Professional Publications.

Lave, J. (1991). Situating learning in communities of practice. In L. B. Resnick, J. M. Levine, & S. D. Teasley (Eds.), *Perspectives on socially shared cognition.* Washington, DC: American Psychological Association.

Lawrence, M. (1994). The use of video technology in science teaching: A vehicle for alternative assessment. *Teaching and Change, 2*(1), 14–30.

National Cable Television Association. (1995). *Taking charge of your TV: A guide to critical viewing for parents and children.* National Cable Television Association.

Orban, C., & McLean, A. M. (1990). A working model for videocamera use in the foreign language classroom. *The French Review*, 63(4), 652–663.

Pelletier, R. J. (1990). Prompting spontaneity by means of the videocamera in the beginning foreign language class. *Foreign Language Annals*, 22(3), 227–232.

Potter, R. L. (1976). *New seasons: The positive use of commercial television with children*. Columbus, OH: Charles Merrill.

Reid, J. C., & MacLennan, D. W. (1967). *Research in instructional television and film*. Washington, DC: U.S. Government Printing Office.

Salomon, G. (1984). Television is "easy" and print is "tough": The differential investment of mental effort in learning as a function of perceptions and attributions. *Journal of Educational Psychology*, 76, 647–658.

Secules, T., Herron, C., & Tomasello M. (1992). The effects of video context on foreign language learning. *The Modern Language Journal*, 76, 480–487.

Stempelski, S., & Tomalin B. (1990). *Video in action: Recipes for using video in language teaching*. New York: Prentice Hall.

Taylor, C. B. (1979, January). Video to teach poetry writing. *Audiovisual Instruction*, 27–29.

Utz, P. (1989). *Video user's handbook: The complete illustrated guide to operating and maintaining video equipment*. New York: Prentice Hall.

Valmont, William J. (1994). Making videos with reluctant learners. *Reading and Writing Quarterly: Overcoming Learning Difficulties*, 10(4), 369–677.

Wagschal, P. H. (1987). Literacy on the electronic age. *Educational Technology*, 27(6): 5–9.

Winn, M. (1980). *The plug-in drug: Televisions, computers, and family life*. New York: Basic Books.

Learning by Constructing Realities With Hypermedia

MULTIMEDIA IN EDUCATION

Multimedia have a rich history in education. Instructional media, such as slide/tape and multi-image presentations, interactive video, and video productions, have used multimedia representations to convey instructional messages for decades. With the advent of inexpensive, high-resolution monitors, sound and video compression technology, and massive memory (random-access and fixed storage) for personal computers, multimedia have become standard modes of representation in software. Multimedia desktop computers (see Figure 6.1) are now able to capture, synthesize, and manipulate sounds, video, and special effects such as animations, and integrate them all into a single multimedia presentation. Multimedia computers are common in schools.

As with most technological innovations, multimedia's first successes were in the commercial sector. Touch-screen videodisk technologies combined graphics, audio, and video in point-of-sale and point-of-use kiosks in shopping malls, museums, corporate headquarters, and retail outlets to provide sales information to potential customers. Some were even connected directly to catalog sales operations to enable customers to do some virtual shopping.

Multimedia have been used extensively in corporations to deliver employee training. The advent of multimedia was largely responsible for a whole new

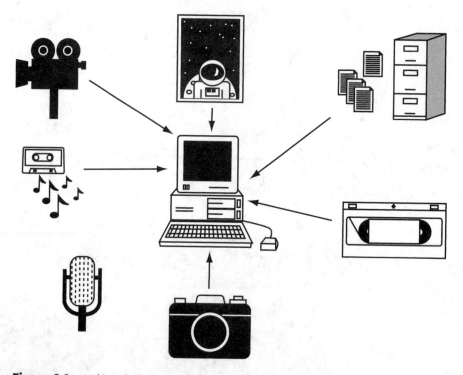

Figure 6.1 Multimedia in a Computer

approach to corporate training, called *electronic performance support systems* (EPSS). Rather than providing training to employees whether they need it or not, EPSS provide just-in-time training using multimedia resources to provide individual employee training at the time they need it, which is the most teachable moment. Andersen Consulting, for instance, developed a business practices multimedia course for all new employees that could be completed at their work site when they need the information. Most commercially viable software packages now provide point-of-use, just-in-time, online training on how to use their software.

In addition to training, multimedia are becoming an essential component of corporate and educational communications. Multimedia are used to enhance group lecture presentations. PowerPoint presentations have become the most ubiquitous form of multimedia in education. PowerPoint presentations integrate multimedia resources and links into their packages to allow presenters to dazzle their audiences. In order to support internal communications, most videoconferencing systems (see chapter 5 for more discussion) allow users to share and interactively manipulate graphics, text, audio, and animation while seeing and talking with each other in real time. Most corporate communications have gone multimedia. Schools are following.

In education, multimedia evolved, as most technologies have, as a technology in search of a problem. In the early 1990s, it seemed that the multimedia computer was the answer to whatever educational question was being asked. After all, that was the MTV generation, so students needed to be entertained by continuously changing, multimodal, multimedia learning shows. Providing information in multiple modes would surely make it more interesting and therefore more understandable to students. Educators, enamored of the multisensory representations afforded by the new multimedia technologies, claimed, as Edison did about motion-picture film, that students could and would eventually learn everything they needed to know from multimedia. That zealous prediction failed, in part, because commercial multimedia producers were more committed to producing adventure games than educational programs. In the past few years, numerous multimedia reference titles (databases, encyclopedias, and other information programs) and some quality educational software titles have been produced that can support educational objectives; however, multimedia have not substantially affected K–12 schools. Why not?

Multimedia, when used to deliver instruction, too often lack a clear objective or adequate instructional strategies to support any educational goal, because most commercial multimedia producers do not know how to be educators and because multimedia technologies have no implicit or explicit structure for teaching. Although a number of educational multimedia producers have developed fine examples of educational software, using multimedia merely because they provide multisensory representations of ideas is not enough to support meaningful learning. How should multiple media be combined?

Multiple channel research from the past implied that when the channels provide complementary information, learning should increase, but when the information in different channels is redundant, no improvement in learning normally occurs. And when the information in different channels is inconsistent or distracting, decrements in learning will likely occur. When stories were presented verbally, with and without video, and with voice, video, and text, no differences in recall, recognition, or visualization occurred (Ottavianio, 1993). Stamper (1991) showed that even intensive studying from multimedia materials for a two-year period produced no changes in critical thinking skills or attitudes toward school or attendance in sixth and seventh grades. Although little, if any, research exists to support the predicted effects of multimedia on learning, multimedia have become an accepted teaching device, nonetheless.

WHAT ARE MULTIMEDIA?

Multimedia represent the integration of more than one medium into some form of communication. The media represent different modes of experience, including visual, auditory, olfactory (smell), tactile (touch), and even gustatory (taste). For instance, consuming a sizzling plate of fajitas or quaffing a complex beer involves all of the senses—observing the color, feeling the texture, tasting the piquancy, smelling the aromas, and hearing the sizzles or bubbles. These are multimodal, multimedia experiences—stimulating all of the sensory modalities. Instructional multimedia, however, typically involve only the auditory and visual modalities in the integration of media such as text, sound, graphics, animation, video, imaging, and spatial modeling into a computer system (von Wodtke, 1993). Multimedia can also include record-based data, numeric data, animations, and just about any other form of communication that can be digitized (Figure 6.1).

Today multimedia representations in software are taken for granted. Nearly all information, including that on the WWW, uses multimedia representations. Why are multimedia so popular? Multimedia presentations are engaging because they overstimulate the senses with a barrage of sounds and images. For today's video generation, they are attention-getting and attention-holding. But is that enough for meaningful learning? Attention is a necessary condition for learning, but we believe it is not sufficient. Meaningful learning, as we have argued throughout this book, requires much more than attention.

Multimedia Technologies

Just as the contents of multimedia vary a lot, so do the ways that multimedia are stored, retrieved, and delivered. The major disadvantage of multimedia, when compared with text, is the enormous amount of memory required to store multimodal information, especially video. A number of multimedia formats have been developed over the years for storing ever larger computer files.

Videodisks   Multimedia received a major boost from the development of videodisk technologies in the 1980s. Designed initially as a replacement for videotape, it was quickly adopted as a popular medium for instruction because of its random-access and still-frame capabilities. Videodisks hold continuous motion, analog video (at 30 pictures or frames per second), just like videotapes do. However, rather than encoding information magnetically, as on audio- and video-tape, tiny pits corresponding to the strength of the video signal are engraved on videodisks by a high-power laser in a spiral pattern on the disk from the inside out. A low-power laser is used to reflect light off these pits. This reflected signal is converted back into an analog video signal, which is reproduced on a television monitor. This signal-encoding method enables the user to access and play up to 54,000 individual pictures on the disk, which may hold audio, motion video, or still images.

Videodisks can be used in stand-alone mode to replay audio, video, or images, or they may be connected to a computer as a peripheral, visual storage device. The computer program organizes and presents information, calling on the videodisk to supply instructional video in stereo (or bilingual), still slides, computer-generated images, or animation on demand. In these interactive programs, the computer output is typically seen on one screen while the videodisk output is replayed on another screen. By adding a video overlay card to the computer, both the computer output and videodisk output may be seen in combination on the same screen, allowing computer-generated graphics, arrows, or other cues to be overlaid on video images. The digital revolution has rendered videodisks nearly obsolete, because audio and video are now normally digitized and stored in the computer's memory, just like text or other forms of information. Although a number of educational programs produced on videodisks are still being used, very few, if any, educational videodisk programs are now being produced.

Compact Discs   Compact discs (CDs) have emerged, for now, as the dominant multimedia storage device. The tremendous growth of CDs resulted from the replacement of analog audio on phonographs and audiotapes to digital audio on CDs. Music is digitized by sampling the sound up to 44,000 times per second and encoding it as a number that is burned on the disk. Music is recreated by converting those numbers back into the range of sounds that are amplified and replayed through speakers in analog form. These sound bits are recorded onto a CD in much the same way as video was encoded onto videodisks.

Visual information is encoded onto CDs as individual screen pixels. The color and light characteristics of each pixel (dot) on the computer screen (512 pixels by 480 pixels for normal video) are encoded as a number. The number is read off the CD and displayed on the computer screen 30 times per second. One second of normal resolution video at 24 computer bits per pixel requires more than 20 megabytes of storage space, while a full minute would require more than a gigabyte (1 billion bytes). Such massive storage requirements would seem to make digital video impossible to store and replay on any normal computer. However, by reducing the resolution and size of the image or the number of bits per pixel, these massive requirements can be reduced.

More significantly, a number of video compression technologies have emerged. One of the standard compression routines, MPEG (Motion Picture

Experts Group), looks at similarities across pixels and frames and stores only the changes, rather than discrete numbers for each pixel for each frame of video. These compression routines have reduced the storage requirements by factors of 100. Most require the addition of special software and/or hardware (video boards) to be added to computers to compress and decompress video images. Coupled with ever-larger storage devices (hard drives and CDs), digital video has joined digital audio as the standard. Two software standards, QuickTime and Video for Windows, enable reduced-frame (size and motion) video to be played on most Macintosh and Windows computers. These operating system extensions provide a standard format for adding movies to any kind of document. QuickTime, for instance, provides an industry standard for creating or recording video input and playing back that video as movies on any Macintosh. CD-ROMs became popular multimedia storage devices because they could hold 650 megabytes of computer files, which in the early 1990s was significantly larger than any mass storage devices commonly available for personal computers. They became even more popular when inexpensive (less than $1,000) CD recorders became available for most computers, allowing users to record multimedia programs onto a CD. However, as of 1997, with most personal computers sporting multi-gigabyte hard drives, the CD-ROM is being replaced by other disk options (e.g., Jazz drives).

DVDs A new generation of digital disks (digital videodisks, digital versatile disk, or DVDs) look like CDs, but pack a lot more information on the disk. DVD-ROM drives capable of holding 4.7 gigabytes on a standard DVD disk emerged in 1997, and are rapidly becoming the most common form of video and multimedia communications. DVDs can hold 133 minutes of video per side. They deliver extremely high-resolution movies with multiple audio channels and information bases about the film and the actors, but they can also be used as CD-ROMs to store computer files. Inexpensive drives, including an MPEG card to play DVD movies, are available for most computers. Most multimedia computers are being shipped with a DVD drive of one sort or another as a standard feature. These drives can also play standard CDs.

A new generation of writable DVDs are now available. DVD-RAM was the first rewritable format to come to market. It is the best suited of the writable DVD formats for use in computers. Similar in concept to CD-R, DVD-R (DVD-Recordable) is a write-once medium that can contain 4.7 gigabytes per side of any type of information normally stored on mass-produced DVD disks—video, audio, images, data files, multimedia programs, and so on. Depending on the type of information recorded, DVD-R disks are usable on virtually any compatible DVD playback device, including DVD-ROM drives and DVD video players. The DVD-RW formats are now supporting reading and writing information to DVDs. However there are impediments to DVD-RW's full compatibility with existing players. Change is a way of life in computer peripherals. What is certain is that future storage devices will become ever larger and faster.

World Wide Web The WWW emerged in the mid-1990s as a distributed computing option to stand-alone multimedia computers. In the early stages, the Web was used to store largely text-based documents on computers all over the world and to allow users anywhere to access those documents (much more information on the WWW is included in chapter 3). With the evolution of more powerful servers and desktop computers, the Web is rapidly becoming a giant, distributed multimedia knowledge base. Most Internet browsers, such as Netscape or Internet Explorer, can be enhanced with plug-in extensions, such as Real Video, Shockwave, QuickTime, and QuickTime VR, that allow multimedia programs to be accessed, recorded, and replayed on any powerful desktop computer. Although the Web appears to be replacing current CD technologies for education, it is certain that new technologies will once again shift the balance of power in computer storage technology.

Multimedia Production Software Mirroring the exponential growth in computational power and data storage and display in modern desktop computers, sophisticated software that exploits that computing power has emerged to support the design and development of multimedia programs. There is a continuum of tools for producing multimedia and hypermedia, from commercial, high-end multimedia production packages to special-purpose, educational multimedia authoring systems. They vary in power and price.

Commercial multimedia production packages tend to be expensive, powerful packages for producing multimedia programs. Programs like Macromedia Director and Authorware Professional provide sophisticated graphics tools, full animation, video production, and higher levels of interactivity—all at a cost of up to $5,000.

Special-purpose authoring systems make the production of multimedia and hypermedia easier for younger students. Products like HyperStudio, Digital Chisel, and StorySpace are not as flexible or powerful as other authoring tools, but they are friendlier, easy-to-use environments for kids, and they are inexpensive (usually less than $100). We recommend using this type of software because they are easy to learn and, more important, because they are able to produce hypermedia—a special form of multimedia.

CONSTRUCTING, NOT LEARNING FROM, HYPERMEDIA

The remainder of this chapter will describe how multimedia and hypermedia can be used to engage students in design problem solving. Our premise is simple: Students learn much more when they design, construct, and evaluate multimedia and hypermedia than when they study hypermedia programs. Although hypermedia, like multimedia, have traditionally been used to convey instructional messages to learners, we argue that educators should think of hypermedia primarily

Hypermedia vs. Multimedia

Hypermedia is simply the marriage of multimedia and hypertext. Hypertext is an open, user-selectable form of text where readers can move instantly from where they are reading to any other part of the text simply by pointing and clicking on a hot spot or hot button (maybe a highlighted word or set of words or a separate visual button on the screen). This is accomplished by breaking the text into nodes of text and interconnecting the nodes with each other. In hypermedia, nodes may consist of different media forms—text, graphic images, sounds, animation sequences, video clips, or any other form of media. For example, rather than having users point to a hot button to retrieve a textual description of the presidential election, ABC created a hypermedia review of the 1988 election that mixed audio and video clips of speeches, pictures of the candidates, the text of their platforms, and so on.

The organization of hypermedia is open. The same set of nodes can be organized and accessed in many different ways to reflect many different conceptual orientations or perspectives (Jonassen, 1991). The hypermedia author may create a very tight structure, restricting access to information in ways that make it most easily understood. Or the structure may be completely open, with immediate access to any node in the knowledge base. Learners can access any of those nodes at any time or follow theme-oriented links to related information.

Hypermedia possess some or all of these characteristics (Jonassen, 1989):

- Nodes or chunks of information of varying sizes and various media

- Associative links between the nodes that enable the user to travel from one node to another

- Network of ideas formed by the link structure

- Organizational structure that describes the network of ideas (may reflect different models or conceptual structures)

- Ability to represent explicitly the structure of information in the structure of the hypertext

- Dynamic control of information by the user—that is, a high level of interactivity with the user so the user decides where to go

- Multiuser access to the information—many hypertexts are available to many users simultaneously

as an environment to construct personal knowledge and learn *with*, not a form of instruction to learn *from*. Rather than trying to learn from instructor-designed hypermedia, students should be creating and constructing their own hypermedia knowledge bases. In order to construct hypermedia, students are engaged in many kinds of problem solving. They must search for information, model the structure of that information, and then design the multimedia and hypermedia components. Brown (1998) found that this activity permits students to express their creativity and individuality, develop higher-order thinking and cognitive flexibility, and reflect on their communication strategies. That is meaningful learning. The intellectual effects of hypermedia construction, especially intrinsic motivation and design skills, are most prominent with students who are at risk (Liu & Rutledge, 1997) and students with learning disabilities (Okolo & Ferretti, 1996). Constructing hypermedia programs is engaging for all learners.

Another important premise is that construction should focus on the hypermedia, not the multimedia. Hypermedia enables students to impose some kind of knowledge structure on the information that they include in their hypermedia knowledge bases. Deciding which structure to use and modeling that structure are both important forms of problem solving that engage students in critical thinking. Students are naturally enamored of the multimedia features available, so they will readily create videos and integrate graphics and sounds. As a teacher, one of your jobs is to ensure the intellectual integrity of student productions. Be sure they are producing something that makes sense as well as flashes, gurgles, and pops.

Students as Hypermedia Authors

We recently participated in a study with 7th-grade English and social studies students to discover what rhetorical constructions, cognitive strategies, and social negotiations students engage in when constructing their own hypermedia documents (McKillop, 1996). We used ethnography, grounded theory, and phenomenology (including questionnaires, student learning logs, interviews, document analysis, videotaping, and observation as data sources) to study the process of hypermedia construction. The students wrote and edited their own text and incorporated sounds, images, original QuickTime movies, and video. The process included the composing process, construction of hyperpathways, use of media, utilization of potentials and constraints of the technology, and the social construction of the knowledge. We asked: How will students compose? How will they collaborate? How will they approach and deal with the new environment? How will they work through links and spaces? How will they use media? How will they utilize the constraints and potentials of the technology?

Learning Processes   During the course of the study, eight students worked on the poetry unit, and eight worked on a biography unit. They collected multimedia artifacts—sounds, images, videos, and texts—which they digitized for use in constructing a StorySpace (from Eastgate Systems) multimedia document. In addition to this hypermedia tool, each student developed skills in using SoundEdit Pro for digitizing voiceovers and music; Adobe Premiere for digitizing video and creating original QuickTime movies; Adobe Photoshop linked to DeskScan for digitizing images; and ClarisWorks for word processing. Students studying poetry were assigned a scenario:

> The year is 2021, two years after a nuclear holocaust has decimated your community, your country, and life as it was. Although many aspects of your life are still disrupted, your community feels the need for some sort of continuity and beauty. Your computer-consulting firm (a few computers still work) has been assigned the task of bringing the knowledge of poetry to school-age children. Areas that you will need to concentrate on include the following: how a poem looks; how a poem sounds; how a poem expresses an idea; and how a

poem uses language in a special way. Although some poetry still exists from before the attack, you may need to write new poems of different types to provide students with the foundation they need. You may need to integrate or create film, sound, images, or original movies to complete your task. You will be working as a group for some sections of the project and as individuals for other sections. Good luck.

The students divided the topics among themselves, and they shared their poetry so that they could become familiar with what each member was doing. Each group composed its introduction collaboratively, trying to include navigational information, even though they were themselves a bit unclear at that point about how to navigate through StorySpace. One group decided to follow through on the scenario with a picture and an original poem by one of the members of the group. The other group addressed the scenario with an explanation of the purpose for their presentation.

The students concentrated on their poetry, which they wrote at night. One of the groups had decided that all of the poems would be nature poems, so any poem that did not fit that theme was eliminated from the project. This meant that more poems had to be written to serve as examples for each of the different types. The other group decided not to pursue a theme; in fact, they eventually included all the poems written by the group members.

Although the poetry was written by individuals, the groups were very careful about helping each other. For instance, because only one person could work at the computer at a time, the other group members would assist with scanning, digitizing, and locating pictures, sounds, and video for their group to use for their poetry. At this point, there was a lot of activity in the resource room, and the students accumulated great stacks of resources to assist them. Individuals also began to come in to work during their study-hall time.

In one group, the students were eager to include video, still images, and graphics right from the outset. Each day saw an increase to the resource pile. The students very carefully planned and executed original QuickTime movies. One young man even got the inspiration for a poem from several computed graphics on his home computer; he combined these to create a picture for which he wrote an engaging poem, "A Pig and His Marshmallow" (title inspired by the book *A Boy and His Dog*). One girl searched for and, with the teacher's help, found a video clip of bears eating fish in a spring. Not only did she use the clip, but she also, on the suggestion of her group members, changed the title of the poem because the clip focused more on the bears eating the fish—which she had already discussed in the poem. The video clip helped her to focus on the aspect of the poem that she liked the best, thus, the renaming of the poem.

In the other group, only one student started bringing in pictures right from the start. She scanned the picture and then used StorySpace's ability to open a card with the sound playing to recite her poem. In the end, she did not include a written text of the poem, just the picture and the audio reading. She also constructed an original QuickTime movie using still images and her voiceover reading a poem. It wasn't until she created these two pieces that the members of her group got excited about utilizing the capabilities of the computer. After a while, all the members of this group added pictures to their poems, although no one added any more movies.

Known as the "Web view" because it graphically presents links between spaces, Figure 6.2 shows the topical organization of the project. Each space in this Web view has two features: (1) the title of the space, which when clicked on reveals a window for writing text and media called the writing space; and (2) the organizational space, in which subordinate spaces are represented by identical miniature boxes. The strings between boxes indicate author-generated hyperlinks between text and/or media contained in each of the writing spaces. Not all of the links in a document are visible at one time because each space can contain more spaces inside spaces inside spaces, and so on. When the reader double-clicks in the organizational space, a new Web view of the next hierarchical level of spaces and links is displayed. A single click on the title of the space *Language* in Figure 6.2 reveals the writing space in which words, graphics, or video clips can be placed (Figure 6.3) Music can be included in a video clip or can be programmed to play automatically when the writing space is opened. A single group of words or a graphic area can be highlighted to make multiple links going to different destinations. When the author does this, a dialogue box appears with choices for the reader to follow.

Figure 6.3 illustrates this navigational dialogue box because the students linked the word *simile* to two writing spaces: *Language* and *Beluga*. Figure 6.4 shows the result of the reader having chosen to follow the *Beluga* link. As the space opens, the computer highlights the words the students linked to *simile* in the previous window. In this case, the entire poem is highlighted as an example of a simile.

The biography groups were given the task of researching a famous person's life and composing a monologue to be presented in front of their classes. To mirror what their classmates were constructing without the aid of the computer, the students were instructed to write the monologue in first person. They began by brainstorming

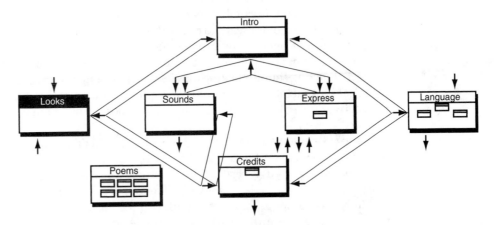

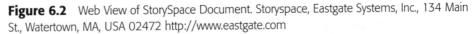

Figure 6.2 Web View of StorySpace Document. Storyspace, Eastgate Systems, Inc., 134 Main St., Watertown, MA, USA 02472 http://www.eastgate.com

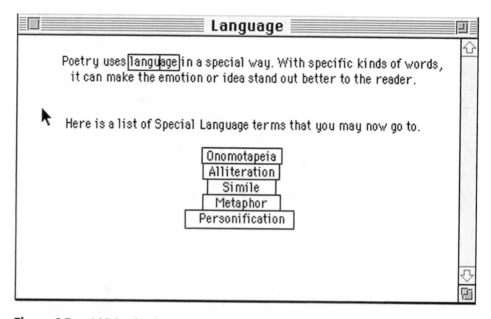

Figure 6.3   Highlighted Links in StorySpace. Storyspace, Eastgate Systems, Inc., 134 Main St., Watertown, MA USA 02472 http://www.eastgate.com

ways to present the projects, such as dressing up as Martin Luther—homemade monk suit and all—sitting Paul Revere atop a horse and filming part of the famous ride, and capturing part of the John F. Kennedy assassination video from the movie *J.F.K.*. One group decided to focus on a family tree to introduce their subjects. While two members of this group decided to introduce their own sections in this fashion, the group as a whole opted for a movie introduction, which included all five students speaking while a picture of their person was shown. The other group also adopted this introductory movie idea, and one of this group's members even created his own introductory first-person movie for his person, Martin Luther.

The students spent the rest of the time writing scripts, scanning images, recording and digitizing sound, creating movies, and planning and executing spaces. Most of the linking that these students did was implicit in the narrative structures that their projects were presented in, and they planned almost no other linking.

Learning Processes   First and foremost, constructing hypermedia knowledge bases is constructive—literally and pedagogically. In the process of constructing hypermedia knowledge bases, students must construct knowledge to represent. The process of constructing knowledge bases is very active and very intentional. It is active, because students are manipulating the various modalities and representations afforded by multimedia programs. And, as evidenced by the students' roles (described next), the process is very intentional, requiring careful planning. Evaluating the fruits of those plans (assessing the effectiveness of the hypermedia

Beluga

Like a fluffy marshmallow,
soft as a pillow.
Like a white cloud,
floating in a blue sky.
With two chubby flippers,
And a twinkle in its eye.
by
Allison Crnic

Figure 6.4 Student Poem as an Example of a Simile. Storyspace, Eastgate Systems, Inc., 134 Main St., Watertown, MA USA 02472 http://www.eastgate.com

knowledge base) requires very incisive reflection and self-regulation. Constructing hypermedia knowledge bases is among students' most complete intellectual activities.

Problem-Solving Processes   Designing hypermedia programs is among the most engaging and complex forms of problem solving that students can accomplish. Design problems engage all of the other forms of problem solving, information searching, decision making, and modeling. Lehrer (1993) carefully described the intellectual activities that students must complete in order to build hypermedia programs. These activities include four major processes:

1. Planning requires that students make decisions about:
    major goals of the knowledge base (who is the audience?, what should
        they learn?)
    topics and content to be included in the knowledge base
    relationships among the topics (how will they be linked?)
    interface design (what functions should be provided to the learner?)
    how the design will collaborate to complete the task

2. Accessing, transforming, and translating information into knowledge includes:

> searching for and collecting relevant information
> selecting and interpreting information sources
> developing new interpretations and perspectives
> allocating information to nodes and deciding how it will be represented, that is, which medium (text, graphic, pictures, video, audio)
> deciding on the nature of the links necessary to interconnect content and create links

3. Evaluating the knowledge base includes:

> assessing compromises in what was represented and how
> assessing the information coverage and their organization testing the browser
> trying it out with users and soliciting their feedback

4. Revising the knowledge base from the feedback includes:

> reorganizing and restructuring the knowledge base to make it more accessible or meaningful

The activities listed under the first major process, planning, all require making decisions.

The activities listed under the second process require a combination of information searching and modeling. Students must not only search for relevant information to include in the program but also model the structure of that information in the hypermedia program. The evaluating activities listed under the third and fourth processes primarily require decision-making kinds of problem solving. Designing engages a complex combination of problem solving.

Teacher Roles   The role of the teacher should be to coach students in these different processes. Coaching is a less directive method of teaching, usually involving prompting or provoking the students with questions about the content and treatment they are using. You may suggest issues but should not recommend answers or treatments. Those are the students' responsibility. Lehrer (1993) suggests questions such as:

- How are you going to organize your presentation, and why?
- How are you going to decide on what to include and what to leave out?
- Can you draw a map of the flow of your program? Does it seem logical?
- Which stories do you want to include, and what do they represent?
- Which are the most important themes in describing your content? How did you determine that they were the most important?

Lehrer also suggests modeling certain processes, such as using notecards to represent nodes and connecting them with pieces of string.

Assessing Learning   Hypermedia knowledge bases are rich indicators of students' understanding. They can be evaluated by asking questions such as:

- How is the presentation organized? How complex is that organization? How appropriate is that organization for describing the content?
- What auditory and visual resources were used? How did those resources complement, explain, or illustrate the ideas being conveyed?
- How many links were provided to interconnect the material? How descriptive were these links? How did they describe the information?
- How was the content conveyed in each of the nodes (expository, stories, questions)?
- How accurate is the information represented?
- Are all important information sources represented in the presentation?

Many more questions should occur to you as you begin to view and evaluate student productions. Student presentations of their programs will usually evince a level of pride seldom seen in classrooms.

In the following four sections, we describe other contexts or settings in which students have produced hypermedia programs. In each of these contexts or situations, the learning processes, problem-solving processes, teacher roles, and assessment processes are very similar to those already described. Therefore, we will not bother repeating that information for each situation.

Storytelling in Shared Spaces

Learners sometimes work in learning and knowledge-building communities, exploiting each others' skills while providing social support, and modeling and observing the contributions of each member. One of the most interesting examples of the intellectual effects of collaborative multimedia production was demonstrated by Smith (1992), where Navajo school children in a reading improvement program collaborated to produce hypermedia programs. The students produced a multimedia version of a familiar, traditional Navajo story, "How Spider Woman Taught Changing Woman to Weave." Third- and sixth-grade students (Figure 6.5) used paint and text editors and picture-capture utilities to develop multimedia interpretations of this important part of their oral tradition.

Smith concluded from the experience that "simply inserting computers and other media into the curriculum without integrating programs and activities into the fabric of the curriculum probably will do little to effect meaningful change" (pp. 292–293). Navajo children lack apparent reasons to learn in traditional learning modes. Producing multimedia materials can help. The key to constructive learning is ownership. Navajo children have no ownership in traditional transmissive approaches to learning, because the context has little meaning in their cultural context. When they use technology to represent their own cultural beliefs, they own the productions and they believe in the products. Perhaps the most interesting conclusion from this study was that collaborative multimedia production was so effective in this situation because the Navajo culture is a cooperative, noncompetitive culture.

Figure 6.5   Navajo Children Working on Multimedia

Designing an Information Kiosk for the Zoo

Contextual learning involves work on meaningful, real-world tasks or simulated tasks in problem-based learning contexts. That is, the students attempt to solve real problems. When this occurs, they understand what they are learning and transfer it more successfully to new situations. Multimedia and hypermedia are powerful tools for engaging learners in meaningful, real-life tasks. For instance, Beichner (1994) reported a project in which highly motivated junior high school students created a touch-sensitive kiosk to be installed in the local zoo. They were commissioned by the zoo to provide an information kiosk to complement the traditional displays of animals.

To prepare the multimedia kiosk, students talked to zoo visitors and staff. They had to work cooperatively to search out content materials from a wide variety of resources and convey that information in a hypermedia program for the kiosk using an on-screen audio recorder, a video tool to operate the videodisk player, color painting and text tools, and a data-linking tool for connecting pieces of information. The multimedia production tools enabled them to grab pictures, video sequences, or audio sequences from the videodisk and place them onto the screen. The students also wrote text and produced colorful drawings by capturing images using a scanner and electronic camera.

They quickly gained independence. Within a few weeks they demonstrated a strong desire to work on their own. Once the students had mastered the editor, roles rapidly changed. Students not only picked out what information and layout designs they would use, they also began showing other students and even their teachers how to best use the equipment and software. The students began skipping study halls and lunch periods in order to work on their screens. They used these tools to create buttons on the kiosk screen. By touching these buttons, zoo visitors could see and hear animals, look for more information, or even print out an information sheet, complete with a map of the zoo and student-generated questions and comments about the animal on the screen.

The students' enthusiasm did not diminish throughout the project. Often the computer coordinator would arrive in the morning to find students who had come in early and were waiting for her to open the door. The students were enthusiastic because they saw that their work had importance because it was a real-world problem. It was worthwhile for them to learn new material and uncover additional resources. By establishing an environment where creative thinking about the content material is combined with real-world assignments, students will learn content, enjoy the learning process, and recognize that they have created something worthwhile that serves the community.

Students as Multimedia Ethnographers

Conversational learners naturally seek out opinions and ideas from others in order to become part of knowledge-building and discourse communities. Reflective learners articulate what they are doing, the decisions they are making, the strategies they are using, and the answers that they are finding, while reflecting on the meaningfulness of it all. Multimedia environments may be used to engage both conversational and reflective learning—in this case, through multimedia ethnography.

Ethnographers are persons who investigate the customs, habits, and social behaviors of races and peoples. Ethnography has traditionally been used to research native, indigenous populations. Ricki Goldman-Segall (1992, 1995), at the University of British Columbia, has developed a multimedia platform called *Learning Constellations* for supporting ethnographic investigations and interpretations by students. *Learning Constellations* allows students to construct multimedia programs, including videos, pictures, and narratives written by them, about the topic of investigation. Her students have used *Learning Constellations*, for instance, to investigate the effects of clear-cutting in the British Columbia rain forests and examining the lives and histories of the First Nations of the Northwest.

Learning Constellations also allows readers to contribute their own interpretations of original stories as well as creating their own stories. These stories come from multiple authors (what Goldman-Segall calls "multiloguing," rather than dialoguing) and are linked together in clusters or constellations of perspectives. These multilogues produce what Clifford Geertz (1973) calls *thick descriptions* of phenomena. The constellations of video and stories that students produce represent larger and different patterns of meaning about the topics being studied (Figure 6.6). "Layers build; stories change; patterns emerge; and inquiry becomes reflexive practice" (Goldman-Segall, 1995). It is that kind of refection that makes *Learning Constellations* a powerful multimedia experience.

The student storytelling afforded by *Learning Constellations* leads to the social construction of knowledge. Students work together to investigate issues in

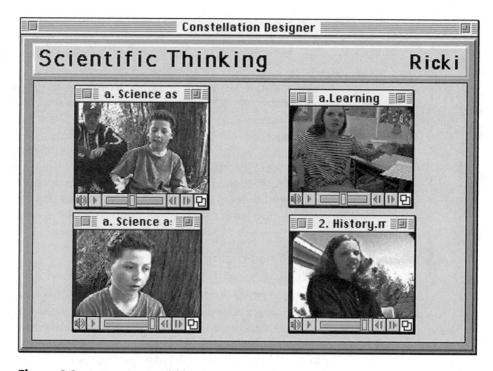

Figure 6.6 Perspectives Available From *Constellations* Knowledge Base. MERLin, The Multimedia Ethnographic Research Lab, University of British Columbia.

multiple levels of conversation. Students go out into the real world and investigate socially relevant problems. They collect evidence about those problems, usually in the form of video interviews and documentaries (see Figure 6.7). They analyze, digitize, and assemble those videos into multivocal story chunks, called *stars*, which include the videos and the student annotations of them. These stars, produced and told by different people to represent their unique points of view, are assembled into larger groupings called *constellations*. As other students or the public examine the students' multimedia database, they add their own views and annotations. Why? Because "the process of making discoveries and the process of recursive reaction, within the data and among the users, that meaning of an event, action, or situation can be negotiated" (Goldman-Segall, 1992, p. 258). Having students design and film their own video narratives creates a video culture in the classroom—not a passive culture of viewing video, but rather, a culture of constructing videos to tell a complex and important story. In becoming video ethnographers, students become friends with the camera; become a participant recorder by training fellow researchers, teachers, and students how to use video for observation; become a storyteller by selecting video chunks and writing narratives; and become a navigator by exploring using video in new situations (Goldman-Segall, 1992).

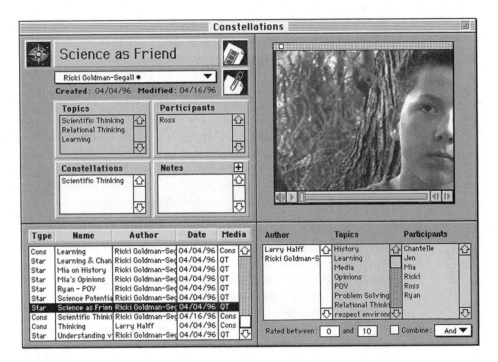

Figure 6.7   Evidence Available in a *Constellations* Knowledge Base. MERLin, The Multimedia Ethnographic Research Lab, University of British Columbia.

Creating Home Pages

Perhaps the most common form of hypermedia development that occurs in schools nowadays focuses on Web page construction. We describe a Web site that elementary students have constructed to represent the activities of their school. It is but one of hundreds of school Web sites that students have produced and maintained. Web pages represent another form of hypermedia, so constructing Web pages is not unlike constructing other forms of hypermedia. The primary difference is that people from around the world can view their productions. Building Web pages is among the most constructivist activities that learners can engage in, primarily because of the ownership that students feel about their products and the publishing effect.

Virtual Schoolhouse   Students at the Andrew Robinson Elementary School in Jacksonville, Florida (with significant support from the faculty and administration), have created an amazing Web site (http://www.rockets.org/) that exemplifies a very comprehensive virtual schoolhouse. It was created and is maintained by students in collaboration with their teachers and principal. The site provides an interesting, easy-to-use tour through the school, with lots of information about what goes on and what students are learning. It features student artwork, and many of the drawings of the building are used as clickable maps, so users of the

Web site can click on pictures to virtually tour the school. Figure 6.8 shows the lobby, which is the first stop on the tour.

When you click on a door, you move through it. When you click on the door to the administrative offices, you see a counter, plants, and labeled doors for the principal, assistant principal, and counselor. When you click on any of those doors, you see a message from the administrator. Each image has many links to other places and information. In the principal's office, for example, clicking on the file drawer labeled "Teachers" brings up a list of links to information and classrooms of the teachers. Follow the link to the computer teacher's lab, and you'll see artwork of a row of computers, the monitors of which show the names of software the students use (HyperStudio, Digital Chisel, etc.). If you click on one of the monitors, you get information about that software, how the students use it, and more.

Consider the knowledge construction that went into this project! In addition to the artwork and writing, so many decisions had to be made: What do we include? What gets linked to what? Who will do what, and by when? How will the work of that group connect to the work of this one? This project illustrates the results of giving students control over an exciting project. The Internet made it attractive, is the source of lots of feedback on their work, and is the source of many possible extensions of this project.

Where will the students take the project in the future? They saw some Web sites that had developed photographic virtual reality tours using a new software product called RealVR. They decided they should add that capability to their site:

> When we decided to add a virtual reality element to our school's Web site this year, we spent a lot of time looking at the various browsers and plug-ins. We

Sketch by Nereus Manning, 5th Grade Student
Please explore our school by clicking on the colored areas.

Figure 6.8 Lobby of the Virtual School Web Site Developed by Students

wanted to build with technology that would be friendly to the user and create the feeling of really being there. We chose RealVR because they fulfilled these requirements. We sent them an e-mail explaining who we were and what we wanted to do. Very quickly, the CEO was back in touch with us. RealSpace has provided us with their software, and been very generous with their time in answering questions and providing support. (http://www.rockets.org)

It is obvious from their Web site that the students responsible for construction of this site have grown intellectually through their use of state-of-the-art tools. This is a great example of how a constructive Internet project gives new meaning to their reading, writing, artwork, communication skills, and computer skills, while causing them to develop in important ways what the traditional classroom ignores. Other good ideas that demonstrate the Internet's constructive potential include: creating student Web pages; creating Web pages on topics from the curriculum; creating Web pages on local points or topics of interest; creating Web-based simulations and games; creating collaborative research projects; and conducting open-ended, student-directed WWW-based research. Thousands of examples of such efforts can be reviewed by searching the Internet.

Personal home pages where students describe themselves are very constructive. Most home pages are an individual's attempt to help others get to know the author. They are sort of an informal resume, through which browsers can get a multimedia understanding of someone's interests and accomplishments. We must unfortunately express caution about student Web pages. Too much information too often attracts the attention of the wrong people. Many educators recommend that students do not include pictures of themselves or any other information that would help someone to locate the child. It is a pity that students must be afraid of fully expressing themselves.

Cognitive Flexibility Hypertexts

An alternative to school Web sites and personal home pages is to produce Web sites about content topics from the curriculum or local topics or points of interest. In order to preclude students from looking up information and cutting and pasting it to their content Web sites, you may want to try to get them to produce Web sites that contain multiple perspectives or beliefs. Such Web sites are examples of cognitive flexibility hypertexts.

Cognitive flexibility theory was developed by Rand Spiro and colleagues (Spiro, Vispoel, Schmitz, Samarapungavan, & Boerger, 1987; Spiro, Coulson, Feltovich, & Anderson, 1988) to promote advanced knowledge acquisition and flexible reasoning in learners. Why is that necessary? Because most learners have an oversimplified understanding of important concepts, especially in knowledge domains that are conceptually complex. So much instruction oversimplifies the content that it transmits; that is, teachers boil down information into its most easily transmissible form in order to help students understand it. In the process, students learn that the world is a simple and orderly place. So, our instruction filters

TECHNIQUE

- Obtain a site license to use an HTML editor, like Claris HomePage, HotMetal Pro, or Web Weaver, or use a word processor, desktop publishing program, or multimedia development program that allows you to save as HTML, such as Microsoft Word, Digital Chisel, or PageMaker.

- Give a home page assignment. Don't be overly directive. There are many sites displaying student home pages in which it is clear that the teachers gave a rather strict assignment, constraining the student's creativity (must have your name at the top, in blue, as a level 1 heading, followed by a hobbies section with three links, etc., etc., etc.!). In the best student pages it is evident that students had a lot of freedom and really got excited about it. In the more directive assignments, students seem to get less excited and simply meet the requirements.

- Give students ample opportunity and training necessary to include media, like images, sounds, and perhaps animations and/or short videos.

- Don't let storage space constrain you. Some teachers don't let kids put up a lot of images because they fear they will run out of disk space. The cost of storage space is decreasing rapidly, and it should be relatively easy to get a local business to donate more disk space, perhaps in exchange for some student work.

- Think about and reach consensus about how you will deal with the risks presented by the public nature of the WWW. It is true that there are strange people in the world, and that when students put their work, addresses, and e-mail contact information on the Web, they might be contacted by undesirable people. How will you deal with this? Some schools allow students to put their work up, but not images of themselves (this is a shame, because students really like to have their photos on the Web). Some schools don't allow students to use their last names, or require that all contact come through the teacher's e-mail account. This, too, limits what students get out of the experience. We recommend that you talk about concerns with parents, and train students to report any unusual contacts to their teachers and parents. By doing so, you can leave students open to the much more likely possibility of hearing from the many warm, healthy Internet users whose feedback can enrich their learning experience.

- When building Web sites, the goal is to a universal source document that is a set of instructions interpreted by the browser software (like Netscape or Internet Explorer) designed for each type of computer. The browser software then creates the attractive display that resembles what the author had in mind. HTML is a coding system in which text-only documents are expanded to include tags that indicate where to put images, links to other Web sites, changes in text formatting, and more. In the Web's early days, we created Web pages by writing the "source document" in a word processor, and manually inserting the hundreds of cryptic tags (a WWW search will reveal many online tutorials that will help you learn to write HTML code). While HTML coding provides lots of opportunities for debugging (a worthwhile cognitive challenge), we are now fortunate to have several HTML editors—for example, Claris HomePage, Page Mill, and Microsoft FrontPage—that simplify the process of Web page development and allow us to concentrate on what we want to say and how we want it to appear, avoiding distractions that force us to determine why we didn't get what we had envisioned.

out the complexity that exists in most applied knowledge domains, causing shallow understanding of domain knowledge to develop.

Another reason for oversimplifying instruction is because often the domain knowledge is ill-structured. Ill-structured knowledge results from ill-defined concepts, which tend to have variable attributes and ambiguous criteria. That is, events and phenomena in the real world tend to be more ill-defined. There are no prototypic cases or they are misleading, and certain aspects of cases are differentially important in different contexts so each case appears novel because of the interactions of effects (Spiro et al., 1987, 1988).

In order to help students to develop cognitive flexibility, cognitive flexibility theory tries to avoid oversimplifying instruction (Spiro et al., 1988). Hypertexts designed using cognitive flexibility theory stress the conceptual interrelatedness of ideas and their interconnectedness in the link structure. Cognitive flexibility theory provides a powerful model for getting students to think about the complexity of the real world. Cognitive flexibility theory intentionally represents multiple perspectives or interpretations of the content that it seeks to teach. Spiro borrows a rich metaphor of "criss-crossing the landscape" from Ludwig Wittgenstein for physically describing this process. The learner criss-crosses the intellectual landscape of the content domain by looking at it from multiple perspectives or through multiple themes.

Like most constructivist approaches to learning, cognitive flexibility theory starts by building cases. In order to build a cognitive flexibility hypertext, it is necessary to identify several prototypic cases that illustrate how content being studied can be applied. The more varied these cases are, the broader the conceptual bases that they are likely to support. And these cases should be authentic, requiring the same thinking that is required in real-world contexts. The interpretation of these cases depends on students discovering relevant perspectives of themes through which cases can be examined. Figure 6.9 shows the introduction to one case in an environmental Web site. The first case that was developed by students examined the reintroduction of the gray wolf into the Arizona desert. The students examined the issue from the perspectives of a half-dozen or so people who actually will be affected by the wolves (as shown in Figure 6.9). They identified various issues interwoven through their comments: local vs. national control of the land, consumption vs. conservation, cooperation vs. cooperation. Links to those issues and perspectives take the reader to those different interpretations or perspectives on the issue. The Wolf-reintroduction hypertext does not tell other learners how to interpret the jumble of voices, but does suggest ways of looking at and listening to the opinions expressed. Other cases that students developed in this environmental Web site include where to locate a new highway through the forest and whether a new sewage treatment plant should be built in the students' hometown. Developing cognitive flexibility hypertexts requires students to understand the complexity of any issue. That is a major step in intellectual development.

Reintroduction of the Wolf into the Southwest

Long before cowboys roamed, before Spaniards rode in conquest, before even the Apache and Navajo arrived, wolves inhabited the ancient Southwest, but as cattle ranching took hold in the 1800s, the predatory wolf became an obstacle to commerce. By the 1920s it was just about exterminated from the Western landscape. But wolves are making a comeback of a kind in part because of shifting public values.

In January 1995, 19 Canadian gray wolves were released into Yellowstone National Park by the U.S. Fish and Wildlife Service. In January 1996 another 20 were brought to Yellowstone and to Idaho, and in early 1997 the Southwest will get its share. Mexican gray wolves are scheduled to be reintroduced into the wilderness of Arizona and New Mexico, but the battle for public acceptance is still being waged. Should the Mexican wolf be reintroduced? You decide.

For more information, you can read this piece by Sandy Tolan of National Public Radio's Weekend Edition.

To help you make up your mind, you can listen to several people in the area who would be affected by the re-introduction:

- Al Schneeberger of the New Mexico Cattle Growers Association
- A Woman of Catron County
- Man in the Field Interviews
- Charmin Russel
- Dutch Salmon, publisher of High Lonesome Books
- Jim Cook

Figure 6.9   Cognitive Flexibility Hypertext

CONCLUSIONS

Throughout this book, we have promoted our belief that students-as-producers-of-technologies engage in much more meaningful learning than students-as-receivers-from-instructional-technologies. With no technology is this belief more obvious than with multimedia. In this chapter, we have described a number of projects that use multimedia as an authoring platform for students to represent their own meaning. For each of the projects that have been reported in the literature, there are surely many more that have not been reported. We are not suggesting that any particular project represents a model for how hypermedia should engage learners. Rather, we have included these descriptions of student productions as exemplars of the powerful effects of producing hypermedia. We do not suggest that it will be effortless. It is difficult for teachers at all levels to relinquish authority (control over the classroom and control of the meaning that is constructed by students). The level of activity that results from student construction of hypermedia can seem frenetic (it is!), and the meaning that is being constructed may not be obvious while the process is going on. The benefits may require reflection by both students and the teacher.

We recommend that these projects incorporate large chunks of time and curriculum—that is, the products need to be complex. More complex representations of students' knowledge yield better learning. These should not be small projects focusing on a single idea. Rather, they should attempt to integrate ideas throughout the curriculum and preferably from different disciplines. Hypermedia construction is an ideal medium for engaging and supporting interdisciplinary learning. The links in the knowledge base can represent different perspectives from different disciplines. In order to help students handle that complexity, we also recommend the use of an explicit hypermedia authoring tool that supports and emphasizes different link structures. Many multimedia authoring platforms emphasize only the presentation aspects, with no explicit linking available. There are many good products out there that foster student linking as an important component of the software. This is a difficult process that will require a good deal of practice. We have successfully used Post-it notes on a whiteboard with a marker to draw the connections. Students pick up the skill readily, and then they run with it—and run and run and run . . .

THINGS TO THINK ABOUT

If you would like to reflect on the ideas presented in this chapter, then articulate your responses to the following questions and compare them with others' responses.

1. Is *multimedia* singular or plural—does it describe many things or a singular phenomenon?
2. Multimedia, like most technologies, achieved its initial success in the commercial sector. Has there ever been a technology developed exclusively for education that emerged first and prospered in the educational sector?
3. Is MTV multimedia? Why or why not? How could MTV be used for teaching?
4. Stories are powerful forms of communication. How would you use multimedia to tell about yourself? Suppose you had every multimedia resource available; how would you produce your life story?
5. How would you produce an ethnographic study about your school (or your town) using a multimedia program like *Constellations*?

REFERENCES

Beichner, R. J. (1994). Multimedia editing to promote science learning. *Journal of Educational Multimedia and Hypermedia, 3*(1), 55–70.

Brown, C. A. (1998). Learning through construction of interactive multimedia. *Dissertation Abstracts International, 59A,* 0139.

Chuckran, D. A. (1992). *Effect of student-produced interactive multimedia models on student learning.* Unpublished doctoral dissertation, Boston University, Boston, MA.

Geertz, C. (1973). *The interpretation of cultures.* New York: Basic Books.

Goldman-Segall, R. (1992). Collaborative virtual communities: Using *Learning Constellations,* a multimedia ethnographic research tool. In E. Barrett (Ed.), *Sociomedia: Multimedia, hypermedia, and the social construction of knowledge.* Cambridge, MA: MIT Press.

Goldman-Segall, R. (1995). Configurational validity: A proposal for analyzing ethnographic multimedia narratives. *Journal of Educational Multimedia and Hypermedia, 4*(2), 98–106.

Gouzouasis, P. (1994). Multimedia constructions of children: An exploratory study. *Journal of Computing in Childhood Education, 5*(3/4): 273–284.

Jeffcoate, J. (1995). *Multimedia in practice: Technology and applications.* New York: Prentice Hall.

Jonassen, D. H. (1989). *Hypertext/hypermedia.* Englewood Cliffs, NJ: Educational Technology Publications.

Jonassen, D. H. (1991). Hypertext as instructional design. *Educational Technology: Research and Development, 39*(1), 83–92.

Lehrer, R. (1993). Authors of knowledge: Patterns of hypermedia design. In S. P. LaJoie & S. J. Derry (Eds.), *Computers as cognitive tools.* Hillsdale, NJ: Lawrence Erlbaum.

Liu, M., & Rutledge, K. (1997). The effect of "learner as multimedia designer" environment on at-risk high school students' motivation and learning of design knowledge. *Journal of Educational Computing Research, 16*(2), 145–177.

McKillop, A. M. (1996). *The pedagogical implications of student-constructed hypermedia.* Unpublished doctoral dissertation, Pennsylvania State University.

Nelson, T. H. (1981). *Literary machines.* Swarthmore, PA: the author.

Okolo, C. M., & Ferretti, R. P. (1996). The impact of multimedia design projects on the knowledge, attitudes, and collaboration of students in inclusive classrooms. *Journal of Computing in Childhood Education, 7*(3–4), 223–251.

Ottavianio, B. F. (1993). *The effects of multimedia presentation formats on the memory of a narrative.* Unpublished doctoral dissertation, Columbia University.

Smith, K. J. (1992). Using multimedia with Navajo children: An effort to alleviate problems of cultural learning style, background of experience, and motivation. *Reading and Writing Quarterly, 8*(3): 287–294.

Spiro, R. J., Coulson, R. L., Feltovich, P. J., & Anderson, D. K. (1988). *Cognitive flexibility theory: Advanced knowledge acquisition in ill-structured domains.* Tech Report No. 441. Champaign, IL: University of Illinois, Center for the Study of Reading.

Spiro, R. J., Vispoel, W., Schmitz, J., Samarapungavan, A., & Boerger, A. (1987). Knowledge acquisition for application: Cognitive flexibility and transfer in complex content domains. In B. C. Britton (Ed.), *Executive control processes.* Hillsdale, NJ: Lawrence Erlbaum Associates.

Stamper, K. N. (1991). *The effects of the use of multimedia on the higher-level thinking skills of seventh-grade students.* Unpublished doctoral dissertation, East Texas State University.

von Wodtke, M. (1993). *Mind over media: Creative thinking skills for electronic media.* New York: McGraw-Hill.

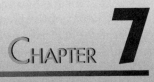
Learning by Exploring Microworlds and Virtual Realities

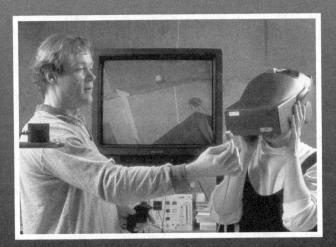

MODELING FOR LEARNING

The putative goal of most education is fostering the development of transferable knowledge in learners. Contemporary research and theory has shown that transfer of learning, particularly higher-order kinds of learning, requires well-developed mental models. Mental models are internal representations of the personal theories that people construct about phenomena. These models are usually underdeveloped because learners are required to understand and represent what they know in only one way. Additionally, learners' mental models are underdeveloped because models are usually conveyed by the teacher to the student with the belief that if the teacher shows the learner how to think, they naturally will be able to. Unfortunately, learning doesn't work that way. Rather, meaningful learning understanding requires that learners construct their own models. In order to construct mental models, learners must explore and manipulate phenomenon, observe the effects, and generate mental representations of those phenomena. The purpose of this chapter is to describe and illustrate learning environments that foster and facilitate modeling building by learners.

Penner (2001) defines two basic classes of models, physical and conceptual. A physical model has a visible or concrete representation of the model. On the other hand, a conceptual model is not visible but known in the human mind. Within these two classes, we can further define a model as expedient or explanatory (Clement, 1989). An expedient model exhibits the behavior of the phenomenon, but does not reveal the causes or influences of the behavior. On the other hand, an explanatory model does provide insight into the behavior. Within learning environments that implement modeling activities, the goal should be to have representation along with explanation. Hence, regardless if it is physical or conceptual, being able to represent the knowledge and explain the behavior is a powerful learning tool.

In chapter 6, we described interactive, hypermedia environments and how to help learners construct and represent a model of the information they encounter (Kinzer & Leu, 1997). In this chapter, we describe how higher levels of realism and interactivity can be embedded in hypermedia environments so that students are better able to construct mental models. In addition to text and traditional graphic material, learners now have access to animation, speech, video, and music. These environments (including microworlds and virtual reality) can provide real-time interactions with physical phenomena or historical figures that enable learners to explore various cause-and-effect relationships. These environments visualize phenomena and relationships among them. These visualizations can provide models for thinking (Denis, 1991).

EXPLORING MICROWORLDS

Seymour Papert and the MIT Media Lab coined the term "microworld" to define an exploratory learning environment that presents a simulation of some real-world phenomena wherein learners can manipulate, explore, and experiment in different ways (Papert, 1980). Learners can generate hypotheses about real-world phenomena and then test them in a microworld. Alternatively, they can design their own experimental environments by creating objects and by manipulating variables and controlling parameters and/or factors when conducting experiments. Microworlds support learning by doing, instead of just watching or listening to a description of how something works. Engaging activities can motivate learners to actively participate and direct their own learning rather than passively receiving knowledge in lecture-based instructional delivery. Eventually, this can lead learners to higher-order thinking skills wherein they construct their own understanding of the underlying principles of the microworld through exploration and by rebuilding their own mental model of the world with which they are experimenting (Jonassen, 2000). In essence, microworlds foster the development of problem-solving strategies, critical thinking skills, and creativity.

Microworlds can assume many forms in different knowledge domains, but the four essential characteristics of a microworld are as follows (Papert, 1980):

- simple to understand
- reflects generic characteristics that can be applied to many areas of life
- presents concepts and ideas that are useful and important to learners in the world
- reflects syntonic characteristics, which allow learners to relate prior knowledge and experience to current phenomenon being studied

Based on these characteristics, a microworld can be naturally found in the world or artificially constructed by means of physical objects or computers. They can exist in the playground, classroom, or anywhere, and they are relative to the learner's age and interests. For example, Burton, Brown, and Fischer (1984) use skiing instruction as a pretext for developing a model for designing skill-based microworlds. They believe that a microworld is a controlled learning environment where a student is able to try out new skills and knowledge. It is a practice-oriented simulation that allows the student to learn about objects in the environment and their relationships. Complexity is controlled by manipulating the equipment (e.g., the length of the skis), the task, and the environment (e.g., making easy turns on the "bunny" slope and later making more difficult turns on steeper terrain). All microworlds, computer-based and other, are exploratory environments that rely on the interest and curiosity of the learner.

Video-based adventure games are microworlds that require players to master each environment before moving on to more complex environments. They are compelling to youngsters, who spend hours transfixed in these adventure worlds. Games can become intrinsically motivating learning environments when they reflect challenge, curiosity, realism, fantasy, and control (Malone & Lepper, 1987). In addition, games can embed cognitive, social, and cultural factors within the environment (Rieber, 1996), which can help learners transfer skills from play and imitation to real situations that they will experience.

Successful microworlds rely on students regulating and controlling their own learning. Among the goals of self-regulated learning is that of encouraging transformational learning as a central tenet of cultivating self-knowledge

(Mezirow, 1985). The awareness of what one knows and the ability to integrate it with new learning that is aligned with the individual's actual past experiences is a valued and essential assumption of constructivist learning environments that utilize modeling as a learning tool.

Computer-Based Microworlds

The most well-known computer-based microworlds are environments created with the Logo programming language. Seymour Papert developed the simple procedural computer language. Logo supports the creation and manipulation of turtle objects that become components of larger, more complex objects. The programming syntax was designed to represent people's understanding of the natural behaviors of the world. For example, the backward and forward movement of the turtle object is used to model simple animal behavior.

StarLogo and Boxer are alternative programming languages to Logo. StarLogo is a microworld programming language developed at MIT Media Lab by Michael Resnick (1994). It is similar to Logo because of the use of turtle icons, but this language allows thousands of turtles to act simultaneously, not independently. In addition, the background screen can be an active part of the model by holding and passing information to the turtles. Boxer, another offspring of Logo, is a more organized program structure than Logo wherein all computational objects within the program are represented by boxes (diSessa & Abelson, 1986).

The MicroWorlds authoring tool is a Logo-based application program that makes the actual process of creating a computer project a rich learning experience. The official MicroWorlds Web site (http://www.microworlds.com) provides resources and examples for creating projects. A major asset is the project library that contains examples and ideas for creating interactive projects within different subject areas, such as language arts, math, and science. The library provides Logo programming tips to assist with creating projects and pedagogical information to assist teachers with, including project creation and experimentation within their instructional activities. In addition, the library includes projects created by students and teachers in the United States and other countries, such as Spain and Canada. The diversity of the projects reflect different languages and cultures. This allows students from all over the world to interact with projects. Another asset is that you do not have to know Logo programming or install the MicroWorlds application on your computer. The MicroWorlds Web Player allows you to view the projects with Internet browsers.

In many cases, students will interact with microworlds designed and created by companies and teachers. Prebuilt microworlds can be limiting to knowledge construction when effective instructional strategies are not built in to the environment. In addition, the level of feedback provided to the learner during critical moments of interaction is important for the knowledge construction process. However, this raises the concern of too much direction rather than allowing the user to explore and make mistakes. Learning environments that reflect more programmed instruction that directs the learner's exploration within the environment may not support constructivist goals within these environments. Rieber (1992,

p. 99) describes the following computer-based microworlds characteristics as essential elements for constructivist learning:

- Provides a meaningful learning context that supports intrinsically motivated and self-regulated learning
- Establishes a pattern whereby the learner goes from the "known to the unknown"
- Provides a balance between deductive and inductive learning
- Emphasizes the usefulness of errors
- Anticipates and nurtures incidental learning

Interactive Physics Many object-oriented microworlds require no programming language in order to manipulate objects in the microworlds. One of our favorites is Interactive Physics (www.InteractivePhysics.com), a research environment for exploring topics in Newtonian mechanics, such as a momentum, force, acceleration, and so on. It consists of several demonstrations, such as a car crash and falling objects, and many experiments, such as particle dynamics, equilibrium, and collisions. The motion in a plane experiment (see Figure 7.1) provides teachers and students with the tools to monitor aspects of the experiment (e.g., normal, friction,

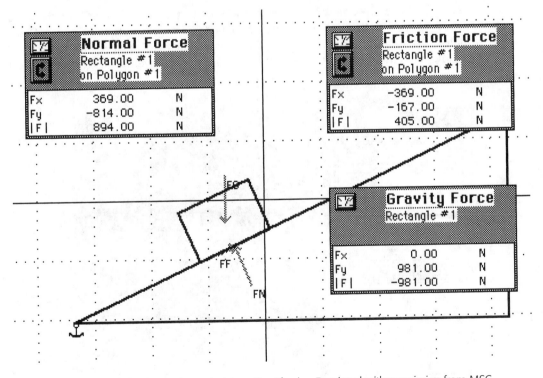

Figure 7.1 Inclined Plane Experiment in Interactive Physics. Reprinted with permission from MSC Software, www.InteractivePhysics.com.

and gravity force) as the block slides down the plane. The user can change any aspect of the microworld (e.g., stickiness of the surface, friction, gravity level) and rerun the experiment to test the effects. This microworld allows learners to create or run an infinite number of different physics and play "what-if" games in order to understand the dynamics of physical objects. Interactive physics engages active and interactive learning by allowing the learner to manipulate any aspect of the environment. That is the essence of interactive learning.

StarLogo   StarLogo is another application that allows students to easily interact and build microworlds. The application offers many examples and demonstrations for exploration in math, biology, and physics. An interesting project is the traffic microworld (Figure 7.2) where students can investigate concepts in social systems. The car traffic is affected by many elements, such as the number of cars, car speeds, and the sighting of police cars. The microworld allows students to manipulate these elements in order to see how traffic patterns develop based on adjustments to the environment. A brief sighting of a police car can cause the "stop-and-go" effect in traffic, without change to the number of cars. When the police car is removed, the slow points in the traffic will "ripple" toward the cars that have not reached the original position of the police car until it eventually disappears from the screen.

SimCalc   The SimCalc project teaches elementary and middle school students calculus concepts through MathWorlds, which is a microworld consisting of animated worlds and dynamic graphs that manipulate actor movement. By exploring the movement of the actors in the simulations and seeing the graphs of their

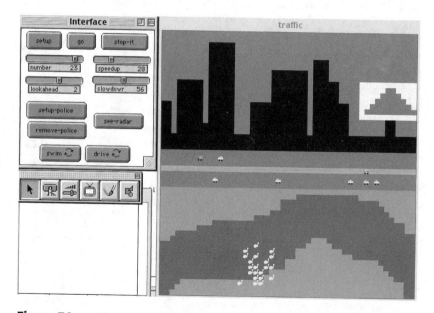

Figure 7.2   Traffic Simulation. StarLogo, http://www.media.mit.edu/starlogo courtesy of MIT.

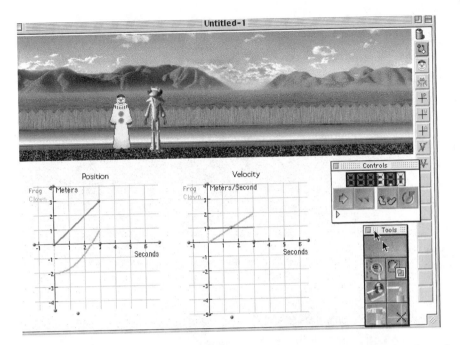

Figure 7.3 Experiment in MathWorlds. Sim Calc Technologies, LLC (www.simcalc.com). The Sim Calc Project, NSF Grants REC-9353507, REC-9619102, and REC-0087771.

activity, students begin to understand important calculus ideas. In the MathWorlds activity illustrated in Figure 7.3, students match two motions. By matching two motions, they learn how velocity and position graphs relate. Students must match the motion of the green and red graphs. To do this, they can change either graph. They iteratively run the simulation to see if they got it right! Students may also use MathWorlds' link to enter their own bodily motion. For example, students can walk across the classroom, and their motions would be entered into MathWorlds through sensing equipment. The microworld would plot their motion, enabling the students to explore the properties of their motion.

Math Cats The Math Cats Web site (http://www.mathcats.com) promotes open-ended exploration of math concepts via MathWorlds projects. As a computer teacher in an elementary school, Wendy Petty developed the Web site to supplement in-class math activities. It has now become a resource for teachers, home-school kids, and students in college-level computer courses. The Web site reflects constructivist approaches to learning by encouraging creativity and collaboration. The Web site provides a gallery of projects created by teachers and students. The projects range from simple to complex, and each is accompanied by the Logo programming code so that students can create their own. A popular project, the Dancing Cat (Figure 7.4), is a beginner's-level activity that allows students to create simple animation while learning the basic Lingo commands. Students learn how to manipulate the movements of objects and create buttons to start the animation.

Figure 7.4 Dancing Cat (Reprinted with permission)

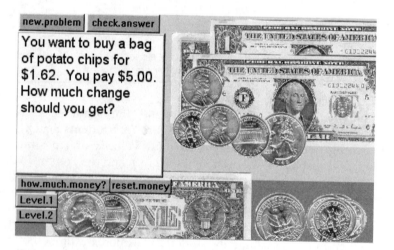

Figure 7.5 Counting Money (Reprinted with permission)

Counting Money A fun math microworld project is the Counting Money example (see Figure 7.5). The program presents the student with a new math problem relating to currency, and the student must drag the appropriate amount of money. There are two levels of difficulty to accommodate the student's level of performance. Providing a difficulty level can be an effective motivational strategy for playing the game, because learners choose to participate in tasks that are neither too easy nor too difficult (Rieber, 1996). The Counting Money project assists with learning addition and subtraction, and recognizing currency.

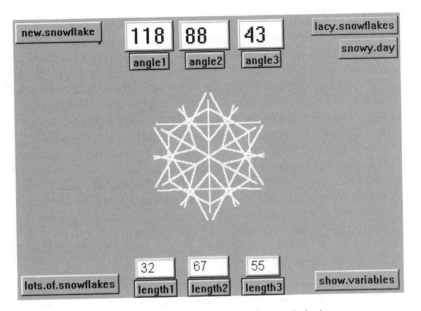

Figure 7.6   Snowflakes Example (Reprinted with permission)

Snowflakes   The Snowflakes project (Figure 7.6) allows the student to create randomly-generated snowflakes by having the student set up variables to determine the angles used to make the snowflakes. In addition, they can control the speed of the snowflakes falling to the ground. This activity assists with understanding angles and how they form patterns when the angles are brought together.

Learning by Constructing Microworlds

When students build physical models to improve understanding of the natural world, the activity helps to express their own understanding that may be different from biased representations (Penner, 2001). The computer is an excellent tool for assisting students with creating microworlds. The creation process is an important component of learning (Papert, 1980), which is supported with students constructing their understanding of a phenomenon in a microworld.

As is the case with most instructional design projects, the people who learn the most are the designers and developers, not the target audience. The gathering, reviewing, and evaluation of content leads to more understanding and "ownership" of the learning than having the instructor lecture the same information. The following examples demonstrate how providing access to computer design tools is an effective strategy for learning and more importantly, motivation to learn.

OWL   OpenWorld Learning (OWL) is a nonprofit organization in Denver, Colorado, that operates after-school and summer computer programs to support the educational and career success of K–12 students. Christopher Myers, founder and executive director of OWL, designed the program to teach core information technology skills to kids in low-income Latino neighborhoods (2001b). The OWL program has served approximately 700 kids who voluntarily participate in an educational program that emphasizes the development of skills for writing, conducting research on the Internet, using word processor and database applications, and creating programming projects using the MicroWorlds authoring tool.

The OWL program recruits and trains college-educated people to serve as teachers and mentors to students. The teachers are the primary facilitators of the learning activities. In addition, the program recruits bilingual paraprofessionals, college work-study students, and community volunteers as additional teachers and coaches. The adult teachers are responsible for training the core of student teachers, who will become mentors to their peers. Student teachers as young as 9 years old develop teamwork and leadership skills along with confidence in their learning. The student teachers must pass certification tests linked to each level in the OWL curriculum in order to prepare for their teaching roles. The six core certification levels are as follows:

1. MicroWorlds Introduction—Basic skills creating MicroWorlds animation, such as creating art, inserting and formatting text, and writing commands for simple movements of an object.

2. Animating graphics from the Internet—Retrieving information and resources from the Internet for MicroWorlds projects and using advanced Logo commands for animation.

3. Beginning Microsoft Word Skills—Inserting, formatting, and editing text along with printing of documents.

4. MicroWorlds Programming: Turtle Geometry—Manipulating turtle movement with objects and Logo commands. Also, write programming procedures with Logo.

5. MicroWorlds Programming: Video Game Design—Programming environment to be manipulated by colors, and advanced programming to manipulate the turtle movement.

6. Microsoft Word: Internet Research Project—Advanced formatting and editing of a document. Also, researching and writing a paper by gathering information from the Internet.

Learning and Assessment Strategies   An important part of the OWL environment is connecting with the needs of the students and making them feel that their work and efforts are valuable. Part of the responsibility of the adult teachers is to have one-on-one conferencing with students about their projects. During these conferencing sessions, importance is placed on the following activities (Myers, 2001a):

- Examining or "receiving" the project which involves spending time reviewing the components with the student and describing some of the elements of the project. This review also includes reading aloud the writing components to the student. Reading aloud can be a powerful method for alerting the student to confusing or problematic aspects of his or her project based on the reviewer's interaction with the material. This method is similar to the "think-aloud" strategies used in usability studies.

- Allowing the student to describe the project in his or her own words
- Asking questions relating to the content, the techniques used for development, and the interests that motivated the student to create the project
- Sharing stories of how the project may relate to personal experiences of your own or another child's project.
- Asking questions relating to how the student can extend this project or a new one and providing suggestions and ideas.

In the end, conferencing provides a means for active reflection and conception of new ideas and information that a student wants to know, rather than what the teacher wants him or her to know. The student is in control of the learning and the adult teacher becomes the facilitator to help reach the goals.

The peer mentoring is the essential component of the collaborative environment. When students are working on their projects, they signal for help by placing a red cup on top of their computer. At this time, a student teacher (peer mentor) comes by to answer the student's questions (see Figure 7.7). If the student teacher cannot assist, then an adult teacher will try to answer the questions. Most of the time, the questions and/or problems are resolved. If not, then the next level is Wendy Petty, an OWL team member, who has extensive experience creating projects in MicroWorlds.

Figure 7.7 Peer Mentor Assisting Student With a Project. Courtesy Open World Learning. Reprinted with permission.

The OWL program provides incentives to increase student participation and progress. After the conferencing with the adult teachers, all students earn points for completed projects. Students are able to check their point balance in a Microsoft Access database, which also contains data on their work progress and participation. Student teachers earn additional points for assisting their peers in the lab. At daily auctions, the kids bid and trade points for donated goods and prizes. The points and prizes are not the only rewards in this program. The most active student teachers are rewarded with donated Pentium computers for their homes, which allows them to further extend their skills to become technology leaders with their families. Because of the collaborative nature of the environment, the OWL program fosters the growth of more students becoming peer mentors. In addition, students are able to receive one-on-one support and develop lifelong relationships with adults as well as peer mentors.

The following description provides an example of how the OWL program starts with the child's interest and helps to create projects that are stimulating and interesting. A 3rd-grade student, struggling in school, became involved with the OWL program. While talking to a volunteer, who is part Native American, they began discussing their history and prominent figures, such as Geronimo the warrior. The student, who happened to have the same name, did not know much about the warrior and became interested. The volunteer provided more information and showed pictures of the warrior, which motivated the student to create a project. The student used the Internet to search for information, and created drawings, music clips, and animations relating to a Native American "blessing" ceremony that he had witnessed. Figure 7.8 shows the work that Geronimo created.

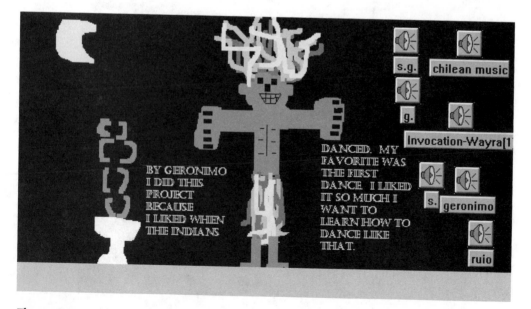

Figure 7.8 Microworld Project Created by Geronimo. Courtesy Open World Learning. Reprinted with permission.

The project increased Geronimo's interest in computer technology and learning. Now, he is an active participant in the after-school program and the program has increased his confidence in learning and interest in computers.

Resources   In collaboration with Wendy Petty, the OWL program is developing a MicroWorlds in Action Web site (http://mia.openworldlearning.org) to support training of teachers and students using the MicroWorlds authoring tool. The Web site will provide a library of projects and lessons that are customized to the skill level of each teacher and student. The instructional activities on the Web site allow students to progress through each project at their own pace. Each project begins with a simple activity, and proceeds to more complex activities that build on the concepts learned in the previous activities. In addition, each project is accompanied by three types of extension projects as a means of applying the student's new skills in creative directions. Figure 7.9 provides an example of a beginner-lever activity that can be used to supplement projects created in MicroWorlds.

EXPLORING VIRTUAL REALITIES

Virtual reality (VR) has many names and definitions, and the term is used to describe everything from three-dimensional (3-D) animation on personal computers to networked simulators. It is often associated with computer games and/or military simulations. Currently, it is being used in different areas such as scientific visualization, medicine, architecture, psychology, and rehabilitation of people with physical disabilities. In some schools, VR is used as a working model for historical or chemical simulations, which can help students understand situations or phenomena that are difficult to comprehend with traditional instructional activities, such as reading and lectures.

For our purposes, we define VR as a type of microworld that provides learners with an interactive, 3-D experience by surrounding them with a moving, simulated world. As an active or "inside" participant of this environment, the user is able to see, hear, touch, speak, manipulate, and interact. The essential characteristic of a "true" VR environment is immersion. It relates to the extent to which the user's senses are isolated from the surrounding environment and the interface is transparent. Within the environment, the learner's senses interpret images as being real which allows him or her to behave like an inhabitant of the environment. In addition, objects appear solid, can be picked up, examined from all sides, and explored in many sensory ways, such as feeling and smelling. Interaction with objects is completely intuitive and matches interactions in the natural world (e.g., grasping, pointing).

Kinds of Virtual Reality

There are different kinds of virtual reality environments that differ in capabilities and functionality.

Activity 1: Make rainbows out of squares.

- Fill an empty shape with one color and place this shape on a turtle.
- Write a procedure to make squares of changing colors. Here is one example, which will repeatedly stamp the circle shape, fill it with a different color, move forward, and turn a tiny bit. You may use this procedure or create your own.

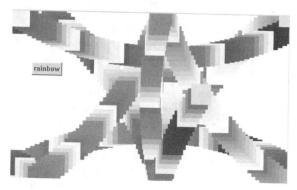

```
to rainbow
repeat 110 [pd stamp setc color + 1 fill
pu fd 10 rt 1]
end
```

Activity 2: Make rainbows out of circles.

- Instead of a solid square, use a solid circle shape to make your rainbow. Make a rainbow button and set it to "many times."
- Experiment with different numbers after *fd*, *rt*, and *setc color +−*.

Activity 3: Add sounds while the rainbow is forming.

Write a procedure to add sounds which get higher and higher while the rainbow is forming. Here is one way. (*Note* needs two inputs, for pitch and length of time to play the note. In this procedure, *note* uses the number of the color for its pitch, but it cannot be higher than 127. Use an *if* command to set the note and color back to 0. Notice the two sets of brackets. Experiment with different numbers for the length of time to play the note.) Make a button set to "many times."

```
to rainbow-with-sound
repeat 110    [if color > 127 [setc 1]
              note color 2
              pd stamp setc color + 1
              fill pu fd 10 rt 1]
end
```

Activity 4: Make a rainbow "worm" which wiggles in different directions.

Use the *random* command to make a wiggly rainbow worm:

```
to rainbow-worm
repeat 110
[if color > 127
    [setc 1]
note color 2
pd stamp setc color + 1
fill pu fd 10
rt −10 + random 20]
end
```

Figure 7.9 Instructions for Making Rainbows (Reprinted with permission. Wendy Petty, All Rights Reserved)

Immersive Virtual Reality Immersive VR, depending on the objective and scope of the project, is the most compelling and, in some cases, the most complicated type of VR environment to create. (Full immersion can be affected by either donning a head-mounted display [HMD], data gloves to gesture and interact with objects, and tracking devices.) Wearing an HMD allows you to look around and view the VR environment as you would the real world. It usually consists of two tiny monitors mounted inside a device that is situated approximately 3–5 inches in front of the user's eyes. The device shields the user's peripheral vision and tracks the movements of the head to simulate directional placement within the virtual space. Thus, when the user turns his or her head left or right, his or her viewpoint within the virtual environment changes accordingly. Mated with some sort of navigational device, either a wand or joystick, the user's movements, both direction and view, are fairly accurately tracked within the environment. Tracking equipment registers head motion and provides signals to a computer in order to make the required changes in viewpoint.

An alternative is a chamber world or room where moving images are projected on the walls. In 1992, the Electronic Visualization Laboratory at the University of Illinois–Chicago developed the Cave Automatic Virtual Environment (CAVE). The CAVE is a theater comprised of three rear-projected screens for walls and a reflective projection for the floor (Cruz-Neira, Sandin, DeFanti, Kenyon, & Hart, 1992). Each wall of the CAVE represents the field of view for the user. Designed for a multiuser experience, the CAVE lends itself perfectly to small groups of 4–8 students, allowing for both intergroup interactions as well as individual exploration because each user can look in any direction.

The level of autonomy, presence, and interaction must be high for the VR environment to be immersive. Zeltzer (1992) defines the three major characteristics of VR as follows:

- Autonomy—extent to which the environment functions, independent of user interaction and input. Environment should evolve and develop.
- Presence—the sense of being a part of the environment, which increases as the interface becomes more natural and intuitive. Presence is also related to cognitive processes such as memory for objects and events in the virtual environment (Hoffman, Hullfish, & Houston, 1995), which can assist learning.
- Interaction—extent to which interaction between participant and environment follow the laws of the environment.

Desktop VR Desktop VR creates a "window to the world" feeling to users, but it does not meet the conditions for immersion as described above. This type of virtual reality allows users with desktop monitors to navigate an environment freely in real time or to navigate a limited environment such as a panorama or a 360-degree circle. Panorama technologies, such as Apple's QuickTime technology and those using iPix technology, assist designers with creating these views. Macromedia Director is another software application that allows you to create 3D objects and environments.

Augmented Reality Augmented reality is a type of VR that has gained popularity within the military and an emerging group of academics who have begun to create compelling projects with it. This sort of VR begins with a real-world perspective and then augments it with various types of virtual artifacts. An example of this sort of technology is a flight simulator for the Air Force that allows the pilot and navigator to view real-world topographical information while also experiencing enemy aircraft that have been placed in the environment with which the pilot can interact.

Educational Applications of Virtual Reality Environments

In the past, immersive virtual reality applications were not very common in K–12 environments, because of the expensive computing equipment needed to create the environments. However, this is slowly changing. Most of the research and applications developed by universities initially focused on higher education, but they are steadily working their way into K–12 classrooms. Stuart and Thomas (1991) define seven uses of VR in the classroom:

- Explore existing places and things that the student would typically not have access to
- Explore real things that could not be effectively examined unless there were alterations based on size and time
- Create places, things, and events with altered qualities
- Interact and collaborate with people at a distance
- Interact with people in nonrealistic ways
- Create and manipulate abstract conceptual representatives, like data structures and mathematical functions
- Interact with avatars (virtual beings), such as historical figures and people representing different races, religions, and viewpoints.

There are plenty of examples of VR environments applied to educational settings. For example, Dede, Salzman, and Loftin (1996) have investigated how ScienceSpace, a collection of virtual worlds for the exploration of Newton's laws of motion, has aided students in learning challenging concepts in science. The visualization and manipulation of objects while working in the environments increased students' understanding of the pheonomenon being studied. Overall, students enjoyed their experience and perceived the virtual world as a fun way to learn.

Bowen Loftin and others at the Johnson Space Center in Houston, Texas, have created the Virtual Physics lab for NASA astronaut training (Delaney, 1992). This VR environment allows students to manipulate physics and science experiments relating to structural imperfections and extrinsic forces, such as friction. Students can interact with different objects and can modify the force of gravity and other physical constraints.

The Human Interface Technology Laboratory (HITL) at the University of Washington has been integrating VR learning environments into the schools via the Virtual Reality Roving Vehicles (VRRV) project. The HITL staff provides guidance to teachers regarding planning, designing, and implementing VR projects for their instructional activities. For one project, the HITL assisted teachers responsible for motivating students who are at risk to stay in school (Byrne, Holland, Moffit, Hodas, & Furness, 1994). The students created their own world in a 3-D-modeling computer application, which was transferred into the VR environment. As the students worked on their projects and later interacted with their designs in an immersive VR, they became more enthusiastic about participating in class.

The University of Missouri's Advanced Technology Center (ATC) developed a project called Virtual Harlem, which consists of approximately 10 square blocks of Harlem, New York, as it existed in the early 20th century (see Figure 7.10). The environment not only allows students to visualize the setting and context of several fictional texts in a computer-generated environment, but also enables them to interact with it by navigating through streets, with historical characters through questions and audio queues, and participate in its design (Carter, 1999). In the Virtual Harlem learning environment, students must navigate and make decisions based on various options presented to them rather than passively receive knowledge from the teacher or text. This active decision making gives students the feeling of participating in a real-world environment, and also transforms learning into exploration. Currently, student research materials help to refine and expand on

Figure 7.10   7th Avenue, Harlem, New York—Circa 1926 (© 2000 Advanced Technology Center, University of Missouri)

this base of knowledge, as students have the pleasure of not only navigating but also performing interdisciplinary research on the time period that provides extra dimensions to the learning environment.

An exciting element of this project is the networked collaborative experience that exists between CAVE units. The units allow collaboration among students who may be located anywhere around the world and who are studying the same material with access to similar hardware and software. The students can be represented as avatars or computer-generated representations of humans within the environment. Participants could interact and communicate with one another as well as with the environment. In the future, avatars will be able to facilitate role-playing within an environment. Students will be able to literally step out of their "selves" to become someone else for a while. This could have implications for studying social behaviors and race relations during the past and present.

The Virtual Harlem project has been used as a resource for students in African-American literature courses. One study found that exploration within the VR learning environment contributed to more descriptive student reflections of the Harlem Renaissance period in comparison to students who did not explore the environment (Carter, Moore, & Amelung, 2000). Even more interesting, the writing samples by the same students indicated a more positive perception of the period after experiencing the Virtual Harlem project. The results of this study lead to other concerns, such as how to accurately and ethically depict another time in history and the prominent figures within the time period. To make the decisions regarding the historical details and characteristics, we will need to include people from different disciplines, such as history and psychology, to examine and represent the "reality" within these worlds. This is a good example of how VR can integrate different disciplines while learning occurs in context.

CONCLUSIONS

Microworlds and virtual reality can be used effectively to engage students in collaborative learning that supports meaningful knowledge construction. Many efforts at collaborative learning in schools fail because the instructional tasks are not situated in appropriate contextual situations that will facilitate the transfer of knowledge to new situations. Requiring students to collaborate in order to study for multiple-choice tests will probably will not result in increased learning for any of the students. This is an issue because recall is an individual activity that is not effectively enhanced by collaboration. In addition, people have different learning styles and these learning environments support those who are more visual or kinesthetic in understanding information.

In microworlds and virtual reality simulations, learners can practice their newly acquired skills and knowledge without the unfortunate results of actual failures. Therefore, they can learn safely by simply doing and experimenting in the environments provided by microworlds and virtual reality simulations.

Furthermore, teachers and students have the ability to change and/or update the microworlds and simulations with new information and scenarios. This allows students to engage in a social construction of concepts and characters, as well as historical events and people.

THINGS TO THINK ABOUT

If you would like to reflect on the ideas presented in this chapter, then articulate your responses to the following questions and compare them with others' responses.

1. What is the relationship between physical models, computer-based models, and internal mental models? How are they alike? How are they different? What is the degree of correspondence among them?
2. How "micro" does a microworld have to be? Stated differently, how large of a task or domain can microworlds represent?
3. Most microworlds have been developed to support math and science. Can you think of what a microworld would look like for understanding political ideas like democracy, capitalism, or sociological ideas like mores, beliefs, etc.?
4. What is reality? How can it be virtual? Aren't things either real or not?
5. What is your favorite thing in the world? Imagine developing an immersive VR world that would enable you to explore that thing.

REFERENCES

Burton, R. R., Brown, J. S., & Fischer, G. (1984). Skiing as a model of instruction. In B. Rogoff & J. Lave (Eds.), *Everyday cognition: Its development in social context*. Cambridge, MA: Harvard University Press.

Byrne, C., Holland, C., Moffit, D., Hodas, S., & Furness, T. (1994). Virtual reality and "at-risk" students. Seattle, WA: Human Interface Technology Laboratory Technical Report HITL-R-94-5.

Carter, B. (1999). From imagination to reality: Using immersion technology in an African-American literature course. *Journal of the Association for Literacy and Linguistic Computing*, 14(1), 55–65.

Carter, B., Moore, J. L., & Amelung, C. (2000). Seeing is believing: Advanced visualization and the use of virtual reality in an African-American literature course. *Consciousness, Literature and the Arts*, 1(3). Retrieved February 1, 2002, from http://www.aber.ac.uk/tfts/journal

Clement, J. (1989). Learning via model construction and criticism. In J. A. Glover, R. R. Ronning, & C. R. Reynolds (Eds.), *Handbook of creativity* (pp. 341–381). New York: Plenum.

Cruz-Neira, C., Sandin, D. J., DeFanti, T. T., Kenyon, R. V., & Hart, J. C. (1992). The CAVE: Audio visual experience automatic virtual environment. *Communications of the ACM, 35*(6), 64–72.

Dede, C. J., Salzman, M., & Loftin, R. B. (1996). The development of a virtual world for learning Newtonian mechanics. In P. Brusilovsky, P. Kommers, & N. Streitz (Eds.), Multimedia, hypermedia, and virtual reality. Models, systems and application. *Proceedings of the First International Conference, MHVR 1994*. Berlin: Springer-Verlag.

Delaney, B. (1992). Virtual physics. *CyberEdge, 11*(1), 5.

Denis, M. (1991). Imagery and thinking. In C. Cornoldi & M. A. McDaniel (Eds.), *Imagery and cognition*. New York: Springer-Verlag.

diSessa, A. A, & Abelson, H. (1986). *Boxer: A reconstructible computational medium. Communications of the ACM, 29*, 859–868.

Hoffman, H. G., Hullfish, K. C., & Houston, S. (1995). Virtual reality monitoring, Seattle, WA: Human Interface Technology Laboratory Technical Report P–95–1.

Jonassen, D. H. (2000). *Computers as mindtools for schools: Engaging critical thinking*. Upper Saddle River, NJ: Merrill/Prentice Hall.

Kinzer, C., & Leu, D. J., Jr. (1997). Focus on research—the challenge of change: Exploring literary and learning in electronic environments. *Language Arts, 74*(2), 126–136.

Lave, J., & Wenger, E. (1990). *Situated learning: Legitimate peripheral participation*. Cambridge, England: Cambridge University Press.

Malone, T. W., & Lepper, M. R. (1987). Making learning fun: A taxonomy of intrinsic motivations for learning. In R. E. Snow & M. J. Farr (Eds.) *Aptitude, learning, and instruction, III: Conative and affective process analysis* (pp. 223–253). Hillsdale, NJ: Lawrence Erlbaum Associates.

Mezirow, J. (1985). A critical theory of self-directed learning. In G. Darkenwald & A. Knox (Series Eds.) & S. Brookfield (Vol. Ed.), *Self-directed learning: From theory to practice* (pp. 17–30). San Francisco: Jossey-Bass.

Myers, C. (2001a). *Thoughts on conferencing*. Denver, Colorado: Open World Learning Lab Internal Report.

Myers, C. (2001b). *Open World Learning: A Colorado non-profit working to close the educational and digital divide*. Denver, Colorado: Open World Learning Lab Internal Report.

Papert, S. (1980). *Mindstorms: Children, computers, and powerful ideas*. New York: Basic Books.

Penner, D. D. (2001). Cognition, computers, and synthetic science: Building knowledge and meaning through modeling. In W. G. Secada (Ed.), *Review of Research in Education, 25*. Washington, DC: AERA.

Reigeluth, C. M. (1983). *Instruction-design theories and models: An overview of their current status*. Hillsdale, NJ: Lawrence Erlbaum Associates.

Rieber, L. P. (1992). Computer-based microworlds: A bridge between constructivism and direct instruction. *Educational Technology Research & Development, 40*(1), 93–106.

Rieber, L. P. (1996). Seriously considering play: Designing interactive learning environments based on the blending of microworlds, simulations, and games. *Educational Technology Research & Development, 44*(2), 43–58.

Resnick, M. (1994). *Turtles, termites and traffic jams*. Cambridge, MA: MIT Press.

Stuart, R., & Thomas, J. C. (1991). *The implications of education in cyberspace. Multimedia Review, 2*, 17–27.

Zeltzer, D. (1992). Autonomy, interaction and presence. *Presence, 1*, 127–132.

Learning in Problem-Based Learning Environments

There are numerous computer-based learning systems that have been developed to engage students in a variety of problem solving. We call these systems problem-based learning environments (PBLEs). These environments engage and support students in different kinds of problem solving, from story problems to open-ended investigations and experiments. Some of these environments consist of prepackaged materials that students cannot manipulate and change, while others provide multiple spaces for student constructions and contributions.

In this chapter, we describe some of these PBLEs. We should point out that our conception of PBLEs is different from other conceptions of PBLs. The term problem-based learning (PBL) was developed by Howard Barrows and colleagues as a curricular approach to medical education (Barrows & Tamblyn, 1980) in which medical students' entire training consists of problems that lead them to a better understanding of the basic sciences in medicine. PBL is probably the single most important innovation in education in the past two decades. It is a powerful and effective method for preparing physicians to be problem solvers. However, PBL as a system entails far greater social and pedagogical changes than are possible in most K–12 schools. Problem-based learning has been generalized in the literature to any number of educational innovations that engage problem solving. In this chapter, we describe some of these technology-enhanced innovations.

STORY PROBLEMS

Although story problems may not be the most interesting kind of problem solving, they are the most prominent. Found especially in math and science courses from 1st grade through graduate school, these problems embed algorithmic problems in some shallow story context. Typically found at the back of textbook chapters, students are required to disembed the information from the story, select the relevant values, and insert them into some formula. Research shows that students are not very successful in transfering their abilities to solve problems to other problems.

There are several instructional approaches to support learning how to solve story problems, and there are numerous problem-based learning environments that employ these different approaches. The most common type of instructional approach is the tutorial. Most of the interactive learning systems that are sold to schools use this kind of approach. Tutorials typically present information in text or graphics on how to solve problems, and then ask the learners to perform part or all of the problem-solving activity in order to assess their comprehension of the method. Students respond, and the tutorial software compares a student's response with the correct answer stored in the computer's memory. Correct responses are rewarded, while incorrect responses result in the presentation of remedial instruction. Sometimes the remediation strategies are fairly sophisticated, with the software providing instruction geared to the nature of the student's error. Following the remediation, the program typically presents the problem again, providing the student another opportunity to respond correctly. Tutorials consist of sequences of these presentation-response-feedback cycles followed by quizzes that assess students' abilities.

Figures 8.1 and 8.2 show two different screens of mathematics instruction from Interactive Mathematics by Academic Systems. After having functions explained to them, students click the Apply button to practice solving problems (see Figure 8.1). Immediate feedback is provided about the correctness of the answer along with some analytical feedback intended to help learners understand their errors. In Figure 8.2, students click on the explore buttons to study a graphical representation of the functions. In tutorials such as these, students are presented with instruction, followed by practice items and feedback. The tutorial approach is effective for well-structured kinds of problems such as story problems. One can easily argue that tutorial instruction is not constructivist. We agree, however, that tutorials remain a popular approach to teaching well-structured problem solving.

Tutorials in Problem Solving (TiPS) is another computer-based learning environment that uses a more conceptual approach to teach story problem solving. Students learn to solve different kinds of math problems, such as change, compare, group, function, and vary problems (Marshall, 1995), by representing the entities in the problems in an problem structure. The TiPS program provides students with a set of diagrammatic tools that represent these different problem structures, and requires students to utilize the tools to diagrammatically analyze

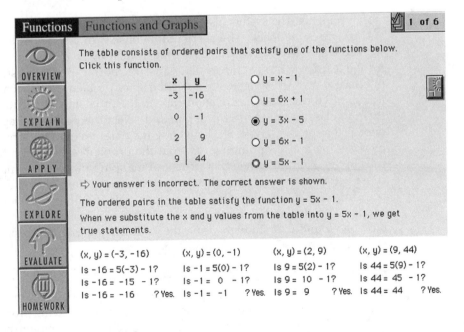

Figure 8.1 Story Problem Tutorial. Copyright 1997–2002 Academic Systems Corporation. All rights reserved.

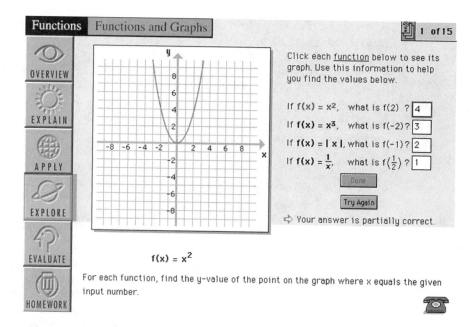

story problems. The system also contains a tutor that assesses students' responses and provides feedback. The curriculum consists of a series of lessons that use worked examples. Worked examples illustrate how an expert solves the problem for the learner to study and emulate. In TiPS, both experts and students use the interface shown in Figure 8.3 to solve the story problems. They read the problem to identify the sets and set relationships in the problem statement. This will help them to classify the type of problem and select the problem diagram that best depicts that problem type. Students drag the diagram onto the screen and fill it in by dragging and dropping words from the problem statement into appropriate cells in the diagram. When this structural mapping process is complete, students construct an arithmetic formula to calculate the solution. They then receive feedback from the computer on the accuracy of their solutions (see Figure 8.3). Derry and the TiPS Research Group (2001) conducted a pair of experiments on the interface. She found that students using the TiPS schema interface resulted in statistically greater gains by students over time.

Problem-Solving Processes   Story problems are well-structured problems that are neither the most interesting nor complicated. Most story problems have an accepted solution and method, so the primary problem-solving process is deciding which method to use. There is little need to search for information, because all necessary information is normally provided. What the TiPS environment adds to the story problem-solving process is conceptual modeling of the task, which is essential

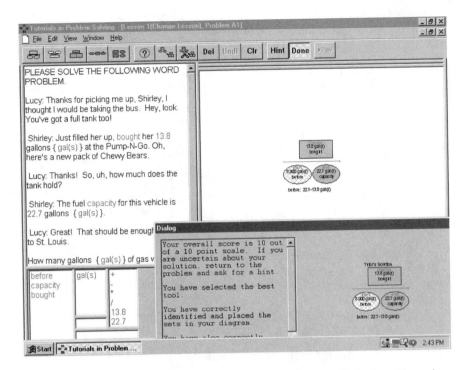

Figure 8.3 TiPS Screen Showing Student Solution and System Evaluation. Wisconsin Center for Education Research, University of Wisconsin–Madison.

for understanding and the ability to transfer that problem-solving ability. The first part of the solution process is to select the most appropriate model from the menu bar that represents the kind of story problem being solved. So, although learners are not constructing their own models, they are using models.

LABORATORY PROBLEMS

In the sciences, solving laboratory problems is a prevalent activity. Laboratory activities normally require following a set of procedures, observing the results and taking measures of the processes, and then inferring what happened. Figure 8.4 shows a screen from volumetric analysis of chlorine in an environment called ChemLab. This environment enables learners to conduct a wide range of chemistry experiments, take notes, make observations, and take measurements. The icons on the top of the screen represent laboratory equipment and processes that can be used in the experiment. Because of inherent dangers in conducting laboratory experiments, many teachers are choosing to use these virtual experiments that faithfully represent most aspects of the experiment, except the smells.

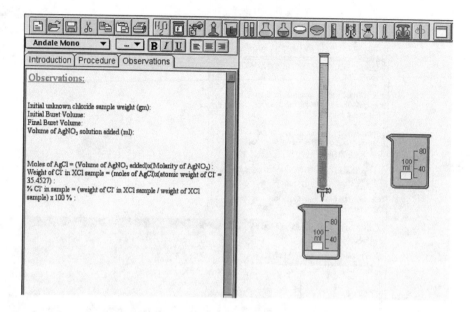

Figure 8.4 Chemistry Experiment in ChemLab. Permission granted by Model Science Software, Waterloo, Ontario.

Problem-Solving Processes Laboratory experiments are slightly more ill-structured and complex problems than story problems. Although most of the processes are predetermined, the experimenter can try new procedures. The labs primarily require decision making. The environment itself allows the learners to construct simulated physical models of the experimental process.

INVESTIGATION PROBLEMS: THE ASTRONOMY VILLAGE

Developed by the National Aeronautics and Space Administration (NASA), The Astronomy Village (AV) provides rich multimedia resources and exploration tools in a virtual observatory community (Figure 8.5) to support exploration and scientific inquiry, data and image analysis, and learning of important concepts and methods of astronomy. In teams of three, students select and carry out up to 10 stellar investigations (each lasting approximately four weeks). To help the students conduct their astronomical investigations, the village provides multimedia resources including more than 100 articles on astronomy, 335 images of stellar phenomena, and video interviews with astronomers. Students also learn to use a powerful suite of tools, including e-mail, a replica browser, an image browser, simulations, image processing software, a calculator, and a Web browser. The AV

Figure 8.5 The Astronomy Village. Copyright © 1995 by Wheeling Jesuit College/Classroom of the Future (WJC/COTF). Taken from *Astronomy Village* CD-ROM.

contains an Orientation Center, Conference Center, Library, Computer Lab, Auditorium, Cafeteria (for informal conversations), and of course the Observatory on the Hill (Figure 8.5).

Like all NASA multimedia products, the AV requires student to select an investigation, develop a plan, and carry it out. The AV supports 10 different investigations, including:

- *Search for a Supernova*—uses neutrino data to locate a supernova
- *Looking for a Stellar Nursery*—views Omega nebula using different wavelengths
- *Variable Stars*—identifies a Cepheid variable star in another galaxy
- *Search for Nearby Stars*—tracks movement of stars' positions as the Earth circles the sun

- *Extragalatic Zoo*—shows different galaxies and clusters
- *Wedges of the Universe*—views depths of space in two wedges of sky
- *Search for a "Wobbler"*—looks for stars that wobble in their motion
- *Search for Planetary Building Blocks*—examines Orion nebula for proplanetary disks
- *Search for Earth-Crossing Objects*—looks for asteroids that cross Earth's path
- *Observatory Site Selection*—selects a site for an observatory

Selecting an investigation begins in the Conference Center, which contains text and video descriptions of each investigation, or in the Auditorium to listen to lectures on each investigation. Having selected an interesting investigation, students develop a plan using the Research Path Diagram, which provides a path to guide them through their investigation, including background research that is needed, data collection, data analysis, data interpretation, and presentation. Students use the Auditorium, Library, and Replica Viewer to gather background research and then go to the Observatory to collect data. In the Observatory (Figure 8.6), they can use an image browser (Figure 8.7) or select a particular observatory from which to view the sky. Observations must be carefully planned in order to provide the best data.

At the completion of an investigation, students must make a presentation to their class and other astronomers about their findings. The presentation summarizes all of the data that they have collected and analyzed. Scoring rubrics and evaluation sheets are provided to help guide the evaluation of these presentations and all other student activities.

Problem-Solving Processes   The Astronomy Village supports a wide variety of well-structured and ill-structured problems. In a study conducted recently, students joined a "research team" and chose Nearby Star, 1 of 10 investigations to complete (Shin, Jonassen, & McGee, in press). The goal of the project was to determine the distance of a nearby star from the Earth. In the background research, students collected relevant information by reading articles in the AV Library and listening to lectures at the AV Conferences. The background research included the parallax principle, Earth motion, characteristics of nearby stars, principles of trigonometry, and measurement of distance of nearby stars. After collecting appropriate information, the students observed images in the AV observatory to identify Nearby Stars in our galaxy. Based on the recorded images, they observed the movement of stars in the sky and calculated the positional shift during the 6-month period at the Image Processing Lab. This process is called the Data Collection phase.

The students analyzed the collected data to calculate the parallax angle of the Nearby Star and used it to calculate the distance of the Nearby Star from the Earth. Based on the results, the students interpreted how star movements in the sky can be employed to measure the distance of Nearby Stars. These phases were called Data Analysis and Data Interpretation. Finally, each student team presented its procedures and results to the class.

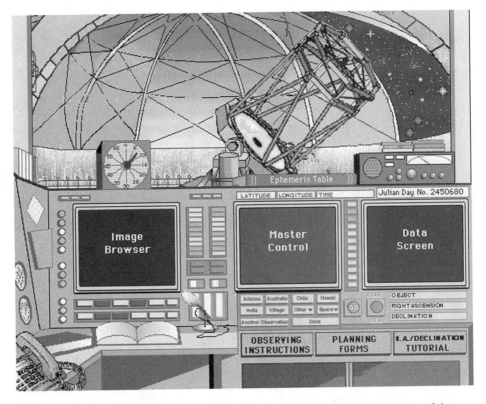

Figure 8.6   Observatory. Copyright © 1995 by Wheeling Jesuit College/Classroom of the Future (WJC/COTF). Taken from *Astronomy Village* CD-ROM.

These activities consisted of information searching, a lot of decision making, and some designing. Students had to design the nature of the experiment. We also found that the skills required to solve more well-structured problems were different from the skills required to solve more ill-structured problems.

INVESTIGATION PROBLEMS: EXPLORING THE NARDOO

The Nardoo is an imaginary river in Australia that provides a rich context for ecological investigations to support biology, geography, social science, and language and media studies. While it is focused on ecology, the Nardoo's more general purpose is to engage skills in problem solving, measuring, collating, and communicating. While exploring the Nardoo, students study the interactions between living organisms and the physical and chemical environment in which they operate,

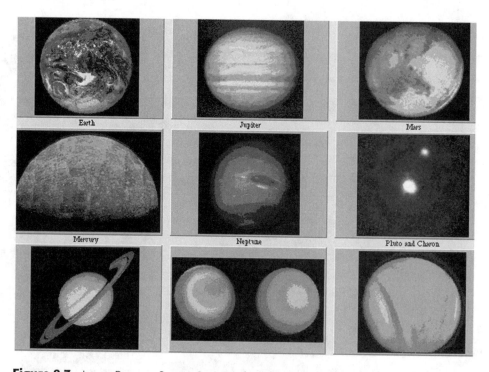

Earth   Jupiter   Mars

Mercury   Neptune   Pluto and Charon

Figure 8.7 Image Browser. Screen Capture of NASA Images Taken From *Astronomy Village* CD-ROM. Copyright © 1995 by Wheeling Jesuit College/Classroom of the Future (WJC/COTF).

with particular emphasis on the role and impact of the human species at both a macro and micro level. It is an active learning environment in which students participate in teams, investigate issues (take measurements, interpret maps and graphs, analyze data), and communicate their results.

Students begin their investigation of the Nardoo River in the Water Research Centre (Figure 8.8), where three different specialists describe the investigations and provide help when requested. Items in the Centre are hot buttons providing access to investigations (clicking on the River Investigation board takes students to a visual identification of the different investigations [Figure 8.9], a file cabinet full of information, video and radio clipboards, computer catalog, plant and animal book, text tablet, and a clippings folder).

Each investigation focuses on a different problem with different issues. They include flood problems, dams and catchment basins, algae blooms, coal mining, wildlife changes, logging, overgrown water plants and weeds, wetlands degradation, and farming impacts. One of the investigations focuses on how chemical pollution has affected the Nardoo River ecosystem:

Many of the children of Pilliga Crossing enjoyed fishing from the banks of the Nardoo River during their spare time. They noticed an increasing number of dead

Figure 8.8 Water Research Centre. Courtesy Interactive Multimedia Learning Laboratory, University of Wollongong, Australia. Reprinted with permission.

Figure 8.9 River Investigations. Courtesy Interactive Multimedia Learning Laboratory, University of Wollongong, Australia. Reprinted with permission.

fish floating around their favorite fishing holes. Local media carried news reports dealing with this and other incidents which may be related.

Your task: Find possible reasons for the fish kill. Prepare a report that details your findings, as well as any procedures that the community might adopt to fix the problem.

In this investigation, students may access a rich variety of information sources about the investigation, including television reports (e.g., *Fish found dead in river, Chemical dumping to be fined, Chemical dumping witnessed*), radio reports (e.g., *Chemical disposal policy outlined, Tip poisons nearby river*), and newspaper articles (e.g., *Keep out of river, Acid burns school boys at local tip, Industry suspected of dumping acid*). Students also have access to a plant and animal book to see how changes to the wetlands will affect the flora and fauna of the region. Students can sample the river at any point (see Figure 8.10) for a variety of pollutants (phosphorus, nitrogen, pesticides, oil), as well as for indicators of the stream's health (pH, water temperature, flow rate, turbidity, algae, oxygen). Their task is to identify the sources of pollution along the river, as well as to predict the effects of those pollutants on the river animals and plants. It is hoped that the students will form

Figure 8.10 Chemical Pollution Investigation With PDA. Courtesy Interactive Multimedia Learning Laboratory, University of Wollongong, Australia. Reprinted with permission.

an opinion about the need for environmental pollution controls. To navigate and manipulate the multimedia environment, students use their PDA (personal digital assistant). The PDA (see Figure 8.10) provides access to information, navigation, and exploration tools, permitting students to take measurements, manipulate data and text, research multimedia information, and plan activities.

To support various investigations, the Nardoo program provides a number of simulators. For example, in order to learn about water usage, students can access the simulator in Figure 8.11. In this simulator, students identify the number

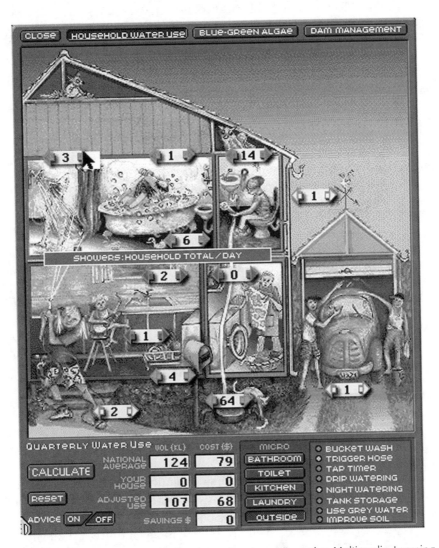

Figure 8.11 Water Usage Simulator. Courtesy Interactive Multimedia Learning Laboratory, University of Wollongong, Australia. Reprinted with permission.

of baths, showers, toilet flushes, dish washings, car washings, lawn waterings, and so on, their family uses per day. The simulator calculates the volume of water usage and compares it with national averages. Students can then implement various water-saving features in each of the rooms (bathroom, kitchen, laundry), rerun the simulation, and determine the level of savings attributable to these devices.

The Nardoo River multimedia program provides a problem-solving environment that enables students to actively manipulate a complex environment, seek information, and conduct investigations in order to construct their own knowledge about ecological issues. The teacher's guide provides a number of activities for both individual and collaborative use. This environment is another excellent example of a multimedia-based learning environment that can be used to engage learners in meaning making. It possesses most of the attributes of the learning environments described in chapter 7.

INVESTIGATION PROBLEMS: SAILING ON THE *MIMI*

One of the best known and most revered of educational programs, *The Voyages of the Mimi* (*Voyage* and *Second Voyage of the Mimi*), combines video, software, and print materials, along with a real sailboat, into an interdisciplinary science and math curriculum for the middle grades (4–8). Developed at the Bank Street College of Education, the Voyages, like anchored instruction described in chapter 5, contextualize and anchor learning in a series of video adventures. Students conduct open-ended and interdisciplinary investigations and scientific explorations. In the first series of the *Mimi* adventures, a video tells a series of adventure stories about a scientific expedition to study whales on the *Mimi*. The second series of stories tells of archaeologists in search of a lost Mayan city. The adventures encountered by the *Mimi* on the videos include (among others):

Whalewatch—provides a firsthand look at whale researchers at work and explores the variety of whale species

On the Shoals—an electrical failure leaves the *Mimi* in danger of running aground in the shallow waters of George's Shoals

Mapping the Blue Part—scientists map the ocean floor using data collected by ship and by satellite

Counting Whales—the crew conducts a whale census, using the computer to help analyze the data

Whale Bones—fossil records, evolution, field research methods, and the natural history of whales are the focus of work at the Smithsonian Institution

Going Fishing—the crew observes humpback whale feeding behavior, and students get a glimpse of day-to-day life on a seagoing research expedition

Songs in the Sea—an expedition to the studio of Katy Payne, whose work is the study of whale songs

The Second Voyage of the Mimi continues the adventure with a group of archaeologists wintering off Mexico's Yucatan peninsula in order to study the Mayan civilization. Like the first series, it combines dramatic episodes and documentary expeditions to develop mathematical and scientific concepts in grades 4 through 8.

Replete with information about whales, ships, the sea, marine science, and survival techniques, the adventures in *The Voyage of the Mimi* provoke students' interest in scientific and mathematical concepts by observing their use in real-life situations. The adventures take place aboard the sailboat *Mimi* in the North Atlantic. Like the *Scientists in Action* series described in chapter 5, the Voyages introduce scientists who use science and math in their work. A series of documentaries explain the science and math themes from the adventure, such as global weather patterns, sampling techniques, and navigation.

Each adventure is supplemented with a wealth of print materials (lesson plans, activities, and projects) that help to integrate the video programs into science, math, social studies, language arts, music, and art classrooms. Additionally, software provides students with problem-solving games and simulations to enable them to practice the skills and concepts explored in the video material. For instance, Pirate's Gold challenges you, as the captain of a ship searching for treasure, to locate sunken treasure so that your diver can recover it. (*Note:* You have only three tanks of air to dive with.) Using chart books that show the latitude and longitude of the treasure, the students must navigate the ship most efficiently among hazards to locate the treasure.

Additionally, many students have the opportunity to experience the *Mimi* firsthand. The *Mimi*, a 70-foot ketch, docks in ports up and down the Atlantic Coast. Over the past 6 years more than 150,000 school children have attended dockside learning festivals that included hands-on demonstrations of *Mimi*-related science and technology. The students get to visit the *Mimi* and ask Captain Granville questions. Some classes share their firsthand experiences via the Internet with other land-locked classrooms unable to attend the *Mimi* Fest. They ask students from around the country to e-mail their questions for the class to ask the experts at the *Mimi* Fest about the *Mimi*. The host class students ask the questions for their partner guest class and, after the *Mimi* Fest, formulate the answers and send all the questions and answers to each participating classroom. They also transport a banner from the guest class to the *Mimi* Fest and display them.

Problem-Solving Processes   The Nardoo River and the Voyages of the *Mimi* are both great environments that engage and support problem solving in students. Most of these investigations in these environments are open-ended. That is, the students get to make decisions about what to investigate and how to investigate it. In such experiments, students solve design problems, the most complex kind. Designing investigations requires a great deal of information searching within and outside these environments, and significant decision making in order to determine appropriate methods. Like the Astronomy Village, these environments function as a virtual model of a physical environment. These

PBLEs represent one of the most complete and compelling kinds of activities that students can engage in—simulations. It would be more engaging for students to be discovering and planning their own investigations; however, that kind of activity is beyond the scope of most schools.

CONCLUSIONS

These PBLEs are examples of a kind of problem-based software that is becoming more available to schools. These environments engage students in a wide variety of kinds of problem solving, from simple story problems to complex design experiments. Unfortunately, these kinds of environments are not available in all disciplines or for all content domains. Finding these activities may require some digging. We believe that when you find them and allow your students to exploit the environments fully, the reward will be obvious.

THINGS TO THINK ABOUT

If you would like to reflect on the ideas presented in this chapter, then articulate your responses to the following questions and compare them with others' responses.

1. Story problems are the most common kind of problems that students encounter. Why? What is it about schooling that makes more complex and ill-structured kinds of problems so difficult to implement?
2. Developing conceptual models of problem types is so important to being able to transfer problem-solving skills. Are there other technologies described in this book that could help students to construct models of different kinds of problems?
3. What would a laboratory in health education, foreign languages, or English literature look like? What kinds of problems would students solve? What kinds of tools would they need?
4. Astronomy Village shows that the same environment with a set of tools can support a large number of investigations. What are the problem-solving tools that make this possible? Can you think of similar tools in other domains?
5. The Nardoo River includes a simulation that students can manipulate to test different hypotheses. How does such a simulation differ from laboratory activities?
6. The *Mimi* combines computer-based with real-life adventure. Can you think of other activities that do this or should do this?

REFERENCES

Barrows, H. S., & Tamblyn, R. M. (1980). *Problem-based learning: An approach to medical education.* New York: Springer Publishing Company.

Derry, S. J., & the TiPS Research Group. (2001). *Development and assessment of tutorials in problem solving* (TiPS): *A remedial mathematics tutor.* Final Report to the Office of Naval Research (N00014–93–1–0310). Madison, WI: Wisconsin Center for Education Research, University of Wisconsin–Madison.

Marshall, S. P. (1995). *Schemas in problem solving.* Cambridge: Cambridge University Press.

Shin, N., Jonassen, D. H., & McGee, S. (in press). Predictors of well-structured and ill-structured problem solving in an astronomy simulation. *Journal of Research in Science Teaching.*

Assessing Constructive Learning and Problem Solving With Technology

Throughout this book, we have provided guidance for assessing each type of learning activity. However, we recognize how important it is for educators to be able to construct quality assessments for these nontraditional learning experiences. This final chapter more thoroughly addresses how to assess the constructive learning and problem solving activities described in this book.

ASSESSING MEANINGFUL LEARNING: AUTHENTIC AND PERFORMANCE ASSESSMENT

This entire book has focused on developing meaningful learning activities based on the effective use of technology to support problem-solving activities. We have argued throughout this book that meaningful learning should be authentic and therefore complex. Just as the learning activities we have described engage learners in meaningful experiences as manifested by the problem-solving activities described, so must our assessments as well. Educators are finally beginning to understand that in order to evaluate authentic learning, we must use *authentic assessments*. In the last decade, calls for authentic assessment have encouraged educators to discard outdated evaluative methods designed to *sort* students, in favor of *assessment systems* designed to provide important information required to *improve performance*. Similarly, for our assessments to be "congruent" or in alignment with the activities we have described, we must adopt authentic and/or performance assessment practices.

Performance assessment refers to the process of assessing a student's skills by asking the student to perform tasks that require those skills. Performances in science might examine the ability to design a device to perform a particular function or to mount an argument supported by experimental evidence.

One source (Wiggins, 1990) defines performance assessment as having these elements:

- Students must construct a response or a product, rather than simply select from a set of pre-defined alternatives or answers. So, in chapter 5 we saw that students can create or "construct" a news broadcast rather than completing a multiple choice test on current events.
- Assessment then consists of direct observation or assessment of student behavior on tasks or on the product that they produced, and further, the tasks or products are designed to resemble activities commonly required for functioning in the world outside school.

In essence, the performance of the learning task and the assessment tasks are interwoven and inseparable. Rather than assessing an activity that is completely separate from the activity that learners engage in, we assess the product of that very same learning activity; we assess the learners' performance.

Other terms—authentic assessment, alternative assessment—are sometimes used for performance assessment. These terms however, are not interchangeable. Alternative assessment generally refers to assessments that are in opposition to standardized achievement tests (e.g., the SAT or ACT exam) and to objective test item formats. On the other hand, authentic assessment is closely related to performance assessment and means that learners engage in educational tasks that are meaningful and directly related to real tasks that they may need to perform in the future. For example, having social studies students engage in an activity to poll public opinion on a local issue would be an authentic assessment task as compared to having these same social studies students take a closed-book exam on principles of democracy.

Performance assessment activities can take many forms including all those described in this book, plus more traditional activities such as conducting experiments, computing mathematical problems in authentic contexts, or writing extended essays. In all cases, the students should be aware of the scoring system and the criteria used to determine the assessment scores for the activity. This leads to the main tool used in performance assessments to define and communicate those assessment criteria—rubrics.

ASSESSING PERFORMANCE AND CONSTRUCTIVE LEARNING WITH TECHNOLOGY: RUBRICS

The focus of this chapter is to help you learn to develop and use performance assessments that will provide you with the data you need for assessment purposes, and also provide students with feedback vital to improving their performance on the authentic and complex activities presented in this book. How do we improve performance while assessing it? The simplest answer is that complex learning cannot be assessed or evaluated using any single measure. Rather, we must examine both the processes and products of student learning. Throughout this book, we have provided criteria for evaluating students' uses of different technologies. These criteria can be used to develop rubrics for evaluating performance. Rubrics have become a popular method for authentic assessment.

Rubrics and Meaningful Learning Environments

Many terms are used to name the documents or methods we use to assess learner performance. These include scoring grids (because they are often in grid form), scoring schemes, rating scales and, perhaps the most commonly used term—rubrics.

By definition, a *rubric* is a code, or a set of codes, designed to govern action. In educational settings, the term has evolved to mean a tool to be used for assessing a complex performance. In schools, rubrics often take the form of a scale or set of scales. In a typical classroom, for example, oral reports are mysteriously *graded* (neither students nor teachers can really tell you where the grades come from) and a few comments generally accompany the grade. Little substantive feedback about the performance is made available to the student, who cares only about the grade received.

Consider, instead, a meaningful learning environment in which the students and teachers work together to develop a rubric that will promote intentional learning by identifying important aspects of the performance, use the rubric to gather information about the learner's performance, and use the information as input for reflection on the performance. That reflection provides evidence to improve the performance. Although rubrics can be an important tool for innovative educators who set out to create and enhance technology-rich, meaningful learning environments, rubrics are often created and used in ways that defeat their purpose. In this section we will show you how to develop good rubrics and to think about using rubrics to assess not only student performance but also the power of the learning environments you create.

The Anatomy of a Rubric   A rubric is generally represented as a set of scales used to assess a complex performance and to provide rich information used to improve performance. For example, consider the task of making an effective oral presentation. There are several elements (components) that combine to form an effective oral presentation, including (but not limited to) organization, pace, vocal qualities, and use of visual aids. So, a simplified, but useful, rubric used to assess a group discussion might include scales for different elements, something like:

Student Participation in Group Discussions		
Inadequately Never participates; quiet/passive	. . . **Adequately** Participates as much as other group members	. . . **Exceptionally** Participates more than any other group member
Comments Related to Topic Under Discussion		
Inadequately Comments ramble, distract from topic	. . . **Adequately** Comments are usually pertinent, occasionally wander from topic	. . . **Exceptionally** Comments are always related to topic

These rubrics are clearer and more informative than simply assigning a letter grade, but there are several ways to enhance the value of this rubric. First, let's establish a common vocabulary to use when discussing rubrics: A rubric is a set of scales, one for each criterion that is considered important. The scale for each element consists of several *ratings* that describe the different levels of performance that might be expected.

Characteristics of a Good Rubric   The most effective and useful rubrics tend to display certain important characteristics. We will discuss these characteristics briefly, along with the most common pitfalls experienced by novices. Finally, we will develop a Rubric for Developing Effective Rubrics in order to demonstrate these characteristics.

- **In an effective rubric, all important elements are included**. If something is important enough to assess, consider it an element and develop a scale with ratings that describe it. By definition, the rubric identifies (both for the assessor and the student) the aspects of the performance that are considered important. Consider the rubric a sort of contract between educator and student, and resist the temptation to assess anything not included in the rubric. If you forgot an important element, then renegotiate the rubric.

- **In an effective rubric, each element is unidimensional**. Avoid using elements that are really *molecules*. In chemistry, an *element* is irreducible. Water is a molecule, composed of both hydrogen and oxygen—it can be separated into these elements, which cannot be further separated. Likewise, in the preliminary example presented in our first rubric, the so-called element "Voice Qualities" is really a combination of things that should be broken down more completely, perhaps into separate elements of "Volume" and "Intonation." The penalty for attempting to assess molecules rather than elements is that assigning ratings is more difficult, as is deriving specific feedback on which to base attempts to improve performance. Just what was it about the voice quality that was not adequate?

- **In an effective rubric, ratings are distinct, comprehensive, and descriptive**. The ratings should cover the range of expected performances. Some elements are best assessed in a simple, 2-rating scale—a yes/no distinction—while others might require as many as seven distinct ratings. For example, the "Volume" element in an oral report might simply be assessed as "too quiet" or "loud enough," while an element like "social interaction" might justifiably involve 5 or more ratings.

A common problem in rubric design involves an attempt to use a similar scale for all elements; for example, using a standard 5-point scale.

Weak	Poor	Acceptable	Good	Excellent

Although it might seem simpler and cleaner to use such a scale for each element, can you really describe the difference between ratings of "Weak" and "Poor," or between "Good" and "Excellent," say, for example, for the pace of an oral presentation? Would these assessments be defensible, or too subjective? Also, when a standard scale is used for multiple elements, you lose a lot of information that is better transmitted by descriptive ratings rather than generic labels. For example, a student might learn more from a presentation that had been rated as "Boring" than from one that received a "Weak" rating in an element titled "Motivation." Use labels that make sense and describe the behaviors, and use just enough of them to cover the range of possibilities.

- **An effective rubric communicates clearly with both students and parents**. The ultimate purpose of a rubric is to improve performance. This is accomplished by clarifying expectations and by providing important information about progress toward the desired goal states. Rubrics convey the complexity of the task and focus intentional learning. The feedback their use provides serves as an important baseline for reflection by both learners and educators. For these purposes to be realized, the rubric must communicate clearly with those it is to serve. Make sure that all who use the rubric (learners, parents, and educators) share a common understanding of all of the terms used. This common understanding is often achieved as the educators and students develop the rubric collaboratively, after which students explain it to their parents. This is a great way to develop metacognition (understanding of cognitive processes used), and it helps students regulate their learning as they proceed through the complex tasks offered by meaningful learning environments. Avoid educational jargon and words with weak or several meanings. Consider developing, preferably with students, descriptions of each element and each rating, or using elaborate, full-sentence rating labels instead of single terms.

• **An effective rubric provides rich information about the multiple aspects of the performance and avoids the temptation to create a contrived summary score.** Despite the fact that the real value of a rubric lies in its ability to provide information on the separate elements that comprise a complex task, novice users (especially teachers in the public schools) seem compelled to turn the ratings given on individual *elements* into *scores* for each element, and then to combine these scores to form a total score and then, worse yet, a *grade*. When individual elements are combined, information that could improve performance is lost. When ratings are treated as numeric scores and combined, elements of more and less importance are generally treated as if they were of equal value, and an inaccurate picture of the performance is created. For example, suppose that ratings for "Organization" and "Intonation" are combined after using a rubric to assess an oral presentation. Generally, the scores are added in a way that makes the two appear equally important. Even when the different elements are combined using some sort of weighting system that assigns different numbers of points based on the importance of the element, when scores are combined, attention is paid to the total at the expense of the information about how to improve performance on each element.

Heuristics for Developing an Effective Rubric   Developing rubrics is a complex task. As is the case in most complex tasks, there's no single "right answer." For most activities for which a rubric might be an appropriate assessment device, it is quite likely that different people would develop different rubrics, each with its own set of advantages and shortcomings. Although there is not a single right way to go about developing a rubric, the following set of heuristics will help to provide some direction to your initial rubric development activities. As you become more proficient, you will no doubt refine these heuristics to meet your own needs. We've presented the heuristics as a sequential list, but it is likely you will need to revisit steps as needed.

• Start by writing a few sentences that define the importance of the topic of the rubric. Why should learners perform this activity? This will help as you move through the rest of the rubric development process.

- Make a list of the major "elements" of the activity or topic. An element is essentially an important component or criterion of the overall task or activity. You should create elements for every aspect of the activity that you wish to assess. Additionally, as described in the characteristics of a good rubric, your elements should be *unidimensional*. That means they should be single items that can't be reduced to a set of other items. When your elements are not unidimensional, you will have a hard time defining the actual performance activities that define the element. A general rule of thumb would be that you should have somewhere between 3 and 7 elements. If you feel you need more than that, you may need to consider separate rubrics. For example, for a rubric for multimedia presentations, we might define 3 elements: organization, content and delivery.

- For each element, you have several activities to develop your rubric:

    ✓ Define the element—what activities define that element? What is it you wish to see in the students' performance relative to that element? For instance for the multimedia presentation example, we might define organization as the thoughtful structuring of the elements of the presentation in order to achieve the stated objectives.

    ✓ Define the rating scale for each element—remember that you shouldn't necessarily use the same rating scale for all elements. Refer to the characteristics of an effective rubric for more hints on defining a rating scale. You'll want to make sure that the scale is descriptive of the element in question. For the organization of the multimedia presentation, the scale might be: inadequate, adequate, and excellent.

    ✓ Define the meanings of each scale item—each must be defined in action- or behavior-oriented terms. This is probably the hardest work involved in rubric creation. It isn't very difficult to decide that you will have a rating scale of three levels, but clearly defining what each level of the scale means can be hard work. It is in many senses like writing a good instructional objective—and if, in fact, you have already specified very clear objectives for the performance task, you'll definitely want to refer to those objectives for guidance on the content of your rubrics.

- Here's a definition in specific action- and product-oriented terms of an "inadequate organization" for a multimedia presentation:

    ✓ The presentation was untitled
    ✓ The objective was not stated
    ✓ The objective was unclear
    ✓ The outline or storyboard was not provided
    ✓ The outline or storyboard provided did not match the content of the presentation

✓ The speaker notes were not prepared

✓ The speaker notes were present, but were not well enough prepared to allow for a smooth, polished speaking role

✓ Rehearse the presentation using the speaker notes until a smooth delivery is attained

On the other end of the spectrum, here's a description of "excellent."

- ✓ All the descriptors of an effective organization were presented
- ✓ The sequencing of events built a compelling, even artistic expression of the idea, opinion, or argument being presented

- All aspects of a rubric should be focused on providing useful feedback to students that will help them to improve performance. As you develop the definitions of each scale item, it is also useful to develop recommendations that are appropriate for students when they achieve that particular rating. Returning to our organization element for the "inadequate" performance, the recommendations might include:

✓ Select a title after writing the objective and make choices about content and organization

✓ Rewrite the objective after a rough draft of the presentation

✓ Utilize peer editing to get feedback concerning the sequence of storyboard elements

✓ Rewrite speaker notes in a way that effectively prompts the speaker to deliver a smooth performance

Creating these recommendations up front will help you to provide students with consistent feedback based on the rubric definition.

Once you've followed these guidelines, you'll want to revisit the rubric you've created. The next section describes a rubric for examining the effectiveness of the rubric you've just created.

A RUBRIC FOR ASSESSING THE EFFECTIVENESS OF A RUBRIC

Even when you follow the heuristics described in the previous section, developing rubrics is still a difficult task. A rubric is effective to the extent that it helps learners focus on the important elements of a performance and provides information on which they can reflect and base strategies for growth. Most rubrics can be improved by a sincere attempt to assess them against the rubric in Figure 9.1 on page 235.

ELEMENTS
_____

Comprehensiveness: Are all of the important elements of the performance identified?

Important elements are missing (attach list of missing elements). | All important elements are identified.

Unidimensionality: Are the elements irreducible, or do they represent factors that are better addressed separately?

More than one element should be broken down (attach list). | One element should be broken down. | All elements are unidimensional.

RATINGS
_____

Distinctiveness: Do the ratings represent clearly different categories, or is there overlap or ambiguity?

Ratings for one or more elements seem to overlap (attach list of elements). | Ratings for each element are distinct from one another.

Comprehensiveness: Do the ratings cover the full range of expected performances?

Ratings are missing (attach list of suggested additions). | All important ratings are identified.

Descriptiveness: Do the ratings provide meaningful input for reflection?

Several ratings have generic or minimally useful labels (attach list). | Few ratings have generic or minimally useful labels (attach list). | All ratings communicate clearly.

CLARITY
_____

(the extent to which key stakeholders will understand)

Few students will understand all of the terms used in elements and ratings (attach list of suggestions). | Most students will understand most of the terms used in elements and ratings (attach list of suggestions). | All students will understand.

Among Parents

Few parents will understand all of the terms used in elements and ratings (attach list of suggestions). | Most parents will understand most of the terms used in elements and ratings (attach list of suggestions). | All parents will understand.

Quality of Information Provided

Misses many opportunities for information to communicate clearly about the quality of the performance. | Adequate information is provided to serve as the basis for growth. | Lots of specifics are provided to facilitate development.

Resists Temptation of Generic Scales

"Generic" scales seem to compromise the value of the rubric (attach list of offending elements). | The scale for each element reflects a sincere effort to identify distinctive ratings.

Resists Temptation to Summarize

Information of value may be overlooked because a summary collapsing categories is used (attach list of suggested additions). | No attempt to create an overall score or grade is evident.

Figure 9.1   Rubric for Assessing Rubrics

USING ASSESSMENT RUBRICS

In order to gain the maximum power that rubrics offer, innovative educators creating meaningful learning environments should consider the following tips:

- Develop rubrics collaboratively with learners. This is an outstanding opportunity to get students thinking about what expert performance looks like, and to help students learn how to learn.
- Encourage learners to use the rubrics to guide them during the learning process. Throughout this book, we have promoted the idea of intentional learning. When rubrics are made public before the learning activity begins, students can use the content of rubrics to focus their activities.
- Encourage students to explain the rubrics to parents and other interested individuals, perhaps in the context of student-led conferences during which they describe the progress they're making and the lessons they have learned.
- View rubrics as providing important information educators and learners can use to select learning activities, rather than as evaluative devices with which to label, sort, or grade students. Gaps between what is reported and what is desired on a single element should be viewed as opportunities for growth.
- View rubrics as powerful tools in your own professional development. Consider designing a rubric that will help you become a more effective educator in promoting meaningful learning. Ask peers to develop it with you, and perhaps to use it to assess your progress from time to time. These assessments, combined with your own, can be the most important factor in your development as an innovative educator.
- Use rubrics to help you assess the quality and power of the learning environments you create, as well as the progress of individuals. In the following section, we create a rubric you might wish to modify and use to help you assess the environments you create. Using such a tool, you are likely to identify additional ways to enhance the educational experience you provide for your students.

ASSESSING CONSTRUCTIVIST USES OF TECHNOLOGY

Technologies should be used in the pursuit of meaningful learning. Nearly a century's worth of research and experience in implementing learning technologies have proven that they teach no better than teachers. That is, when used to deliver instructional messages, students generally learn no differently from technologies or teachers. Richard Clark has for many years argued that technologies are "mere vehicles" that deliver instructional messages to learners, much the same as trucks deliver groceries to supermarkets (Morrison, 1994). It doesn't matter which vehicles you use; they are all equivalent in their ability to deliver instructional groceries.

In contrast, we have claimed that instructional delivery is the wrong issue. We argue that technologies should not be used as conveyors and deliverers of the designer's message to a passive learner. Rather, they should be used as tools that students learn with (Jonassen, Campbell, & Davidson, 1994). Why? Because when learners are passive receptacles of technology-delivered messages to be consumed and regurgitated, they are not learning meaningfully. Alternatively, when students learn by using technologies as tools for growing and sharing their own groceries, they are learning meaningfully. We have argued throughout this book that technologies should engage students in meaningful learning, where they are intentionally and actively processing information while pursuing authentic tasks together in order to construct personal and socially shared meaning for the phenomena they are exploring and manipulating. Using technologies to help them articulate and reflect on what they know is the glue that holds personally constructed knowledge together.

Now, we offer a rubric you might find useful in refining the learning activities you create. In doing so, we are asking you to assess how constructive students' learning is. That is, are students active, constructive, authentic, intentional, and collaborative? We offer it as a starting point, not as a definitive answer. We anticipate that you will modify this rubric to help you answer the questions of greatest importance to you, to your students, and to their parents.

Assessing Active Learning, where learners explore and manipulate the components and parameters of technology-based environments and observe the results of their activities. If your learning activity or environment includes active learning, to what extent does the environment promote manipulation of real-world objects and observations based on these activities? Figure 9.2 provides a rubric for assessing active learning.

Assessing Constructive Learning, where learners articulate what they know and have learned and reflect on its meaning and importance in larger social and intellectual contexts. If your learning activity or environment requires constructive learning, to what extent does the environment cause learners to perceive puzzling dissonance and form mental models to explain incongruity? Figure 9.3 provides a rubric for assessing constructive learning.

Assessing Intentional Learning, where learners determine their own goals and regulate and manage their activities. If your learning activity or environment requires intentional learning, to what extent does the environment cause learners to pursue important, well-articulated goals to which they are

Learner Interaction With Real-World Objects		
Little of the learner's time is spent engaged with tools and objects found outside school.		Learners are often engaged in activities involving tools and objects found outside school.
Observation and Reflection		
Students rarely think about or record the results of actions taken during activities.	Students often stop and think about the activities in which they are engaged.	Students share frequent observations about their activity with peers and interested adults.
Learner Interactions		
Students manipulated none of the variables or controls in environment.	Students manipulated some variables and controls in environment.	Students manipulated all or nearly all variables/controls in environment.
Tool Use		
Students used no cognitive tools.	Students used some cognitive tools to support explorations/ manipulations.	Students used nearly all cognitive tools effectively.

Figure 9.2   Rubrics for Assessing Active Learning

Dissonance/Puzzling		
Students engage in learning activities disparity because activities are required, rather than an intrinsic interest.	Learners frequently seem to be operating based on a sincere curiosity about the topic of study.	Learners are consistently striving to resolve between observed and what is known, operating on a sincere desire to know.
Constructing Mental Models and Making Meaning		
Learners rarely create their own understandings of how things work.	Learners are often expected to make sense of new experiences and develop theories.	Learners routinely wrestle with new experiences, becoming experts at identifying and solving problems.

Figure 9.3   Rubrics for Assessing Constructive Learning

intrinsically committed? To what extent can learners explain their activity in terms of how the activities relate to the attainment of their goals? Figure 9.4 provides a rubric for assessing intentional learning.

Assessing Authentic Learning, where learners examine and attempt to solve complex, ill-structured, and real-world problems. If your learning activity

Goal-Directedness		
Learners are often pursuing activities that have little to do with the attainment of specified goals.		Learners are generally engaged in activities that contribute to the attainment of specified goals.

Setting Own Goals		
Learning goals are provided by educators.	Learners are sometimes involved in the establishment of learning goals.	Learners are routinely responsible for developing and expressing learning goals.

Regulating Own Learning		
Learners' progress is monitored by others.	Learners are involved as partners in monitoring and reporting progress toward goals.	Learners are responsible for monitoring and reporting progress toward goals.

Tool Learning—How to Learn		
Little emphasis is placed on metacognition. There are few opportunities to discuss the learning process with peers or educators.		The culture of the learning environment promotes frequent discussion of the processes and strategies (both successful and unsuccessful) involved in learning.

Tool Articulation of Goals as Focus of Activity		
Learners don't see the relationship between the activities in which they are engaged and specified learning goals.		Learners describe the activities in which they are engaged in terms that relate directly to the specified learning goals.

Tool Technology Use in Support of Learning Goals		
The use of technology seems unrelated to the specified learning goals.	The use of technology contributes to the attainment of specified learning goals.	The use of technology makes a powerful contribution to the attainment of specified learning goals.

Figure 9.4   Rubric for Assessing Intentional Learning

or environment includes authentic problem solving, to what extent does the environment present learners with problems that are naturally complex and embedded in a real-world context? To what extent do the problems you present cause higher-order thinking? Figure 9.5 provides a rubric for assessing authentic learning.

Assessing Cooperative Learning, where learners collaborate with others and socially negotiate the meanings they have constructed. If your environment or activity includes cooperative learning, to what extent does the environment promote meaningful interaction among students and between students and experts outside of school? To what extent are learners developing skills related to social negotiation in learning to accept and share responsibility? Figure 9.6 provides a rubric for assessing collaborative learning.

Complexity		
The tasks learners face have been designed for schools (i.e., separated into "subjects" and developed to simplify learning.	The tasks learners face are embedded in theme-based units that cross disciplines and present issues in context.	Students accept challenges as they exist in real world, using language, math, science, and technologies to accomplish important tasks.
Higher-Order Thinking		
A large percentage of what is expected is memorization. Students are rarely asked to evaluate, synthesize, or create.	Students are often asked to develop ideas and solutions, often in groups, and demonstrate the abilities to create and reason.	Learners routinely generate hypotheses, conduct investigations, assess results, and make predictions.
Recognizing Problems		
Students are not expected to be problem finders, but are instead expected to be able to solve occasional well-structured problems presented to them.	Students occasionally face ill-structured challenges and are expected to refine their problem as well as solve it.	Students frequently face ill-structured challenges and develop proficiency in identifying and defining problems.
"Right Answers"		
The "problems" presented to learners tend to have "right answers," "correct" solutions that the students are expected to eventually reach.	The problems presented are new to the learners, and generally involve complex solutions of varying quality, rather than "right answers."	

Figure 9.5   Rubric for Assessing Authentic Learning

Interaction Among Learners		
Little of the learners' time is spent gainfully engaged with other students.	Learners are often immersed in activities in which collaboration with peers results in success.	
Interaction With People Outside of School		
Little of the learners' time is spent gainfully engaged with experts outside of school.	Learners are often involved in activities in which there is significant collaboration with experts from outside of school.	
Social Negotiation		
Little evidence that learners work together to develop shared understanding of tasks or of solution strategies.	Learners are often observed in the process of coming to agreement on the nature of problems and on best courses of action.	Learners collaborate with ease. Negotiations become almost invisible, yet the ideas of all team members are valued.
Acceptance and Distribution of Roles and Responsibility		
Roles and responsibilities are shifted infrequently; most capable learners accept more responsibility than the less capable.	Roles and responsibilities are shifted often, and such changes are accepted by both the most and least capable.	Students make their own decisions concerning roles and responsibilities, freely giving and accepting assistance as necessary.

Figure 9.6   Rubric for Assessing Collaborative Learning

ASSESSING PROBLEM SOLVING WITH TECHNOLOGY

In chapter 2 of this book, we introduced several types of problem solving. Then throughout the book, we associated these problem-solving skills with the technology-based activities we have suggested. Just as previous rubrics represented a set of rubrics for assessing the constructivist aspects of meaningful learning environments, the next set of rubrics can be used to assess the 5 elements of problem solving we have discussed throughout this book. In the following rubrics, the rightmost performance descriptions represent the best learner performance, and the leftmost, the poorest learner performance.

Assessing Information Searching

If your activity or environment requires learners to do information searching, then to what extent do learner's searches demonstrate a cohesive plan, and how well have they evaluated their sources of information (Jonassen & Colaric, 2001)? Figure 9.7 provides a rubric for assessing information searching.

Assessing Modeling

If your activity or environment requires learners to do modeling, then to what extent are learner's modeling activities based on sound information seeking strategies, and representative of deep understanding of the target domain? Figure 9.8 provides a rubric for assessing modeling.

Assessing Decision Making

If your activity or environment requires learners to do decision-making (and most meaningful activities will require this), then to what extent do learner's decision-making processes demonstrate the development of alternative solutions, factors by which to judge the decision, and consider multiple perspectives? Figure 9.9 provides a rubric for assessing decision making.

Notice that these rubrics are necessarily interrelated. To determine if the evidence is sound, one must return to the rubric for information searching and examine the credibility evaluation elements!

Assessing Designing

If your activity or environment requires learners to do design, then to what extent do learner's design processes demonstrate clear communication of design, definition of reasonable problem constraints and appropriate design functionality? Figure 9.10 provides a rubric for assessing designing.

Note that designing is the most complex problem-solving process addressed throughout this book. To design necessarily draws on the other problem-solving skills we have been addressing. Thus, this rubric refers you to the prior rubrics for decision making, modeling, and information seeking.

Information searching plan		
Learners do not have a search plan or their plan does not identify what they need to know and why.		Learners have a search plan that identifies what they need to know and why they need to know it.
Strategies for searching the World Wide Web—Search Terms		
Students rarely use relevant search terms in their searches.	Students often use relevant search terms in their searches.	Students always use relevant search terms in their searches.
Strategies for searching the World Wide Web—Search Strings		
Students rarely construct valid search strings and don't use Boolean operators correctly.	Students often construct valid search strings using Boolean operators correctly.	Students always construct valid search strings using Boolean operators correctly.
Relevance evaluation		
Most of students' located resources are irrelevant and not pertinent to the problem.	Most of students' located resources are related and/or pertinent to the problem.	All of students' located resources are related and/or are pertinent to the problem.
Credibility evaluation—source—author		
Students identify sources with authors who do not have authority in the relevant field.		Students identify sources with authors who have authority in the relevant field.
Credibility evaluation—source—organization		
Students identify sources from unauthoritative or biased organizations.		Students identify sources from authoritative and unbiased organizations.
Credibility evaluation—source—dated		
Students identify sources that do not indicate when site was developed or last updated.		Students identify sources that clearly indicated when site was developed and last updated.
Credibility evaluation—source—bibliography/references		
Students identify sources that do not include a reference list, or have an uncredible reference list.		Students identify sources that include a credible reference list developed and last updated.
Credibility evaluation—content—factual		
Students identify sources that use content that is opinion.		Students identify sources that include factual content.
Credibility evaluation—content—completeness		
Students identify sources that are incomplete or have gaps of information on the topic.		Students identify sources that are complete in terms of their content on the topic.
Credibility evaluation—content—objective language		
Students identify sources that use biased or extreme statements.		Students identify sources that use unbiased and unextreme language.
Credibility evaluation—content—language		
Students identify sources that use poorly written language.		Students identify sources that use well-written language (no misspellings or poor grammar).
Triangulation		
Students rarely identify and cite two sources that verify their information.	Students often identify and cite at least two sources that verify their information.	Students always identify and cite at least two sources that verify their information.

Figure 9.7 Rubric for Assessing Information Searching

Model is based on sound information seeking

Refer to information-seeking rubrics.

Output of the model

Students produce modeling output that is confusing and does not support interpretation	Students produce modeling output that includes some unimportant variables; some interrelationships among variables are missing	Students produce modeling output that includes most important variables; show interrelationships among variables

Selection of variables

Model uses incorrect variables that are not relevant or accurate in terms of system behavior	Model uses mostly variables that are accurate and relevant in determining and predicting the behavior of the system	Model uses only variables that are accurate and relevant in determining and predicting the behavior of the system

Use of variables

Model inaccurately represents variable interrelationships	Model shows some relationships between variables accurately; representation is not complete enough for system	Model shows relationships between variables accurate and also completely to represent the target system

Model represents understanding of a real system

Model inaccurately simulates the system and represents naïve understanding; makes inappropriate assumptions	Model mostly simulates a real system accurately; uses some questionable assumptions; supports few predictions	Model faithfully simulates a real system and makes appropriate assumptions about that system

Model supports testing

Model cannot support predictions or hypothesis testing by users	Model supports some/few predictions, hypotheses, and speculations by manipulating variables	Model supports a range of predictions, hypotheses, are speculations by manipulate variables

Figure 9.8 Rubric for Assessing Modeling

Development of relevant alternative solutions		
No alternative solutions are considered, or they are not based on sound evidence or are not relevant to the current problem.	Most alternative solutions are based on sound evidence and relevant to the current problem.	All alternative solutions are based on sound evidence and relevant to the current problem.
Choosing relevant factors/information from which to judge the decision		
Students rarely define relevant factors to judge decisions based on the context in which it must operate (including all audiences for the decision).	Students often define relevant factors to judge decisions based on the context in which the decision must operate (including all audiences for the decision).	Students always define relevant factors to judge decisions based on the context in which the decision must operate (including all audiences for the decision).
Decision process considers multiple perspectives		
Students rarely show evidence of having deeply considered alternative points of view.	Students often show evidence of having deeply considered alternative points of view.	Students always show evidence of having deeply considered alternative points of view.
Decision articulation		
Students rarely articulate their decision in a clear way.	Students often clearly articulate their decision.	Students always clearly articulate their decision.
Decision justification		
Students rarely justify their decision relative to alternate solutions and the defined relevant factors.	Students often justify their decisions relative to alternate solutions and the defined relevant factors.	Students always justify their decisions relative to alternate solutions and the defined relevant factors.

Figure 9.9 Rubric for Assessing Decision Making

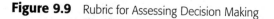

THINGS TO THINK ABOUT

1. If meaningful learning should be authentic, so should assessments. How do we design authentic assessments in the classroom (assuming that the classroom is not an authentic environment)?
2. Performance assessments are designed to assess if learners know how to do something? What do tests assess?
3. There are many kinds of knowledge: declarative knowledge, structural knowledge, procedural knowledge, situational knowledge, conceptual knowledge, strategic knowledge, sociocultural knowledge, world knowledge, experiential knowledge. Is it worth assessing all of these kinds of knowledge in learners? If so, when?
4. Much of what people who are very skilled (experts) know is tacit (not readily accessible). How can we assess that kind of knowledge if it is not consciously known? When should we try?

Design is based on research and information seeking		
Refer to prior rubric on information seeking.		
Design reflects reasonable problem constraints (budget, constituents, extent of functionality, schedule)		
Design solution does not state reasonable constraints for the design.	Design solution partially states reasonable constraints for the design.	Design solution clearly states reasonable constraints for the design.
Design reflects sound decision making among viable alternatives		
Refer to decision-making rubric above.		
Communication of design		
Design is not clearly articulated and/or the communication media is inappropriate for this design.	Design is mostly articulated in clear fashion that is appropriate for the design media.	Articulates design in skilled and clear fashion that is appropriate for the design media.
Systemic understanding of design content		
Refer to prior rubric on modeling.		
Creativity/originality of design		
Design does not suggest any new approaches to the problem.	Design minimally suggests new approaches or challenges way things are normally done.	Design suggests new approaches or challenges way things are normally done.
Design functionality		
Design does not solve intended problem.	Design mostly functions so as to solve intended problem within constraints previously defined.	Design functions so as to solve intended problem within constraints previously defined.
Constituent appropriateness		
Students create design that is not appropriate for identified constituents.	Students create design that is appropriate for most identified constituents.	Students create design that is appropriate for all identified constituents.
Plans for revisions of design		
Students rarely or do not create plan for design revision; or plan has no basis.	Students create plan for revision of design somewhat based on testing and feedback.	Students create sound plan for revision of design based on testing and feedback.
Media-specific implementation elements		
Based on the actual design medium, there will be other assessment elements. For instance, if students engaged in a hypermedia design task, you would want to consider elements for: navigation, use of graphics, use of multimedia, layout, use of fonts, use of color, use of sound, etc.		

Figure 9.10 Rubric for Assessing Designing

5. What are the differences between measurement, assessment, and evaluation?
6. What are the differences between assessment criteria and assessment rubrics?
7. Tests look for correct answers. Rubrics look for what are deemed correct or desirable performances. Are they different? How?
8. Is it fair or appropriate to use rubrics to evaluate students?
9. How can rubrics be used as learning tools?
10. Intentions (motivations) are internal to the learner(s). How can we assess learners' intentions if we cannot see inside their heads?
11. The most important outcome of an information search is meaningful material. Can you write a rubric for what it means to be meaningful?

REFERENCES

Elliott, S. N. (1995). *Creating Meaningful Performance Assessments*. Retrieved from http://www.ed.gov/databases/ERIC_Digests/ed381985.html; ERIC Digest E531; ERIC Identifier: No. ED381985.

Jonassen, D. H., & Colaric, S. (2001). Information landfills contain knowledge; searching equals learning; Hyperlinking is good instruction; and other myths about learning from the Internet. *Computers in Schools, 17*(3/4), Part I, 159–170.

Jonassen, D. H., Campbell, J., & Davidson, M. (1994). Learning with media; restructuring the debate. *Educational Technology Research and Development, 42*(2), 31–39.

Morrison, G. R. (1994). The media effects question: "Unresolveable" or asking the right question. *Educational Technology Research and Development, 42*(2), 41–44.

Wiggins, G. (1990). *The Case for Authentic Assessment*. Practical Assessment Research and Evaluation 2(2). Retrieved from http://ericae.net/db/edo/ ED328611.htm

INDEX

Note: Page numbers in italics with an "i"—such as *193i*—indicate an illustration.

Abelson, H., 192, 208
access provider, Internet, 33
accessing information. *See* information searching
Action for Children's Television, 123–124
active learning
    activity driving learning, 20
    anchored instruction, 135–137
    documentaries, 151
    learning as goal, 84
    learning theory, 4–5
    meaningful learning, *6i*, 7, 13
    rubric assessment, 237
    scientific inquiry, 54
    StorySpace project, 174
    virtual travel, 64
activity, driving learning, 53
activity structures, 80, *81–82i*
adaptation, within learning communities, 112
ADSL, Asynchronous Digital Subscriber Line, 35
Advanced Technology Center (ATC), 205
adventure games, 101–104, 191
AirPort wireless communication, 37
algorithmic problems, 21, 210
Allen, Steve, 145
Amazon Quest, 62
Amelung, C., 206, 207
analog video, 127, 129–133, 167
anchored instruction, 135–137
Anderson, D. K., 183, 185, 188
Andres, Y. M., 99, 118
argument, 91, 112–113
articulation. *See* constructive learning; constructivism
assessing learning
    anchored instruction, 137
    The Astronomy Village, 216
    documentaries, 152
    global telecommunities, 101

    knowledge co-construction, 107–108
    Learning Circles, 92
    within learning communities, 74, *75i*
    modeling and feedback, 154–155
    MUDs and MOOs, 104
    newsroom videography project, 144–145
    one-act videography, 152–153
    OWL project, 198–199
    performance assessment, 228–229
    press conference, 141
    scientific inquiry, 54
    StorySpace project, 176–177
    structured online communications, 91–92
    talk shows, 146
    virtual travel, 64–65
    Web publishing, 59–60
    WebQuest creation, 49
The Astronomy Village, 214–218, *215i, 217i, 218i*
asynchronism/synchronism, 75, 78, 80
Asynchronous Digital Subscriber Line (ADSL), 35
at-risk students
    cybermentoring, 108–111
    hypermedia creation, 171
    OWL project, 198
    virtual reality creation, 205
ATC, Advanced Technology Center, 205
attachments, e-mail, 76
attention span and TV viewing, 124–125
augmented (virtual) reality, 204
authentic learning
    anchored instruction, 135
    documentaries, 151
    learning assessment, 228–229
    meaningful learning, *6i*, 8
    rubric assessment, 238
    scientific inquiry, 54
    technology and, 13, 57
    video press conference, 137–138

    virtual reality, 205
    zoo kiosk project, 178
authorship, collaborative, 87–88, 106–107
avatars in adventure games, 206

Bailey, Lisa, 142
bandwidth, 35
Barab, S. A., 119
Barn Owl cam, 36, *36i*
Barnes, C. A., 17
Barrett, E., 188
Barrows, H. S., 210, 225
Basili, A., 21, 30
Bauwens, Mary, 142
Becker, H. J., 10, 16
Beentjes, J., 124, 160
behavioral psychology, 2
Beichner, R. J., 178, 188
Bereiter, C., 32, 68, 72, 83, 85, *88i*, 120
Biological Timing Online Science Experiment, 51
Blumenfeld, P., 68
Boerger, A., 183, 185, 188
Boolean logic, 42
Booth, K. S., 38, 67
Bowen, Mrs. (5th-grade teacher), 56
Boxer programming language, 192
brain activity, 2
Bransford, J. D., 134, 160
"Bread Baking Field Trip," 60–61
Britton, B. C., 188
broadcast TV vs. videography, 122–126
Brookfield, S., 208
Brown, C. A., 170, 188
Brown, J. S., 4, 16, 191, 207
browser, defined, 33
Bruckerman, A., 102, 118
Brusilovsky, P., 207
The Buddy Project, 108–111
bulletin boards, electronic, 77–78
Burton, R. R., 191, 207
Bush, G. W., 67
Bush, President George, 32
Byrne, C., 205, 207